OUTRAGEOUS
RUGBY
MOMENTS

Keith Quinn

OUTRAGEOUS RUGBY MOMENTS

Stories of controversy, humour, scandal and disgrace

Edited by Joseph Romanos

Hodder Moa Beckett

This book is dedicated to my sports broadcasting colleague and
friend, Peter Sellers of Dunedin. In my very earliest days as a cadet
reporter Peter inspired me to respect the sporting history and stories
of our country and to always pay detailed attention to sports record
keeping. I have always regarded it a serious compliment to be told
you've got memory for detail like Peter Sellers has.

ISBN 1-86958-884-3

© 2002 Original text — Keith Quinn and Joseph Romanos
The moral rights of the authors have been asserted

© 2002 Design and format — Hodder Moa Beckett Publishers Ltd

Published in 2001 by Hodder Moa Beckett Publishers Ltd
[a member of the Hodder Headline Group],
4 Whetu Place, Mairangi Bay, Auckland, New Zealand

Designed and produced by Hodder Moa Beckett Publishers Ltd
Film and printing by Oliver Young, Auckland

Contents

LADIES DRESSING ROOM

An outrageous start to an outrageously long tour almost 30 years ago. Ian Kirkpatrick's 1972-73 All Blacks — the pride of New Zealand maledom — forced to use the 'Ladies Dressing Room' for their opening match against British Columbia in Vancouver, en route to Britain and France. This match was played on October 10 and, almost four months later, the tour finished with a test against France. For the record, Kirky's men won this game 31–3. Pictured here, from left, are: Peter Whiting, Bob Burgess and Kirkpatrick.

Introduction

Outrageous Rugby Moments . . . hmmm. I'm not really an outrageous person, or at least I don't think I am. My dictionary gives the word outrageous several meanings, including immoderate, shocking, grossly cruel, immoral and offensive. During my time as a rugby broadcaster I have received some correspondence describing me in even less flattering terms than that, but, overall, I hope they weren't correct. Like any journalist worth his salt, I like a good scandal, but I have always tried to balance my coverage, telling it like it is without twisting the knife that one revolution further than necessary.

Having watched a fair bit of rugby over the past few decades, and read about a lot more, I wanted to write a book that related some of the bizarre and unusual moments in New Zealand's rugby history. *Outrageous Rugby Moments* seemed a catchy title, so there it is. I suppose I could have called this book *Interesting Rugby Moments*, but *Outrageous Rugby Moments* somehow seemed catchier.

What to include? I mean, when you think about it, there are almost endless examples of shocking moments in New Zealand rugby. Jonah Lomu's four tries against England in the 1995 World Cup semi-final certainly shocked the English. Ian Kirkpatrick coming into the test in Sydney in 1968 as a reserve after 22 minutes and then peeling off three tries shocked rugby followers who were still trying to get used to the game's new substitute rules. I watched Eric Watson coaching the All Blacks in 1980 and saw them passing bricks, not balls — Watson's logic was that with the threat of imminent pain should they drop the brick, they might be more inclined to be careful with their passing and catching. That sight was a shock.

So you can see that by using wide parameters, I could have included many thousands of stories about New Zealand rugby. Far too many for one book.

What I've done, therefore, is restrict myself to a balance between the obvious musts for this type of book — the Deans 'try' of 1905, the Murdoch sending home in 1972, the 1986 Cavaliers tour, Wayne Shelford's axing in 1990, Richard Loe's stormy career, South African journalist Charles Blackett's clearly racist telegram in 1921, the formation of the All Golds in 1907–08, Andy Haden's 1978 lineout dive at Cardiff Arms Park, 'Suzy' and the food poisoning of 1995 — and the zany and off-beat.

Not all rugby followers will know the story of New Zealander Ross Cullen, sent home from an international rugby tour for ear-biting. Perhaps it is timely to examine again the shameful way that fine All Black fullback Mike Gilbert was treated after he signed to play rugby league. I've dealt with two famous sendings-off, those of Cyril Brownlie and Colin Meads, perhaps bringing to light some details not known or at least long since forgotten. The 1981 Springbok tour of New Zealand had to be included, but instead of regurgitating it match by match, I've tried to focus on the tour more through the eyes of one of the most prominent objectors, Graham Mourie.

There have been minor outrages dotted between the big ones. The way Liam Barry was snubbed during the All Blacks' tour of Britain in 1993, Vic Cavanagh being overlooked as All Black coach, John Ashworth's stomping of J.P.R. Williams at Bridgend in 1978, Kit Fawcett's unconventional and misinterpreted behaviour in South Africa in 1976. At the time they all rated a big heading, or a lead item in the radio or television bulletins of the day.

Then there were stories I was particularly keen to discuss. John Hart, despite what on paper is an impressive career in rugby coaching, has become a controversial figure in New Zealand rugby. Why? What really happened during the rush to professional rugby in 1995? Do we understand the impact the constant drain of leading players for overseas shores is having on New Zealand rugby? What have been the juiciest rugby books produced in New Zealand? Was there ever a player more wronged than All Black Ron Rangi? Do people realise how badly we treat our All Black captains once they are no longer required?

Between these stories, I've included dozens of short anecdotes, ranging from the curious to the humorous. Hopefully it all adds up to an entertaining and informative book, one that reflects my lifetime's interest in this great game.

There are a few people I would like to thank for helping with the book. First, my co-author Joseph Romanos, for his ideas and energy, and particularly for picking up the slack when I shot off overseas with the All Blacks in the crucial final weeks of this book's production. The illustrations in this book come from many sources, including my own files that now date back nearly 40 years. But it would be hard to illustrate a book of this nature without reprinting at least a few of Peter Bush's photos. He has been my mate on many an overseas tour. He was the New Zealand journalist who, sniffing a sensational story, followed Keith Murdoch to Heathrow Airport in 1972. His picture from that day is included in these pages.

I have included a full bibliography at the end of this book, but should say a special thank you to some of New Zealand's leading rugby historians down the years, men like Arthur Carman, Arthur Swan, Rod Chester, Neville McMillan and Ron Palenski. Their writing has not only given me hours of pleasurable reading, but has helped immensely in researching various segments of this book. Lindsay Knight has assisted by proofreading the book and giving me the benefit of his own deep rugby knowledge, and Warren Adler, commissioning editor at Hodder Moa Beckett has, as ever, been enthusiastic, resourceful and full of innovative ideas.

Keith Quinn
January 2002

1. Of all the Loe acts

The fall and rise of Richard Loe

One of the more intriguing pieces of rugby history to be reshaped and reworked concerns the career of the Waikato, Canterbury and All Black prop Richard Loe. In much of the rugby world, this man is rubbished and reviled when his career is discussed. At the same time in many parts of New Zealand, those same issues about Loe's playing days are hardly ever raised. To many rugby followers within New Zealand, Loe is something of a rollicking folk hero.

Yes, Loe might have been a fine prop in many a test match scrum battle, but for thinking people, discussion about his playing prowess must inevitably return to the numerous scraps and squabbles in which he was involved that went way beyond the bounds of rugby decency.

Like the 1992 test match at Brisbane when Wallaby winger Paul Carozza slid in for a try and Loe appeared to dash his forearm across the Australian's upturned face. The result was a broken nose for Carozza and heavy criticism for the New Zealander from the Australian press (and even some New Zealanders). Film of the incident seemed damning, but Loe was quoted in one paper as saying the whole business was just a storm in a teacup.

Thankfully Terry McLean was one writer who coined a memorable line at the time — 'Some storm, some teacup.'

Yet many thousands of the New Zealand sports public, perhaps encouraged by the way All Black coach Laurie Mains appeared to absolve Loe of any wrong-doing, also believed nothing too bad had been done to Carozza.

A few months later in 1992, it was harder to come down on the soft side of sympathy for Loe in the New Zealand NPC rugby final when Waikato played Otago in Hamilton. This was the game in which Otago fullback Greg Cooper had to leave the field early on after suffering injuries to his eyes. The expression 'eye-gouged' was

Richard Loe (right) finished up his representative career in Canterbury.

used. The videotape clearly showed the damage had occurred after Cooper had been in contact with Loe's searching fingers. Loe received a nine-month suspension for the incident, later reduced to six months.

After that game I got an indication of the off-field backing for Loe. Many Waikato supporters believed that Loe was not the bad guy. As 1992 was the early days of judiciary video analysis, many of Loe's supporters concluded that television was to blame, through excessive coverage and replays of the incident.

What happened was somewhat convoluted, but it went something like this. In the live telecast, nothing was seen of the way Cooper had fallen in the tackle and nothing could be seen of the way Loe had been near him when he fell. I was on the sideline with cameraman Roger Duncan, and we were not part of the telecast. (We were actually filming for a slow-motion sequence of the rugby action, trying to capture images to the strains of the slow movement of the Ravel Piano Concerto!)

After the game, when the telecast crew were standing around the Outside Broadcast van sipping coffee and talking about the game, the question was asked: 'Why *did* Greg Cooper wander off the field holding his eyes?' A young female staff member from the video replay area was standing in this circle of colleagues, and mentioned that she might have seen something on her machines, but that her replay shots had not been cut into the telecast.

Several of us crowded into her booth in the van and she spun back her videotapes. She replayed to us the video segment that later was to become famous or infamous — depending on your standpoint. It showed Loe grasping at Cooper, leaving the fullback sprawling on the ground holding his face. In the van we played it over and over and, believing it was a significant incident that had not been seen before, it was fed up to the Auckland newsroom. It was then replayed in the 6 pm news and in the days afterwards many, many times.

As a result of that piece of videotape and an operator's vigilance, Loe appeared before the New Zealand Rugby Union judiciary the following week and copped his long suspension.

For being part of a few staffers who watched the after-match video, I paid the price with word-of-mouth accusation. On several occasions, people who wanted to know why, in essence, I had dobbed in Loe accosted me in Hamilton, once in a bar and several times at Rugby Park. I hope I stood firm with those people. My usual reply when charged by angry people about rugby fighting and incidents is to say: 'Ask him — he did it, not me.'

What is curious, though, is that in the years after Loe's retirement he has been reborn in the public eye. For several years he wrote a column for the *Sunday News*. He is in demand as a guest speaker and he appears regularly as a commentator and studio guest on various television shows. I appeared several times with him on the 1999 TV show *Tight Five*. He is a jovial fellow, full of good cheer and bonhomie.

In other words, he is absolved of all that went on in his often-fiery rugby career. It makes you wonder about the psyche of the average New Zealand rugby watcher. Many of them are prepared to forgive and forget those two very questionable incidents. And from them a tough guy has emerged, a man who can now speak with authority on the good points of the game.

News Media Auckland

'I have no regrets,' says former All Black hard man Richard Loe.

For myself, I had hoped that deep down Loe, when he reflected on his career, deeply regretted some of the things he did on the rugby field.

Apparently not, though. On November 4, 2001, Loe wrote his final column for the *Sunday News*. Under a heading of 'It Was Part of the Job', he wrote in part: 'I have no regrets. I probably deserved some of the criticism about my playing style during my career . . . Sure I played close to the wire sometimes for the All Blacks and Waikato. But I believed I was doing what was expected of me and to benefit my team in those days. I had a job to do and went out and did it.'

This was a sad piece of writing. It was incredible that all these years later, Loe was still unable to accept his thuggery on the field for what it had been, and was still defending it.

But, as I say, his rugby rehabilitation is complete. He coached with the Front Row Factory campaign after he retired, ironically with the stated goal of making the front row a safer place. In 1999, he became a New Zealand Rugby Union resource coach. He helped John Mitchell prepare the Chiefs team and now he has been appointed, again by Mitchell, as a consultant with the All Blacks. He travelled with the All Blacks in Britain and Argentina at the end of 2001, offering specific advice on aspects of forward play.

I never thought I'd live to see it, but Richard Loe is now a pillar of the rugby establishment.

2. Refs to remember

Twelve referees that All Black teams have good or bad cause to remember:

1. **John Dewar Dallas, 1905.** Declined New Zealand claims that centre Bob Deans had scored a try against Wales at Cardiff Arms, meaning the Originals lost the test 3–0, their only defeat on that long tour.

2. **Albert Freethy, 1925.** Ordered Cyril Brownlie from the field in the test against England at Twickenham.

News Media Auckland

Allan Fleury . . . six penalties.

3. **Allan Fleury, 1959.** Awarded the six penalties that Don Clarke kicked to steer the All Blacks to an 18–17 win over the British Lions at Carisbrook, Dunedin. The Lions had scored four tries. Fleury was never offered another test match to control.

4. **Ralph Burmeister, 1960.** Decreed that All Black centre Frank McMullen had played a tackled ball when scoring what might have been the decisive try in the fourth test against South Africa at Boet Erasmus Stadium, Port Elizabeth. South Africa won the match 8–3 and the series 2–1.

5. **Kevin Kelleher, 1967.** Sent Colin Meads from the field in the test against Scotland at Murrayfield, Edinburgh. Kelleher has kept in social contact with Meads. The two had their most recent meeting in 2000 while Meads was on a visit to Britain.

6. Kevin Crowe, 1968. Awarded All Black centre Bill Davis a disputed penalty try in the closing minutes of the test against Australia at Ballymore, Brisbane. This enabled the All Blacks to win 19–18.

7. Gert Bezuidenhout, 1976. Declined to award at least one and possibly two penalty tries — involving interference on All Black centre Bruce Robertson — in the decisive fourth test against South Africa at Ellis Park, Johannesburg in 1976. New Zealand lost the test 15–14.

8. Roger Quittenton, 1978. Awarded New Zealand a last-minute penalty against Wales at Cardiff Arms Park. Brian McKechnie landed the kick and New Zealand won 13–12. Many claimed Quittenton had awarded the penalty after being fooled by Andy Haden's blatant dive out of the lineout. Quittenton has always maintained he awarded the penalty for an offence by the Welsh lock forward Geoff Wheel, who appeared to push his All Black marker, Frank Oliver, out of the lineout.

9. Clive Norling, 1981. Awarded a penalty to New Zealand eight minutes into injury time against South Africa at Eden Park, Auckland. Allan Hewson kicked the goal to give New Zealand a 25–22 victory and with it the series 2–1. While South Africans have always claimed the injury time of eight minutes was far too long, Norling says with halts to injuries and flour-bomb protests, his duration of the second half was spot on.

10. Derek Bevan, 1986. Declined to award Steve Tuynman what appeared to be a legitimate try, enabling the All Blacks to beat Australia 13–12 at Carisbrook, Dunedin, to keep the series alive.

11. Peter Marshall, 1998. Issued debatable penalty against Jonah Lomu in the dying moments of the test at Kings Park, Durban. From the ensuing tap and drive, James Dalton was awarded a hotly disputed try to give South Africa a 24–23 victory.

12. Jonathan Kaplan, 2000. Allowed several minutes of injury time in the crucial Bledisloe Cup match at the Wellington Stadium, then ruled an All Black lineout infringement. Wallaby captain John Eales kicked the penalty to earn Australia a 24–23 victory. Kaplan had bottles and cans thrown at him and was booed as he left the field.

News Media Auckland

Derek Bevan . . . kept the All Blacks in the series hunt back in 1986.

3. Hartless and hurtful

The great John Hart debate

Let me be clear right at the outset: I am a great admirer of John Hart, as a person and a coach. I've always got on well with him personally and I liked the way he conducted himself when he held the most high-profile job in New Zealand sport. But it must be said that, for all sorts of reasons, he has been the coach who most split the New Zealand rugby public.

The bile and poison directed at Hart when he stepped down from his position after the 1999 World Cup was shameful. Talkback callers feasted on him for weeks. He received some poisonous mail, even death threats. Hell — his horse was even spat at! The result is that these days, Hart is not really seen around rugby very much. I know, having been to his house and watched test rugby with him on television, that he still loves the game and cares about the players. But to all intents and purposes, he has largely been lost to rugby since that traumatic departure in 1999.

As best I can judge, the reasons so many people in New Zealand either never liked Hart or turned on him so venomously are:

- He was never an All Black himself.
- He was an Aucklander.
- He was from the corporate world.
- He was well-spoken and assured.
- He was seen to be too ambitious.
- His team lost in the 1999 World Cup semi-finals.

It can be seen that few of these reasons have much to do with rugby. Indeed, if we look at the test records of the past five All Black coaches, it becomes obvious Hart's performance was nothing to be ashamed of.

John Hart . . . his test record stacks up well alongside other All Black coaches.

	P	W	D	L	Percentage of Wins
Brian Lochore (1985–87)	18	14	1	3	77.7%
Alex Wyllie (1988–91)	29	25	1	3	86.2%
Laurie Mains (1992–95)	34	23	1	10	67.6%
John Hart (1996–99)	40	30	1	9	75.0%
Wayne Smith (2000–2001)	17	12	0	5	70.5%

A couple of points about the statistics. Hart also coached the 1987 All Black team to Japan. If his two test wins on that tour are counted (some statisticians do, others don't) his winning percentage rises to 76.1. He co-coached, with Wyllie, the All Blacks at the 1991 World Cup, when New Zealand won five and lost one. Hart's winning percentage remains virtually identical whether these World Cup results are included or not.

So it can be seen from Hart's overall coaching record that he produced generally successful teams. Of modern All Black coaches, Wyllie is clearly in front and Mains is last. Hart is a whisker behind Lochore. Further, the All Blacks had some major successes under Hart. In 1996 they became the first All Black team to win a series in South Africa, and I still rate the day in Pretoria, when they sewed up the series, as the greatest in All Black history. Hart's All Blacks also won the Tri Nations Cup in 1996, '97 and '99 and the Bledisloe Cup in 1996 and '97.

In terms of an overall record, Hart had little to be ashamed of. Why the vilification, then?

Well, we do like our New Zealand rugby coaches to have been All Blacks. There can be no doubt about that. The one tour John Mitchell made with an All Black team, in 1993, stood him in good stead when he was seeking the coach's position in 2001. Never mind that Mitchell was never more than a midweek player and never got near the test lineup, and that he played just six matches in all wearing the All Black jersey. The fact that his résumé included the words 'former All Black' greatly enhanced his standing.

Hart was never anywhere near All Black standard. He was a feisty, snappy provincial halfback who had 26 games for Auckland and two for Taranaki from 1967–76 — a rather unremarkable provincial career. There have been other All Black coaches who were not All Blacks, such as Bryce Rope, Jack Gleeson, J.J. Stewart, Eric Watson and Neil McPhail, but there is undoubtedly a perception in New Zealand that it helps if the coach has done it as a player.

It's interesting that Australia and South Africa do not have this hang-up. For instance, Bob Dwyer, Rod Macqueen, Eddie Jones and Harry Viljoen seem to have managed the job of coach well without having first played for their country.

Hart's arrival on the national rugby scene coincided with a period of domination by Auckland. In the five years he coached Auckland, Hart's team won 78 of their 90 matches. It was until then the highest winning percentage of any Auckland coach. Auckland had some outstanding players and dominant personalities at the time — Andy Haden, John Drake, Gary and Alan Whetton, Steve McDowell, Grant Fox, Michael Jones, John Kirwan, Joe Stanley and Terry Wright among them. Auckland held the Ranfurly Shield for a record spell and made the National Provincial Championship their own.

These players became powerful figures on the All Black scene and Hart, as their coach/mentor/friend, wielded a lot of influence, even in the years when he was not the New Zealand coach. Players like Jones and Kirwan continued to turn to him for advice.

Other parts of New Zealand set themselves to beat Auckland, or the Mighty Aucks as they became known. The anti-Auckland sentiment grew and Hart seemed to personify the target.

The way Hart handled himself merely added to the feeling. He worked for Fletcher Challenge from the time he left school until 1995, when he formed his own consultancy. By the time he left the company, he was the senior executive in charge of employee relations. He was a skilled public speaker and dealt comfortably with the media. I spent several seasons with Hart as my co-commentator for Television New Zealand and was continually impressed with his ability to think quickly and clearly and to explain things so simply.

To some people Hart was too slick by half. That never worried me. The more I got to know him, the more I admired his values. He was a happy family man and his stable personal life was in contrast to Wyllie and Mains, whose marriages sadly broke up during their time as All Black coaches.

There is no doubt that Hart was very ambitious, at times nakedly so. That was the factor that grated on many rugby people. But so what? Don't we want our coaches to be ambitious?

Lochore, Wyllie and Hart formed a superb All Black selection panel in 1987. Wyllie and Hart complemented each other and with Lochore obviously in charge, the All Blacks were as well led that season as they have ever been. After Lochore stepped down, many expected Hart to replace him as All Black coach.

He took an All Black side to Japan at the end of 1987 and though the team was vastly superior to any opposition it encountered, Hart did all that could be asked of him. He had plenty of detractors, even then. Such people seized on his decision to allow television cameras to film part of a pre-international team talk he gave as proof of his ego and love of the limelight. That was even though the permission to film was finalised by team manager Malcolm Dick. I know — I was there. I thought it made good television, but it seemed to give critics more ammunition.

(This incident had a precedent. In 1968 All Black coach Fred Allen allowed a reporter, Alex Veysey, into the dressing room for a pre-test talk in Australia. Veysey wrote a brilliant piece, but the Rugby Union authorities took a dim view of Allen's decision. Allen feels his position as All Black coach was shaky from that moment and he stood down the following year.)

Hart and Wyllie vied for the All Black coach's job in 1988 and, in a narrow vote, Wyllie got the job. It was a fair enough decision. Both had done wonderful jobs at provincial level. Wyllie was tough and had a reputation for being an excellent forward coach. Hart was a good communicator and had particular flair. Wyllie was a former All Black and this may have tipped the balance his way. Anyway, it was seen by some as a victory for the rest of New Zealand over Auckland.

Wyllie initially did incredibly well in the job and his team never suffered a defeat until mid-1990. But after that the wheels fell off and to those closely involved with the team, it became obvious he was struggling. Senior All Blacks, including captain Gary Whetton, approached the Rugby Union in the months before the 1991 World Cup to explain the situation. They felt Wyllie's personal uncertainties were having an effect on his ability to do the job.

Rugby Union chairman Eddie Tonks and his council were placed in a quandary. What to do so close to the World Cup? It was decided to ask Hart to assist the team. In hindsight it was a silly decision because Hart and Wyllie, while not enemies, were vastly different people. One was a Canterbury farmer, the other an Auckland city businessman. One was a forward, the other a back. One was blunt and rugged, the other more subtle and refined. Putting them together was

Alex Wyllie and John Hart with 1991 All Black coaching matchmaker Eddie Tonks.

like re-inventing the Odd Couple.

Hart was really put on the spot when Tonks approached him. He was desperately keen to be the All Black coach, and it was obvious Wyllie would not be carrying on after 1991. If he agreed to assist Wyllie, he was in effect entering a lose-lose situation. Wyllie did not want him there. If the All Blacks won, the triumph would be Wyllie's; if they lost, Hart would share the blame.

He asked to be made co-coach. To some this was perceived as power-grabbing. To me, it was Hart's way of trying to ensure he was able to make a meaningful contribution.

It didn't work. The Aucklanders in the All Blacks tended to talk to Hart, the southerners to Wyllie. The camp was divided and the All Blacks lost in the semi-final. I don't feel Hart's presence made any difference to the result. The great All Black team of the late 1980s was ageing and winding down. Hart didn't help or hurt them at the World Cup, but he did taint his image by being associated with a losing side.

That team was led by Gary Whetton, and Hart was blamed for that too. In 1990 Wyllie dropped Buck Shelford as All Black captain. Shelford to this day blames Hart, saying he helped orchestrate a pro-Auckland, anti-Shelford campaign. I don't believe it. Wyllie was the coach and wasn't a person to be pushed into making such a monumental decision. I've no doubt Hart felt Shelford wasn't the player he had been, but to say Shelford's dumping was Hart's doing and exclude Wyllie from the process is illogical.

Nevertheless Shelford had hundreds of thousands of strong admirers in New Zealand. He was an inspiring on-field leader and his sacking caused outrage, leading to the Bring Back Buck signs we see even today. Shelford blamed Hart and therefore so still do legions of his fans.

Before appointing the All Black coach in 1992, the New Zealand Rugby Union formed a sub-committee to examine the leading candidates' credentials. This group recommended Hart get the job, but the Rugby Union overruled it and went for Mains.

The arrival of Mains on the national scene exacerbated the anti-Auckland sentiment. Mains was a southern man. He was the Otago coach for a decade. He was proud of Otago. He was suspicious and parochial.

When Mains got the job, Hart was really on the outer and it seemed his time might have passed. He headed for the commentary box and did some coaching of New Zealand age teams. But Mains was hardly a roaring success. He lost his first test, to an invitation World XV, and lost the Bledisloe Cup that year. The next year the All Blacks beat the Lions 2–1 and were beaten by England. When they lost at home to France twice and away to Australia in 1994, things looked bleak. Mains wore the look of a haunted man.

He tended to be paranoid at the best of times, and his suspicious nature was hardly appeased in 1994 when the Union changed the national selection panel, dropping Peter Thorburn, with whom Mains related well, and opting instead for former All Black halfback Lin Colling. Though Colling had played in Otago with Mains and Kirton in the late 1960s, he was an Aucklander by the 1990s and Mains was concerned that Colling's promotion was part of a plot designed to eventually have Hart replace him as All Black coach.

Hart stood again for the position of All Black coach at the end of 1994. Not only that, but he made it clear he was not available to be a selector unless he was the coach as well. More Hart arrogance, said some. In another close decision, Mains kept his job. Hart was portrayed as disloyal and divisive, too ambitious by far.

Things turned around for the All Blacks through 1994–95. Outstanding players like Jonah Lomu, Andrew Mehrtens and Josh Kronfeld arrived on the scene and New Zealand was the team of the 1995 World Cup, even if South Africa won the final. The New Zealanders played exciting, open, pacy rugby and Mains was able to finish his All Black coaching stint that year with his head held high, even if his overall record was one of the poorest of any All Black coach.

Hart had a crack at the job yet again at the end of 1995. The landscape had changed. Mains stood down. He may have been tempted to try to carry on, but there was some feeling against him from within the Rugby Union because he was seen as having aligned himself too closely with the World Rugby Corporation plans to lure leading players away from the Rugby Union. Rugby had gone professional. The All Blacks seemed less a team than a brand. Marketing was the buzzword. It all seemed to fit in with Hart's corporate background and he duly got the nod.

For a start things went marvellously. In his first two years as coach, Hart's team lost only one of its 22 test matches. Hart smiled his toothy grin, the All Blacks won and New Zealanders decided he wasn't quite the ogre he had been painted. Maybe Aucklanders weren't so bad after all.

Then, in 1998, Hart suddenly found himself without Sean Fitzpatrick, Frank Bunce, Zinzan Brooke and Michael Jones. The wheels fell off and the All Blacks lost five matches in a row, in real terms it was the worst patch ever for New Zealand.

Hart's chirpiness disappeared and the vultures gathered. During this period he had some particularly bitter critics. Influential journalists Phil Gifford and Bob Howitt made no pretence of their feelings. They didn't rate Hart and said so at every opportunity. Radio host Murray Deaker transformed into a vehement Hart critic. Mains chipped in destructively from the sidelines.

Hart was exceedingly lucky to keep his job going into 1999. If Wayne Smith was sacked for losing two matches to Australia in 2000, Hart's survival in 1998 must be rated a miracle.

Though New Zealand won the Tri Nations Cup in 1999, the team was never totally convincing. There was a worrying 28–7 defeat by Australia in the last Bledisloe Cup fixture. Hart made a controversial decision to try to keep his players in cotton wool by excluding them from NPC matches before the World Cup. In hindsight this left them underprepared. The marketing of the team, including having an aeroplane painted in All Black colours, was way over the top, though this was not Hart's doing. The public expectation built massively.

At the World Cup, the All Blacks overcame potentially troublesome England first up, but were eliminated by France in an extraordinary semi-final. Leading 24–10 five minutes into the second half, the All Blacks suddenly fell to pieces, conceding 33 points in 28 minutes. It was a shocking capitulation. The outrage of the New Zealand rugby fans was incredible and it was Hart, not the players, who copped the flak. Things were not helped by a lacklustre defeat by South Africa in the third place playoff.

Hart fell on his sword, quitting before he even arrived back in New Zealand. Back home he did one interview with Paul Holmes on television and then virtually went into seclusion. There was a lot he could have said, about players not performing, about orchestrated media campaigns, about Mains' sniping. But he elected to say nothing.

I admired the way Hart let his successor, Wayne Smith, get on with the job without any public comment. The media would have fed on any Hart criticism of Smith. There was none, which was not a courtesy Mains paid Hart. But then the anti-Hart brigade will say Hart undermined Mains by standing against him.

Such is the nature of Hart. He has become a cause célèbre of New Zealand rugby. He wrote two books that sold hugely.

Even at the end of 2001, two years after he stood down as All Black coach, two

Photosport

Captain Taine Randell and coach John Hart face the media after the All Blacks had crashed out of the 1999 World Cup.

rugby biographies, those of Todd Blackadder and Norm Hewitt, dwelt on Hart, painting him in unflattering terms. He has had a tumultuous couple of decades in the New Zealand rugby spotlight.

When I think of Hart, I see him beaming after the win at Pretoria, looking forlorn after the shattering World Cup defeat by France three years later. I see him speaking confidently and with wit and insight to huge luncheon audiences, and then removing himself totally from the limelight back in his home in Auckland.

Hart is proof of what the All Black coach's job can do. It can lift a person, make him a national hero, and it can overpower him.

I've been pleased to know John Hart. I've listened to him and learnt from him. I know many others who feel the same. But I concede that for every person who admires him, there is another who thinks he was the worst thing to happen to New Zealand rugby. It seems absurd to say it of such an eloquent, friendly, talented person, but he can rightly be regarded as one of the most controversial figures in New Zealand's rugby history.

4. When Snortin' Horton came callin'

Players who have packed a punch

Never let it be said that a rugby writer must always be critical of players who have let fly at some stage with an almighty punch at an opponent. Such players deserve to be looked upon with scorn. But at the same time, those in the media who do have the courage to comment publicly on the 'punch-ers' and the 'punch-ees' have to sometimes be prepared to face those tricky moments when the players involved demand an explanation for what has been said. Let me explain.

In the world of modern rugby there are fewer punches thrown than in the good old days. The reasons for this are simple. Television has its all-seeing eyes glaring down at the play all the time, with stern men watching video replays of any incidents. The worst of these are then referred to judiciary committees that can suspend or fine the player or players involved.

It is simply not worth it to throw punches during games. Yet sometimes players do.

When I think back over infamous punches that were thrown in the good old days, it is not a warm list I come up with:

- Like the one Jack Hazlett threw at Mike Weston in front of the Royal Box at Twickenham when the All Blacks played England in 1967. The Poo-baas of the Rugby Football Union were evidently not impressed.
- Or Colin Meads landing one on the jaw of the Welsh hooker Jeff Young when New Zealand played Wales at Christchurch in 1969. (New Zealanders tried to say, 'But that Young, he deliberately tried to drive his jaw into poor Colin's fist!')
- And, of course, many people claimed Kevin Skinner threw enough punches to swing a test series New Zealand's way against South Africa in 1956. Kevin thinks its all a load of exaggerated hooey.

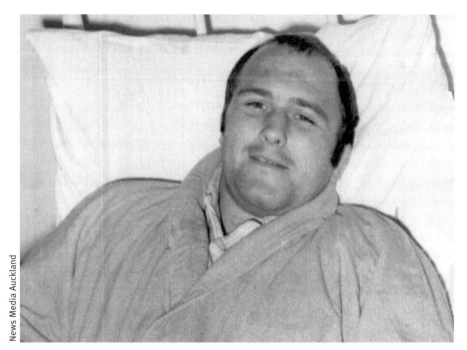

Welsh prop Jeff Young recuperates in Burwood Hospital, Christchurch, after copping one on the jaw from Colin Meads in the first test of the 1969 series.

- How about when Haden was having slight difficulty in the All Blacks match at Perpignan in 1981? He asked the Northland prop forward Wayne Neville to 'sort it out', so the rookie All Black did with a crack that reverberated around the stadium. Thereafter the lineouts went much easier for Haden.
- Remember when Wayne Shelford dispensed some bush justice to Welshman Huw Richards during the 1987 World Cup semi-final at Brisbane? Richards was out to cause trouble and made what seemed to be an unprovoked attack on Gary Whetton. Shelford, with an impressive right cross, floored the Welshman. It was a case of double bad news for Richards because when he came to, he found that referee Kerry Fitzgerald had ordered him from the field.
- Finally, my 'favourite' punch (hush my mouth . . . how can an honest rugby reporter condone violence by having a favourite rugby punch of all time?). This came when the 1977 British Lions began their New Zealand tour of New Zealand on a bitter, slushy day in Masterton, playing Wairarapa-Bush. Included in the Lions team was an imposing lock named Nigel Horton. He came to New Zealand with a big reputation as a strong man, a controlling man and one not to be trifled with, if you get my drift. He had been a copper back home in Birmingham, a town where it was known one had to be tough and rugged to survive.

    Phil Bennett's tourists looked as though they were set to roll over Wairarapa-Bush.

It was a freezing, if not snowy, day and tries and points came with regularity. The local lads gave it heaps, but the points stacked up against them. Eight tries were scored by the tourists (four points for a try in those days) and the visitors won 41–13.

But when I think of the game I cannot recall the tries. What I remember is the crack of a punch landing on cold exposed skin. The thrower was Wairarapa's lock Ian Turley and the man on the receiving end was the Lions' toughest player — Nigel Horton.

Loyal locals watching in the stands said that Horton had asked for it. He had been a frightener right throughout the game until Turley decided to make a point. His punch sliced through the air, Horton took it on the side of the head and was knocked out. The crowd of 9000 cheered. For them, it was the most warming incident of an icy day. Lions manager George Burrell winced: 'It is hard to forgive a punch like that.' But it was a beauty.

After several seconds, Horton tried to raise himself from the mud. He was advised, though, to remain on his knees lest he fall again from his lofty height of 1.98m. Some of the British press noted that it was the first time they had seen Horton decked in such a way. 'Normally,' said one writer, 'he's the one doing the dishing out.' For his part, Turley was known to have been raised as a rugby player of the strong silent type, not given to rough play. The word came down from his dressing room afterwards that he had had a 'gutsful' of Horton's tactics and had decided enough was enough.

Gulp. 'Yes,' I replied, thinking he was much bigger in full physical close-up.

There was an aftermath to my silent admiration of Turley's punch and my scorn for the way Horton had been playing. I reported my views on the incident on TV One's various summary programmes over the next few days and maybe Horton, lying in his Masterton Hospital bed, was watching TV. He must have been.

Fast-forward now two years, to the 1979 All Black tour of England. I was there and commentated a game in which Graham Mourie's team beat Midland Division. In the Midlands second row was Horton. He played well enough and I hope I commentated fairly on his play that day. No problems there. I didn't know the man; indeed I hardly recalled the Turley punch afterwards. At least, not until I was standing in the reception room at Welford Road in Leicester and felt a firm grip on my arm. I turned and looked up at the imposing figure of Mr Nigel Looking-Very-Impressive-and-Mean Horton.

'Hello,' he said, 'do you remember me?'

Gulp. 'Yes,' I replied, thinking he was much bigger in full physical close-up.

'Well I remember what you said about me after that Wairarapa game two years ago. So now I want to know just what the hell you know about rugby.'

Ian Turley (left) was the thrower and Nigel Horton —quite obviously — the receiver of the punch during the Lions' match against Wairarapa-Bush in 1977.

This was indeed a tight spot for me. I was feeling vulnerable, especially with several of his large team-mates closing in. They were well primed for a 'kill' of a media man. My mouth opened and shut several times and nothing came out. Suddenly I felt that commentating on punches in rugby matches had not been a sound career path.

'Come on,' he continued, 'you're supposed to be a bloody commentator. You're supposed to be a bloody expert on the game. But you obviously know nothin' that's wot. You know nothin' about me and yet you made those judgements about me. How come?'

As he continued standing over me, I made a snap decision. All I could do was fall back on my own strengths. I drew myself up to my full height (seemingly several feet below his towering authority) and away I went, thinking I had nothing to lose.

'I know more about you than you think,' I said, doing my best to look him in the eye. 'You are Nigel E. Horton, you are ex-Moseley club, and now you play in Toulouse in France. You began your test career in 1969 and have played 19 tests for England. You actually have been dropped several times in your 10 years, but have always managed to win your way back into favour. You've never played a test against the All Blacks, but you toured New Zealand with the British Lions in 1977. You only played a couple of games

Quinn has "converted" one of his knockers

TELEVISION One's much travelled Rugby commentator, Keith Quinn, has copped plenty of flak this last year or two.

From PETER REILLY

The genial Quinn has conceded on tour that he gets his fair share of letters informing him of a preference for Radio NZ's John Howson's commentary over-riding his filming.

But 'Quinny' takes it all good-humouredly in his stride, bides his time then strikes a telling blow in his own defence which wins him most times a friend and admirer for life.

Last week on tour Quinn got off-stride in an after-match verbal tussle with the extrovert Midlands Counties lock, Nigel Horton.

"As the 'going' quickened I got the impression young Quinn was in for a hard ride. At the finish he won in a canter."

The crowded, jostling scene was set in the Leicester club-rooms after that stunning, five tries to one win over the Midlands side.

In a jammed tight group Quinn started small talk about the game with Horton and inadvertently stumbled over just what number in the lineout the lanky and sometimes controversial Horton had jumped at that day.

Horton: "Hey, wot d'you know about th' game, aye? You're s'posed to be a commentater, you're s'posed to be a bluddy expert on th' game. But y'know nothin', y'don't even know wot number I jump at."

Quinn: "Listen to me mate, I'm a pro. I know more about you than you know yourself."

Horton: "Garn, y'know nothin' mate. Wot d'you know about me?"

Quinn: "Nigel E. Horton, 31, ex Moseley and now Toulouse, began Test career 1969, capped 19 times for England, dropped five times by the England selectors, has never toured for England, has never played against the All Blacks in a Test, toured New Zealand with 1977 British Lions, played against Wairarapa-Bush in tour opener, stopped big punch and had to leave the field, played against Taranaki and then against Otago where he broke his thumb, returned home to England and replaced on tour by Bill Beaumont. I've seen a photograph of him standing with an attractive woman and a small boy outside a big house in Toulouse where he runs a bar having served previously as a Birmingham policeman — and is a specialist No. 5 lineout jumper.

"Take that."

Like a machine gun Quinn rapid-fired bullet after bullet. In amazement Horton's head swung like a pendulum around our little group.

His jaw gaped open, his eyes widened in awe. Then Horton broke the short silence prompted by Quinn's oration, by tipping forward over his pint of bitter and said, almost reverently: "I bow to you Quinn, I bow to you."

Subsequently I overheard Horton introducing Quinn to his mates as "The Mighty Quinn."

Given the chance, the bespectacled Quinn's

KEITH QUINN

smile would have beamed all the way back to his detractors in New Zealand — without need of the satellite link that has the unfortunate habit of leaving his commentaries high and dry on occasions.

How the 8 O'clock newspaper treated the Horton-Quinn 'reunion'.

before you broke your thumb and had to return home. I have seen a photograph of you standing outside a large villa in Toulouse with an attractive blonde woman and a small boy. I think you run a restaurant there now after you used to be a policeman in Birmingham. You wore No. 5 today and you are a specialist in that position.'

I stopped and finished and looked at my man. What would the man with the tough-guy reputation do to me next, me a mere puny sportscaster?

I waited. The others in the group, standing by menacingly, waited as well.

Horton stared into his pint for what seemed like an eternity. He looked up at me, paused and grinned. Then he spoke the most beautiful words. 'I bow to you, Quinn, I bow to you. You *do* know a bit about me. So now let's go and have a drink.'

Rugby, the family game

There are two recorded instances of five brothers playing for one New Zealand team in a first class match.

In July 1903 the Smith family had five brothers in the Bush team that played Wairarapa at Greytown. They were fullback George, centre Bill and forwards Gordon, Bob and Campbell. The Smiths did Bush no good for Wairarapa won the match 16–0.

Then in 1961 five Clarke brothers represented Waikato against Thames Valley at Te Aroha. Two of the Clarkes, Don (fullback) and Ian (prop), were very well known All Blacks. The other members of the family were Doug (centre), Graeme and Brian (locks). Waikato won the match 11–8.

5. Louis the Lip
Luyt's 1995 World Cup speech

June 24, 1995 is definitely not a day New Zealand rugby supporters rate very highly. Not only did their team's dreams come clattering down from the lofty expectation of winning the World Cup final against the Springboks, but there were other critical factors that now make that day's memories disagreeable for New Zealanders to recall.

We know now that the All Blacks went onto the field for the final, for what should have been the game of their lives, in a less-than-perfect physical state. We will never know if it was 'innocent' food poisoning the team suffered at their hotel two days before the final, or whether they were they maliciously poisoned, as some, including All Blacks coach Laurie Mains, have suggested. The food poisoning of so many in the team and the suggestion that South Africa people were responsible acted as an unfortunate backdrop to what should have been a day of true glory for world rugby.

But there was a third factor, which added to the day's misery, and it perhaps topped off the torture for all New Zealanders. Not only were many of the All Blacks ill, not only did they lose the game, in extra time by 15–12, but there is also the recollection of the speech made by the President of the South African Rugby Football Union, Dr Louis Luyt, at the official aftermatch dinner.

To some New Zealanders, the displeasure at what was said that night to the assembled throng has irritated them almost as much as the food poisoning, or the match result.

Feelings of deep anger and exasperation were added to previous disappointments when details of what Luyt said in his address in Johannesburg filtered back home. It was reported that what he said so horrified the All Black players that a momentum of anger rose up which led to a team walkout in front of hundreds at the function.

However, seen in a cold light and with the passage of time, we can now judge more clearly what it was that was so irritating to the All Black players. And there is a balance. We must now ask whether the New Zealand team was legitimately angry or

The Webb Ellis Cup.

just blind with disappointment at having been sick and having lost the final.

The circumstances of the function and the controversial speech by Luyt had some background. It was the Saturday night after the dramatic final. The dinner was held at the Gallagher Estate on the edge of Johannesburg. It was the official post-Rugby World Cup dinner. Some of the news media were invited to attend but what with newspaper deadlines or broadcast arrangements, or maybe even because of the difficulties and risk of night transport in that tough city, there were very few reporters present. Certainly there were no New Zealand news media present. So what happened, in terms of the New Zealand team's behaviour at the dinner, has gone unchallenged since.

We know it was certainly appropriate that Luyt spoke after dinner had been served. He was after all the President of the host nation for the World Cup. What was not appropriate was the delay in getting the dinner started. The South African team, perhaps swept along with celebrations in other parts of Johannesburg, was extremely late in arriving. This certainly irritated a number of people present, not the least being members of the New Zealand side.

Added to that, when the Springboks did appear, what Luyt said grievously offended some members of the All Black team, so much so that several players approached their manager, Colin Meads, and asked his permission to remonstrate in some way with 'that bastard'.

However, I have a full transcript of the Luyt speech and, with due respect, it is hardly packed with insults, as All Blacks present have led us to believe.

In various newspaper quotes and in several books by All Black players since, we have been told that two things upset the players that night. First was an inferred claim in the Luyt speech that South Africa would have won the World Cups in 1987 and 1991 if they had participated, and that somehow the first two World Cups were hollow victories for New Zealand (1987) and Australia (1991).

The other thing to cause agitation was the awarding of a gold watch by Luyt to the Welsh referee Derek Bevan, the insinuation being that Bevan was in some way being rewarded by South Africa for easing their passage through to the winning of the Cup. Let us deal with the first affront. What Luyt actually said was this (taken

Welcome to my world . . . Louis Luyt hosts author Keith Quinn at Ellis Park, his own private stadium in Johannesburg.

from a sound tape recording):

'. . . This is a great day. This is what we have been waiting for so many years. We boasted in '87 that the real World Cup was not won by New Zealand because we were not there. Then again in '91, we boasted again. We were not there. Now in '95 we proved if we were there we would have won.'

With no other references in the transcript to the insult which was so upsetting to the New Zealanders, that must be the part of the address which caused so much offence.

But why were the All Blacks so upset? Elsewhere in the address Luyt pays handsome tribute to the New Zealand team: 'It was wonderful to play against the All Blacks today. I believe today we saw the two best teams on the planet . . . the All Blacks are the greatest rugby nation with us. Not next to us, with us. Because next time they will beat us and the time after that we will beat them.'

Nice words, I would have thought, but the All Blacks, overall, were angry at what was said, especially one has to presume about the demeaning of the 1987 win in the final in Auckland.

Now, years later, let's imagine the excitement of South Africa on that great night for them. They had waited so long for that moment, through years of disconnection and isolation from the rest of the world, especially from their rugby brothers. And that night they were triumphant at their first entry into the World Cup arena.

Wouldn't it be understandable that their praise of themselves be excessive in their hour of reflective glory? Even mightily so?

But even if we allow for some of the words to be totally celebratory of the Springbok win, just how insulting was the whole thing to the All Blacks? Looking at the speech on balance, I, for one, do not think it was.

Dare it be asked: was it not just a case, as one player of the New Zealand team has confided to me since, of the team just not wanting to be at the dinner at all? Did they perhaps prefer to be away from the raucous and yes, perhaps overstated, words of celebration spoken by Luyt? Maybe even some of the All Blacks were still ill? Or, whisper, whisper, maybe when several of the team approached Luyt and remonstrated with him afterwards they showed they were not very good losers.

As for the gold watch presentation to Derek Bevan, Dr Luyt told me himself, when I interviewed him for *Legends of the All Blacks* in 1999, that he had thought at the function that his only task would be to make the welcoming dinner remarks. At the last minute, however, he was asked by (on the tape the name sounds like Jan Vorster of the Gauteng Lions Referees) the South African Rugby Referees Association to present an award for the Best Referee at the Tournament. Luyt agreed to do this and Derek Bevan of Wales was called up. The presentation was in the form of a gold watch. Such an award is subjective, of course, but at the time Bevan was the world's highest 'capped' referee.

There might have been an even bigger uproar had the watch gone to England's Ed Morrison, who had controlled the final earlier that day. Believe me, the New Zealanders were scathing in their opinions of his performance, too!

Luyt told me: 'I should have refused to do it [hand the watch to Bevan], but stupidly I did it, and people now think I gave him the watch. I didn't. The referees decided I should give it to him and it was handed to me just before I went up.'

In truth, only by the widest conspiracy theory could it be claimed that Derek Bevan somehow 'assisted' the South Africans to win the World Cup. Bevan had always been a man of impeccable rugby personality. Certainly at that World Cup he had refereed the Springboks in their very close, wind-swept and rainy semi-final win over France in Durban, but using the New Zealand fans' logic of scorn it could be said he also assisted the All Blacks at the tournament. After all, he controlled one of their games as well, the quarterfinal against Scotland at Pretoria.

Concerning the whole dinner party, All Black manager Colin Meads has told me: '. . . Louis [Luyt] was full of pride and enjoyment at the thrill of winning the World Cup, which I can understand . . . I recall that before the dinner I said [to the All Blacks] that we were going to do everything right with it. Win or lose we were going to wear bow ties and maintain our dignity. Then the South African team was an hour late in getting there. We ended up just waiting around for them to come. Then with Louis' speech on top of all [the other] things, it was a bit hard to take for some of the players and two of the players came to me and asked if they could go and tell him what they think of him. I said, "As long as you do it politely".'

'Everyone says the All Blacks walked out in disgust, but that wasn't quite right because other teams were going then, too. I know the French were gone before us. So a fantastic occasion ended up a sad affair and I felt very sorry. . . . I rang Louis the next day. I didn't apologise for the team, but I said to him . . . we weren't happy with his words and thanking the referee like he did. Being New Zealanders, I told him we took umbrage at that.'

Luyt told me: 'I should have refused to do it [hand the watch to Bevan], but stupidly I did it, and people now think I gave him the watch. I didn't.'

My own view, having read the transcript of the Luyt address, and having spoken to a number of people who were there, is that the All Blacks were, by the lateness of the hour, possibly suffering from the very human condition of deep distress after their loss in the final that day. By then it might also be assumed that their displeasure had been assisted by liquid comfort. Therefore their logic streams might not have been functioning in the clearest way. Luyt also expressed that view to me.

To this day some of those All Blacks will not talk about what happened in the World Cup final that June afternoon. They prefer only to mention other factors, including the food poisoning, the after-dinner function and Louis Luyt's role in it. No one seems to want to recall that in a furiously tough World Cup climax, which went into extra time, and from which it was always known one team had to lose, it was the New Zealanders who suffered the defeat.

There seems enough evidence to conclude that despite the obvious and understandable disappointments of the final and the dinner which followed, there are still a number of members of the 1995 All Black party who have been in a state of denial about what happened that fateful day.

6. Keeping abreast of the times

Streakers arrive in the garden of Eden

Streaking is not generally a pastime that we associate with rugby. It seems more suited to summer sports watching . . . sun, beer, sun-block, picnic baskets, sun-hats — that sort of thing. Thus cricketers have over the years got used to seeing semi-naked, or even fully naked, men and women in various stages of insobriety haring towards them. Rugby, with more of an overcoats, scarves and thermos flasks image, doesn't really lend itself to streaking.

There have been some memorable exceptions, though. The most famous rugby streaker, and maybe even the most famous streaker of all, was a well-endowed 24-year-old woman named Erica Roe who used the halftime interval in the England-Australia test at Twickenham in January 1982 to display her wares.

The Brits loved it. 'Titters at Twickers' type headlines abounded. Even the generally sober *Rothmans Rugby Yearbook* referred to a highlight of the season as being 'when a lady named Erica erupted onto the field like a galleon in full sail, but minus her spinnakers'.

The streak came while beefy England captain Bill Beaumont was imploring his men to greater endeavours. Beaumont felt some of his team, looking past him, seemed somehow distracted, and asked one of them what was the matter. 'Everyone's watching a girl over there who seems to have your bum on her chest, Bill,' came the reply. I don't know if that's a genuine quote, but it has been reported at various times down the years, and I love it, as will anyone who can recall Beaumont's ample hind quarters.

One of the first streaks recorded, at least at a major sports event, was performed by Michael O'Brien at Twickenham in 1974 while England and Wales were locked in mortal combat. There was a famous photo taken that day, of a local policeman, PC

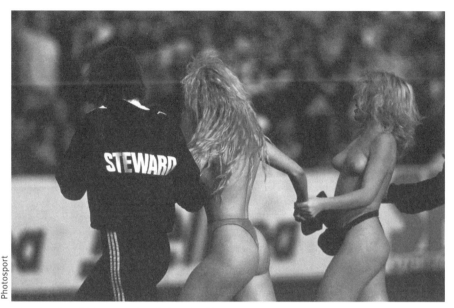

Photosport

The Cheeky Chicks provided light relief in a dull test match at Eden Park in 1991.

Perry, leading away O'Brien and thoughtfully covering the offending body parts with his helmet.

New Zealand has had the odd memorable rugby streaking moment, but the one that really stands out occurred on August 24, 1991, during the Bledisloe Cup match at Eden Park. New Zealand won a generally uninspiring match 6–3, but those at the ground may well recall the occasion more for the appearance of two female streakers than for the quality of the rugby.

The two impressively endowed blondes, Samantha Carroll and Kelly Hawkins, were Australians who were part of the touring Cheeky Chicks strip troupe and the stunt was great publicity for their business.

Their streak proved a huge hit. The players seemed shocked and then amused, while the police and security officials took the incident in good spirit.

Meanwhile, up in the commentary box, Television New Zealand's Keith Quinn and Earle Kirton could not believe what they were seeing. Said Kirton on air: 'Gee, I wonder who they are?' This was followed by Quinn's: 'More importantly Earle, what are their phone numbers?'

Keith's mother was not impressed, but fortunately his wife was not watching!

The streakers' free spirits did nothing to help Australian kicker Michael Lynagh, who managed to successfully kick only one of seven attempts. 'If the four "points" we added to the match had counted, the Australians would have won seven to six,' joked Samantha afterwards.

7. Enough to make you sick

The 1995 food poisoning saga

Of the many controversies that the All Blacks have become embroiled in during a century of test matches, few were as strange as the case of the food poisoning before the 1995 World Cup final against South Africa. And it's a subject that has not gone away.

Late in 2001, two major New Zealand rugby biographies were published. In Norm Hewitt's book, *Gladiator*, he rubbishes the notion that the All Blacks were deliberately poisoned and seems to feel certain members of the All Black management raised the poisoning as an excuse after the defeat. Yet in Todd Blackadder's biography, *Loyal*, author Phil Gifford has a different view. (Quite why the issue needed to be raised is beyond me as Blackadder was not even in the All Black team at that World Cup.) He writes: 'It's a sad reflection more of personal animosity than reality that Keith Quinn, for example, in his autobiography suggested that he doubted the World Cup All Blacks "were affected too much in the playing of that epic final" by the vicious gastric illness that swept through the team.'

So opinion on the issue remains as sharply divided as ever. I covered the entire World Cup, saw the All Blacks in the lead-up to the final, commentated on the final and spoke to the team management immediately afterwards. I can report only what I saw. This is how I saw it . . .

The news media was first alerted to illness within the All Black camp on the Friday morning before the final. We were at a press conference at Ellis Park, where Louis Luyt was announcing the establishment of SANZAR rugby and the Tri Nations tournament. Leon Hagen was filming the press conference for TVNZ, but was pulled away to film the arrival of the All Blacks for their familiar Friday pre-test walkabout on the field.

At a speech later that year, I heard Laurie Mains tell an attentive Dunedin audience that his players were so sick they could not leave their hotel to visit Ellis Park that day. In an interview I did with Mains in 1999, Laurie's version had changed. The

Desperately seeking Suzy . . . coach Laurie Mains had no doubt about who was responsible for the All Blacks' World Cup final loss to South Africa in 1995.

players had indeed visited Ellis Park, but were 'not there long' because of the illness.

At Ellis Park before the final, I interviewed Brian Lochore, one of the All Black team management, as he arrived on the field. His words to the New Zealand audience were to the effect that, 'Yes, there were stomach problems two days ago, but today everyone is OK.' I took those remarks to be absolute fact, as anyone would coming from a man such as Lochore.

The match, a tough, grim affair, went to extra time where Joel Stransky succeeded with a drop kick and Andrew Mehrtens narrowly missed with his attempt. The Springboks won 15–12 after two hours of bruising, rugged football.

Straight after the game I rushed to the door of the All Black dressing room. First out were assistant coach Earle Kirton and manager Colin Meads. Both were visibly disappointed, but neither mentioned any loss of power from the All Blacks because of food poisoning or illness. They were more concerned with what they felt was a less than satisfactory performance by referee Ed Morrison.

In the TV interviews immediately after the game, All Black captain Sean Fitzpatrick made no mention of sickness within the team, and neither did Mains or Meads.

As far as I can recall, the first time a strong assertion was made that the All Blacks might have become ill from the effects of eating or drinking something suspect came on Paul Holmes' show on NewstalkZB on the Monday morning in New Zealand. Holmes apparently phoned Johannesburg, where the All Blacks had had a tired and emotional day around their hotel pool and bar. He interviewed Mains and it was at that point that the story really broke, and the wording around the story changed too. 'Sickness'

Nelson Mandela in the now famous No 6 Springbok jersey.

became 'food poisoning' and finally 'poisoned'.

The clear suggestion was that something had afflicted the All Blacks in the team hotel. Were they affected by bad water, bad hamburgers, bad coffee, bad tea . . . or what? All four were mentioned along the way as, shall we say, definite possibilities.

In his book, *Laurie Mains*, Mains also mentioned a black woman working in the hotel around the time of the final. Her name, apparently, was Suzy, though nobody ever pinned down her identity further. According to Mains' book, she was possibly worthy of investigation by rugby authorities, but, when I talked to Laurie at Ellis Park in 1999 while researching *Legends of the All Blacks*, he did not mention the Suzy story in detail. In fact he said: 'That name should never have made it into the book.'

Things became even murkier in 2000 when one of the South African security guards who followed the 1995 team, Rory Steyn, wrote that Suzy had indeed 'poisoned' the team. Mains was then quoted as saying this 'effectively vindicated' his version of what had happened and that he didn't know 'why on earth Keith Quinn continues to attempt to discredit me'.

But, hang on. In Laurie's book he says there was a Suzy. In 1999, he said to me it was 'unfortunate' that the name went into his book because 'that wasn't a name that was given to me'. Then in 2000 he agrees with Mr Steyn that there was a Suzy!

To add to the confusion, Steyn declared that it was not water, tea, coffee or hamburger but 'a bad fish lunch'. I have heard Colin Meads reckon it was the milk that made him crook!

I gain some nourishment for my views by the number of times that I have heard Sean Fitzpatrick speak at dinners and functions since 1995. When he is asked to comment on the food poisoning story, his reply usually begins along the lines of, 'You'll have to ask Laurie about all that.' I have never heard Fitzy offer much more.

Fitzpatrick says in his book *Turning Point: the Making of a Captain*, 'Mains had become paranoid, perhaps justifiably so. But it was rubbing off on his players, who had to wait to have the team room swept for electronic bugs each session in case the South Africans were recording the All Blacks talks and tactics. Mains had ordered a separate dining room, too, to get the team out of the public glare. It was all adding to the pressure.'

Mains is a great worrier, there is no doubt about that. And he is ever one for conspiracy theories. Since that World Cup I have read about his 'investigation' of the food poisoning incident, of links he has discovered via a prominent New Zealand businessman, to English bookies wanting South Africa to win. From there it's only a short hop to deliberate poisoning.

In the end, you believe what you want. I'm sure some of the All Blacks were sick in the day or two before the final. But I doubt they were affected too much during the final. It was a long, close match. The South Africans out-thought New Zealand, who had been the form team of the tournament, and, spurred on by Nelson Mandela in the grandstand, wearing François Pienaar's No 6 jersey, a stadium full of supporters and 43 million more South Africans desperately hoping they would win, they scraped home.

The All Blacks departed South Africa having played wonderfully well throughout the tournament, and having taken part in a great occasion. Why not leave it at that, instead of claiming sabotage by way of food poisoning?

And as for my own interest in the story, let me put it this way: I am a reporter. As such, I have always wanted to get to the bottom of the so-called 'food poisoning'. That's all. Just to find a clear, direct and definitive version of what actually happened that famous/infamous day. It played a huge part in New Zealand rugby history and so far I have not had it cleared up satisfactorily. With to date six different ways the team is reported to have been afflicted, I am still searching.

No laughing matter

New Zealand v South Africa test matches are no laughing matter, never have been.

Bruce McLeod, the All Black hooker from 1964–70, told me a story not long before his death in 1996. McLeod, Angus to his team-mates, said he always liked to take the field next to Colin Meads. It made him feel more confident to have the indomitable Pinetree nearby.

According to McLeod, the superstition dated back to the fourth test against the Springboks, at Eden Park in 1965. 'There was a big build-up to the test. They'd won the third test with a big comeback so the series stood at 2–1 to us before that last match. I was pretty nervous. The players happened to be standing in a line just before running onto Eden Park. I looked across to the Springboks and they looked very big and grim. I whispered to Piney, "Geez, they look ready." He never even blinked. He just said, "I'm f... ready too." I felt so good when I heard him say that. I've never forgotten that feeling of comfort.'

To Springboks, the feeling going into a test against the All Blacks is equally intense, as is illustrated by this story of Joggie Jansen, the dynamic centre who had such a devastating impact on Brian Lochore's team during the 1970 series in South Africa. Jansen was still on the test scene six years later, when Andy Leslie's All Blacks arrived in South Africa, and was named as a reserve. During a pre-test photo session, he was asked to smile for the camera. Jansen refused, saying: 'You don't smile when you may be playing the All Blacks.'

8. Selections, salutations and sedition

All Black team announcements

The announcement of an All Black team, especially the first one of a season, and even more so when there is a new coach in charge, is dramatic and provokes much discussion.

Sometimes, the inclusion of one player will stir the talkback callers and Letters to the Editor writers into action. For instance, through much of the 1990s, whenever Auckland loose forward Mark Carter was named, there would be howls of derision. I always thought of Carter as a talented and effective flanker, but somehow his presence in the All Blacks used to signify (to those poor souls who look for these things) an Auckland bias.

There have been some heated debates, often spanning provincial boundaries and several seasons, over All Black selections. Whether it's over who is the better halfback, Sid Going or Chris Laidlaw, or the better fullback, Allan Hewson or Robbie Deans, or who would make the best captain, the many rugby experts in New Zealand have strong opinions.

All Black team announcements used to be made soon after the final trial matches at Athletic Park. Players, officials, the media and other hangers-on would gather in the lounge under the main grandstand and wait while the selectors met in another room, just along the corridor. This was a time of great tension. Beer would be drunk, sausage rolls and sandwiches eaten, and the merits and demerits of various players would be discussed. Players would try to relax and chat, but their eyes would return repeatedly to the doorway. 'How much longer?' they'd think.

Sometimes a player would force his way into the team after an exceptional trial, as did Grahame Thorne in 1967 and Eric Tindill in 1935. Sometimes it became clear an old favourite might struggle to make the team, as happened when George Nepia

News Media Auckland

Mick Williment (left) and Fergie McCormick, the man who displaced him for the 1967 All Blacks tour of the British Isles and France.

was outplayed by Mike Gilbert in 1935.

Eventually the chairman of the New Zealand union would call for silence and prepare to announce the team, and there would be a hush of expectation. He'd rattle through the team in that formal initials-not-first-names style and we'd try to quickly work out who was in, and who wasn't.

Two team announcements I particularly recall occurred in 1967 and 1974. In 1967, Wellington fullback Mick Williment was omitted from the team Fred Allen and his co-selectors chose to tour Britain. In his place went Fergie McCormick. This was a sensation because Williment, a fine kicker and solid player, was the incumbent. But Allen liked the running ability and sure tackling of McCormick and went with him. It turned out to be an inspired selection.

We'd have had even more to talk about that day if we'd known what went on behind the scenes. It has since transpired that the selectors inadvertently chose 31 players and it was only a check by chairman Tom Morrison that revealed the fact, just before he read out the names.

Back into a huddle went the selectors and Williment was the unfortunate player who had his name deleted, the Unlucky No 31.

In 1974, likeable John (J.J.) Stewart was into his second season as All Black coach. There had been rumblings that he wasn't happy with what he was seeing from the All Blacks, and all sorts of names were being tossed about as candidates for the tour of Australia that year.

But no one was prepared for the brutal way he discarded so many incumbents.

Andy Leslie . . . sensational '74 selection.

By the time the dust had settled that afternoon at Athletic Park, we realised that Stewart, and his co-selectors Jack Gleeson and Eric Watson, had drafted in 15 new All Blacks to their 25-man squad.

Wellington No 8 Andy Leslie, who had never appeared for the All Blacks, had replaced Ian Kirkpatrick as captain. It was a mark of Kirkpatrick's quality that he was the first to tap Leslie on the shoulder and congratulate him. At the time, it was widely believed that Leslie was chosen primarily to be captain, but Stewart has since told me that was not the case. He was chosen as a player and only after the 25 names were finalised did the selectors set about naming their captain.

'I didn't feel Kirky really enjoyed the captaincy, so I floated the idea of going for someone else. When they asked me who, I thought of Andy Leslie, who seemed to do a good job in Wellington and looked to have the maturity for the role.'

Wellingtonians at least had long considered Leslie would make a fine New Zealand representative and, as early as 1967, he had been tipped as potential All Black material. *Evening Post* sports editor Gabriel David had him in his touring team the night before the 1967 team to tour Britain and France was announced. David was right — he was just seven years early!

Kirkpatrick, while no longer captain, at least kept his place. Gone were leading figures Sid Going, Alex Wyllie, Kent Lambert, Hamish Macdonald, Sam Strachan and Andy Haden. In their place came such players as Bob Barber, Joe Morgan, Duncan Robertson, Graeme Crossman, Kerry Tanner, Doug Bruce, Ash Gardiner, Kevin Eveleigh, Bruce Gemmell, John Callesen, Jon McLachlan, Greg Kane and Billy Bush.

Interestingly, Going wasn't off the scene long. By the end of the year, Stewart was so keen to have the champion from Northland back that he arranged to have Sid's farm managed in his absence and also picked Sid's older brother, fullback Ken, when the team to tour Britain was named. Hamish Macdonald and Kent Lambert were also recalled.

In its way, Laurie Mains' first All Black team, chosen in 1992, was nearly as incredible. Mains seemed similarly determined to make his mark immediately. He dumped the captain Gary Whetton, and also, among others, Alan Whetton, Terry Wright, Zinzan Brooke — all Aucklanders. In came new All Blacks Frank Bunce, Richard Turner, Arran Pene, Mark Cooksley, and also Greg Cooper, who had worn the New Zealand jersey briefly in 1986. Bunce, who had established his reputation when representing Manu Samoa at the 1991 World Cup, provided great service to the All Blacks, but the other changes were not particularly successful and eventually Mains returned to Brooke. He was to drop Kirwan, Michael Jones and Grant Fox — three more Aucklanders — before the next test, only to reselect them soon after.

There was further drama when Mains had to cast about at the last moment for a captain. Having decided to discard Gary Whetton, he intended putting Mike Brewer into the captain's job. He knew Brewer well, having worked with him in the Otago side. But Brewer was hurt during the final trial and could not be selected. This placed Mains in a quandary. After discussing the matter with some trusted advisers, including Brian Lochore, he went for Sean Fitzpatrick, even though Fitzpatrick was one of the Aucklanders of whom Mains was so suspicious.

It turned out to be a happy decision, because Fitzpatrick captained New Zealand for the next six seasons and grew into a wonderful leader.

There does seem to be a tendency for All Black coaches to favour the players with whom they are familiar. Thus Mains was keen to have Brewer as his captain and when he became All Black coach the number of Otago players increased. Brian Lochore, when he took over the coach's job in 1985, came from a background of having coached Wairarapa-Bush. New Zealand trial teams and All Black selections soon included such names as Anderson, Harvey and Kapene, all solid Wairarapa-Bush performers who previously had not attracted much attention nationally.

But new All Black coaches also often seem determined to prove their point. They want to show they are calling the shots. We saw that at the end of 2001 when John Mitchell, having risen meteorically to be the All Black coach, named his 30-man squad to tour Britain. Mitchell had promised it would be his team and lived up to that promise. He dropped Christian Cullen, Jeff Wilson and Taine Randell. When he had the opportunity to let Cullen off lightly by saying he was not considered because of injury, he did not do so. It was as if he wanted to make the point that the new 'Gaffer', as Mitchell described himself, had dropped Cullen.

In one swoop, Mitchell got rid of two genuine All Black legends in Cullen and Wilson, and also Randell, a former captain and player who had appeared in all three loose forward positions since his international debut in 1995.

During the tour in 2001, Mitchell confided that he had left a couple of players at home so

Photosport

John Mitchell was true to his word when he chose his first All Black team.

that they might hopefully get back their desire to be All Blacks. This led to speculation about whom he might be referring. Cullen? Wilson? Randell?

There will always be debates when All Black teams are named. In 2001 we asked if David Hill of Waikato was truly better than Carlos Spencer of Auckland, and whether Roger Randle of Waikato was truly better than Jeff Wilson. In 1962, the New Zealand selectors dropped Ian Clarke, Dennis Young, Kel Tremain and Colin Meads for their second test team against Australia at Carisbrook. With all due respect to the four replacements, Keith Nelson, Stan Meads, John Creighton and Jules Le Lievre, many rugby followers were bewildered. If there'd been talkback radio back then, callers would have had a field day. It would surely have been the same in 1977 when Ian Kirkpatrick was dropped from the team to tour France, the replacement loose forward being Waikato loose forward Dick Myers. While Myers built a solid provincial record, he never had the impact on a game that Kirkpatrick could.

But such is the way with All Black teams. If everyone agreed, there would be no need for selectors.

Mitchell confided that he had left a couple of players at home so that they might hopefully get back their desire to be All Blacks.

One aspect of All Black selections has changed. We no longer have Athletic Park, and very rarely have trials. There is so much big rugby now, what with the Super 12 and the NPC, that there is not really a need. So the chance for all the players to gather in one place to strut their stuff does not present itself.

All Black team announcements are just as important and create just as much debate. But in recent years the announcement tends to be made at a press conference, or be timed to coincide with a major news bulletin, such as television's 6 pm news.

By 2001 All Black teams were coming out on the internet, even to the point where on tour in Ireland and Scotland, the release of the test teams went to the internet first and reporters whose companies had paid plenty for them to go on tour would be waiting at the grounds watching the All Black teams train and yet would be second to find out the test teams!

Incidentally, that 2001 touring team was released at 8.30 on a Sunday morning by telephone hook-up to Christchurch. The media could dial a code and join the hook-up for a press conference from their homes. It might be assumed that some reporters did so while still in bed!

9. Bring back Buck

The sacking which rocked a nation

The 1990 All Black trials were held in early May at the Palmerston North Showgrounds. In keeping with New Zealand rugby's traditions, the players bidding for places in the national team were placed in either the Possibles or the Probables team. The incumbent All Black captain was Wayne Shelford. His Probables team won the 'main' trial 39–25. Having led New Zealand in 12 consecutive test wins over the previous two seasons Shelford was a logical choice to continue captaining the All Blacks.

By that season an aura of invincibility had built around the hard-nosed No 8 from the fledgling province of North Harbour. It stemmed from his winning test record, and also from his aggressive, no-nonsense play. He was a man who played every game with great pride in wearing the famous colours. His leading of a very forceful rendition of the Maori haka, which preceded every test, helped too. He projected a fearsome image to the opposition before any game even kicked off. The fans loved him. To a solid percentage of New Zealand rugby fans, Shelford had become akin to a rugby god. Nothing less. It seemed a formality that his leadership would be required by the All Blacks on their way to retaining the World Cup in 1991.

But Shelford never completed the 1990 season as leader of the famous New Zealand rugby team. The man universally known as Buck was axed from the team altogether. And he completely dropped out of sight as an All Black player.

Precisely what happened when Shelford was dropped as player and captain of the All Blacks is still shrouded in the mists of New Zealand rugby's closed ranks. After those trials in Palmerston North, Shelford was duly named as skipper for the tests against the first touring team of that year, Scotland. By the time the later tests against Australia were being played, he was gone. The Shelford sacking caused one of the biggest debates in New Zealand rugby history.

Though I was closely involved in rugby events around New Zealand at the time, and have subsequently scrutinised what has been said and written about Shelford's

Buck Shelford . . . the true story may never be known.

exit, I can still only get close to the nub of what happened. The true story of why Shelford was dismissed so abruptly might never be known.

One thing we know for sure: Shelford could only have been dismissed so finally because something serious happened to his once solid relationship with the All Black coach, the gruff, equally well-known Alex Wyllie. It seems the confidence that existed between the two as they won test after test through 1988–89 evaporated quickly.

In tracing the sequence of events around Shelford's sensational dumping, you must remember that lurking in the background of this story was the emergence of the fast-improving Aucklander who played in the same No 8 position, Zinzan Brooke. The 25-year-old had a rising brilliance, which any reasonable judge of rugby could see was going to take him, sooner or later, into the test arena. With Michael Jones on the openside flank position and the immovable Alan Whetton on the other side, the only opportunity for Brooke to break in would be at No 8. But dropping Shelford? It was inconceivable.

Brooke had been on the tour in 1989 to Wales and Ireland and had shown qualities in the minor matches for which he was selected to indicate that he was of test calibre. During the tour, Shelford had produced good rugby in the two tests. Brooke had been very good, but had missed out. To many of us, it was only a matter of time before Brooke had to be given the top spot.

When the 1990 team to play the first test against Scotland was announced, Shelford was duly named as captain, and Brooke in the reserves, as he had been intermittently since 1987.

But there was another aspect to this story. Don't forget: during 1990 there had been an exodus of leading rugby players to rugby league. Matthew Ridge, the reserve fullback on the 1989 tour of Britain, switched to play professionally at Manly in Sydney. Then Alex Wyllie gasped: 'You're joking!' when told by reporters that his test fullback, John Gallagher, was also changing to play for money at Leeds in England. Three weeks later there was further disaster. John Schuster crossed over, joining the Newcastle Knights in Australia. Days later it was Frano Botica's turn to head to the new world of playing for money, his destination Wigan in the north of England. These departures rocked the staid and tranquil world of amateur New Zealand rugby.

There were hints of more to come. Rumours swirled while more prominent players switched to league — Brett Iti, Daryl Halligan, Darral Shelford (one of the extended family from Bay of Plenty) and Paul Simonsson (a 1987 All Black). The most sensational of the rumours aligned Zinzan Brooke with Graham Lowe's Manly club. A big man with a fat chequebook was fast approaching Zinny, it was said.

The next phase of the story changes a little and I have strong recollections of part of an incident that involved Wyllie and Wayne Shelford. Being an on-duty rugby reporter for TVNZ on the Scotland tour of New Zealand, I was in Dunedin prior to the first test at Carisbrook. The TVNZ Newsroom in Auckland asked me to interview some leading personalities for the upcoming test. I phoned Wyllie at the All Blacks hotel and set up a time on the Friday for a 9.30am interview. Wyllie sounded fine concerning the interview and we even discussed whether I was going to be part of a 'session' he was to have in a couple of local bars with other news media members that evening. I declined with thanks.

The next morning I arrived at the Shoreline Hotel in south Dunedin at the appointed interview time. Mr Wyllie was not in sight. I waited with the film crew for about a quarter of an hour and then phoned his room. The voice on the other end muttered 'hello'. It was obvious the coach had just woken up. When I told him what time it was he sounded startled and within minutes was bounding down the stairs to meet me. All around us in the hotel foyer were players waiting to go into a team meeting and then onto training. I ushered Wyllie from the noisy foyer to a quieter place outside to more easily conduct my interview.

In speaking to Alex, it became obvious that he was truly just out of bed. He was unshaven and definitely bleary-eyed, his replies were shorter even than the usual brusque Wyllie style and he had an odour of a heavy dose of a good night out, later confirmed by some of my media colleagues who had been with him.

As I prepared to ask my questions the All Black players filed out behind us and climbed onto their waiting bus. They were off to their last pre-test training session. The bus moved off slowly, leaving the All Black coach with my crew and me.

Soon enough I finished my questions and Wyllie moved away looking for a ride to follow the bus to the secret training destination. Former All Black Jeff Matheson, a liaison officer for the team, drove Wyllie away.

I mention the exchange in detail because evidence emerged in various conversations in later years that later that morning Wyllie and Shelford exchanged words at the training session. Shelford, it is said, was annoyed that Wyllie was late to training. When Wyllie arrived he leant on a car at the side of the field in the sunshine while the team played an endless game of their version of touch football, a version that had been invented for the All Blacks by Warren Gatland, who was then a school teacher. The All Blacks used the game at their training warm-ups for years.

Shelford became exasperated with the lack of planning in the practice and, it is said, berated Wyllie. One has to suppose Wyllie did not enjoy that experience.

The next day, the All Blacks won 31–16 but it was far from convincing. Scotland scored three tries and in the first half they looked as if they might cause an upset. Shelford played a solid game, not flashy, but well enough. He was retained for the second test, of course. You don't drop a winning captain. Or do you?

The second Scotland test was just a week later. There were 45,000 at Eden Park and the All Blacks squeaked a win 21–18. Scotland outscored the home team in tries and only five penalties and one conversion by Grant Fox made the winning difference for New Zealand. The tries the Scots scored and a number of other moves in the game resulted from the Scottish backs being allowed a lot of freedom by the All Black loose forwards. Shelford in particular wasn't, as they say, 'getting out wide'.

The gap until the next test team announcement was three weeks. That gave the selectors, Wyllie, John Hart and Lane Penn, time to consider their options before the Bledisloe Cup series against Australia. In that time, also, the buzz about Zinzan Brooke heading for Manly continued to zoom about New Zealand.

At that time I had a Sunday spot on TV called *The Write Stuff*. It was a three or four-minute studio commentary piece in which I spoke my piece on topical sports issues. After the disappointing second Scottish test, I called for changes to be made to improve the All Black team. 'It is essential that there are changes,' I opined, 'and if that means changing the captain, then so be it.'

Such a comment didn't win me any kudos. Shelford really was popular and his record run of test victories had extended to 14 by then. A week later in Sydney I mentioned the remark in conversation to John Hart while getting ready to broadcast a commentary on his New Zealand Colts game with their Australian counterparts. Hart replied with something like, 'Well, you might be surprised to know you're not far off the mark.' The selectors had obviously been talking about Shelford's lack of form.

The following Thursday all hell broke loose. The team to play Australia was released and Shelford's name was missing. In his place was Zinzan Brooke. I for one was not surprised.

Shelford had been playing in a midweek match in Whangerei. His North Harbour team had battled to a 9–6 win over North Auckland and he, like All Black contenders all over the country, would have gone to bed hoping his name would be read out in the test team the next day. As it turned out, Shelford was to be told by his provincial coach, Peter Thorburn, that he was not in the team. The All Black coach of the time did not ring him until Buck had reached his home on Auckland's North Shore.

The late team announcement led to much comment on breakfast radio programmes the next morning. The team's content provoked a stormy reaction. I was working at Independent Radio Sports in Wellington and we rightly headlined the story with bold words. 'All Black captain dumped!' The news that Gary Whetton had been elevated to be the new All Black leader was insignificant compared to the great man's omission.

Photosport

From Feilding to Flushing Meadow, the 'Bring Back Buck' placards sprung up everywhere after the dumping of Shelford.

Buck Shelford was given a final opportunity to regain his All Black spot in 1991 when he opposed Zinzan Brooke in the final All Black trial at Rotorua. He never made it back.

Curiously, in the moments immediately after one of the newscasts came a call from a furious sounding All Black coach. 'If you don't stop using the word "dumped" I'll never speak to your radio station again,' Wyllie thundered. We in the studio gulped and, mindful that our network would need quotes from the All Black coach in future, slightly changed the bulletin's wording. I think we started reading that he had been 'dropped'. Even down the telephone Wyllie had an imposing aura that we chose not to challenge.

The newspaper headlines were equally strong and Wyllie had to make many appearances and offer quotes justifying his panel's decision. He was not at all convincing.

It's odd how now, with the passage of time, the reasons Shelford was dropped have evolved and changed. There have been many different versions. While the Brooke threat of a switch to league was in the background, and there was a lot of behind-the-hand chatter about the relationship between Wyllie and Shelford having broken down, there were other reasons offered.

Some were simply about his playing form. It was said that Shelford hadn't been 'getting out wide' quickly enough. A leg injury was mentioned. There was also a story which gained strength as the months rolled by, that a small but powerful group of Auckland-based All Blacks had got together and 'plotted' to bring about the rugby equivalent of a coup d'état on Shelford. This version was said to further the promotion of Brooke into the test team, as well as advancing Whetton into the captain's role. Whetton vigorously denied such a group when I interviewed him about the plotting rumour for the *Legends of the All Blacks* TV series in 1999.

Blame was also laid at the feet of John Hart, though he, too, sternly denies being an individual instigator of the selection panel's decision. An alleged dressing-room fight between Shelford and his All Black team-mate Grant Fox was also bandied about. It, too, had little credibility.

And in 2001 it was highly intriguing to hear yet another TV documentary (this one about All Black wives) in which Shelford's wife Joanne told how she was at home with Wayne when Wyllie rang up on the morning after he had been dropped. According to Joanne, as spoken on the TV show, Wyllie wanted to get a story about the dropping straight with Shelford for public acceptance. Wyllie enquired down the phone: 'Wayne, you had an injury didn't you? What was it again?' Joanne said she was in the background shouting: 'There was no injury!' Minutes later the phone rang again and it was Wyllie again asking: 'That injury you had — which leg was it?' Mrs Shelford was not impressed.

Blame was also laid at the feet of John Hart, though he too sternly denies being an individual instigator of the selection panel's decision.

So why was Shelford dropped from the All Black picture? Was it lack of form, the presence of a rising star who was better than him, his criticism of his coach, a lack of control in the dressing room, a leg injury, or the ganging up of team colleagues to oust him? Some of the above theories were as outrageous then as they are now. But the rumour-mongers of New Zealand rugby feasted on them with delight.

To me, the imminent Brooke switch to league seems to have the most truth to it. The story is that Brooke, feeling his international rugby union career was going nowhere, had actually signed for Manly in the days after the Scotland tour. However, when he heard that he was actually in the All Black starting XV for the all-important tests against the Wallabies, he asked that Manly please disregard the signature. Graham Lowe, the coach at Manly, is said to have torn up the contract, to his credit. So Brooke was in the All Blacks (and he stayed there for the next eight seasons). Shelford was out, never to return.

The news caused a ruckus rarely seen in New Zealand rugby. Newspapers reached for their strongest headlines ('NZ passes the Buck and Splits the Nation' and 'Dumping of Skipper Splits Nation' were just two). All over the country you took your stance on the situation and were either for or against the decision. Most people, it has to be said, greatly admired Brooke (who grew to be a genuine All Black great) but Buck was still their favourite.

It has to be said the cult figure status of Shelford rose as a result of the All Black selectors' decision. Somebody somewhere wrote the first placard sign saying 'Bring Back Buck' and waved it in a place at a rugby game where TV cameras could see the message. Soon the clever piece of alliteration was repeated all over the world and not just at rugby games, either. At cricket tests, English Premier division soccer matches, America's Cup yachting and countless other sports events the 'Bring Back Buck' sign was waved. The signs were even seen by TV3 political reporter Jane Young while watching the US Open tennis tournament at Flushing Meadow in 2001.

It has become more than a collective call for Shelford's return to the national rugby team. Instead it has become a national symbol, a kind of beckoning call, declaring that the waver is a Kiwi and that Buck, their hero, will never be forgotten.

Shelford became one of the best-known New Zealand faces of his age. And in the years since, whenever discussions have arisen in bars and workplaces and household gatherings about the Shelford dropping a number of the versions you have just read are discussed. They are, of course, often overblown, overstated, embroidered and exaggerated.

Very rarely does one hear that perhaps the young Zinzan Brooke was by that year a better player in the No 8 position. Some people's views are so strong alleging Shelford was wronged that whenever any problem in New Zealand rugby arises, be it in selection, coaching advice, whatever, the cry of 'Bring in Buck' is heard. Such is the power of his presence he is still strong enough as a personality to fix any problem.

─

Grab the grog!

Here is a classic example of how much respect there is in New Zealand for the rugby World Cup. In 1987, shortly after the All Blacks had won the first Cup tournament, the Webb Ellis Cup was taken from Auckland back to the union's headquarters in Wellington. There the trophy was splendidly mounted behind glass and displayed in the Union's boardroom.

Shortly after, a burglary occurred at those same offices — but the intruders did not touch the World Cup. The burglars took all the booze, which was also securely locked behind glass in the same room.

10. Piney's blackest day

Colin Meads marched at Murrayfield

In 1967 Colin Meads was surely the most commanding figure in world rugby. He was all-powerful as a running tight-loose forward, a solid leaper at lineouts, a workhorse in the scrums and, perhaps most importantly, a player who could unquestionably intimidate most opponents. Certainly he was not shy about throwing a punch in any game when he deemed it necessary. Generally, though, he was an admired figure on the world scene.

As a young lad from the King Country, he had been painfully shy when first chosen for the All Blacks in 1957. In many ways he is still a shy man today, but because he is in heavy demand as a guest speaker he comes out from behind a rural reticence to retain huge popularity.

However, it wasn't always this way for the man they call Pinetree.

On the All Black tour of Britain and France in 1967, Meads ran into several problems during the international matches. Against France, he was on the receiving end of some brutal rugby violence while, in another test, he was seen by one referee to be dishing out some.

Meads was in superb form on that trip. It was almost as though he was taking out on British teams the frustrations of having the 1967 All Black tour of South Africa snatched from him. That trip had been cancelled for political reasons. Nobody was happy. It was a case of coach Fred Allen, captain Brian Lochore and the lads in the New Zealand team saying, 'Right! We'll show you what we could have done in South Africa.' That '67 All Black team was a great one. And that is using the word advisedly.

The French international in Paris was the third test match of four played on the tour. (Britain was then in the grip of foot and mouth epidemic, so a trip to Ireland was ruled out.) The French team was crammed with talent and they gave the All Blacks a torrid time at Colombes Stadium. New Zealand won 21–15 — four tries to one — but in the fighting and scrapping, the contest was much more even. One of the French

Colin Meads begins his long walk at Murrayfield in 1967 after being sent from the field by Irish whistler Kevin Kelleher.

players, whom the French seemed happy to identify afterwards for Meads (no doubt lest the teams meet again at a future date!) aimed a kick in open play that landed fair and square behind the big New Zealander's ear. He refused to go off even though blood poured from the wound. The Frenchman received a rousing cheer from the crowd, though Meads says after the game the home team preferred his company to that of their offending team-mate.

I only mention the fact that Meads had been so badly wronged in the French game because the final international of the tour against Scotland followed a week later and Meads, it was hoped, would be fit to play.

Indeed he was. In those days the man from King Country was well nigh indestructible. He had a heavily bandaged head topped by leather headgear, but nothing was going to keep him from being on the field when the team set out to complete its unbeaten test record at Murrayfield. But from the Scotland game came the incident which was to outrage Meads' millions of fans all over the world.

It also outraged many thousands of Scottish followers. So you took your position depending on whose side you supported.

The Scotland game began on a grey Edinburgh afternoon. Ahead of the All Blacks was a truly tough task. If they won, they could head home with victories in all four tests. Plus they were well on their way to a tour record with all wins from the tour's 17 games. (In the end, that proved not possible as the team drew with East Wales 3–3 in the second-last outing.)

The Scotland match was to be a tough game to handle, with a number of incidents along the bumpy road to the big one, the one that made world headlines. Early on, Meads was spoken to by the referee for a lineout breach. The referee, an Irishman named Kevin Kelleher, later called him out again. For the second offence Meads was formally cautioned for 'walking on a couple of blokes', as Meads was later to describe it. He was surprised at the severity of Kelleher's action.

There were other tussles, too. The Scottish captain, Fisher, was proving a rugged character and at one point he so annoyed his opposite captain, Brian Lochore, that Lochore considered giving him a clip, or something similar. Being a wise leader, Lochore thought better of it, though he did ask his flanker Kel Tremain to do the job for him. Tremain did as his captain bid and Fisher went down for a moment, looking decidedly ill. Lochore chuckles these days about how he had to run across with the First Aid officer and act compassionate and concerned about the Scottish leader whom he had just ordered to be restrained by Tremain.

So it was that kind of game. Plenty of action and quite a bit of niggle. And 60,000 fans screaming at every twist and turn. Meads recalled on TVNZ's *Quinn and McBeth* show in 2001 that the Scottish hooker, Frank Laidlaw, had been yelling strongly throughout the game, attempting to be of maximum assistance to Kelleher.

Near the end of the game, when the outcome had more or less been decided, New Zealand was leading 14–3. Scotland kicked off and the ball was taken into a ruck. When it tumbled out on the Scottish side, Meads was lurking on the edge of the forward gathering. The ball rolled past Hastie, the Scottish scrumhalf, and went towards his flyhalf partner, David Chisholm.

The crowd roared an instantaneous shout of 'Off! Off!' and Kelleher, having blown his whistle, called Meads out.

Meads leapt after the bouncing leather, taking three or four paces in its direction. As with any rugby ball spinning across wet grass, it must eventually sit up on a higher bounce. This time when it did Meads lunged a swinging right leg at it. In New Zealanders' eyes, his intent was clearly to toe the ball ahead. But in that flashpoint, Chisholm was also trying to secure possession. It seems to me, having seen footage of the incident about 3000 times down the years, that Meads' swinging right boot, the ball and Chisholm's body were in a crossroads collision at the same time.

In the next instant the 60,000 spectators, who had been growing increasingly distressed at the prospect of Scotland losing the game, drew an instant conclusion. The crowd roared an instantaneous shout of 'Off! Off!' and Kelleher, having blown his

News Media Auckland

Kevin Kelleher, who 'pointed his finger to the grandstands'.

whistle, called Meads out.

The place went into uproar. At the ground through the darkening gloom it became obvious that stern words were being spoken to Meads. As Lochore stood near, making it a threesome, who fitted neatly into a single TV shot, it was obvious Kelleher was about to do something drastic.

And he did. He pointed his finger to the grandstands of Murrayfield and, as Cyril Brownlie had experienced at Twickenham in 1925, Colin Meads felt the cold, clammy feeling of being sent off in a rugby test.

He walked away, head down, looking for all the world as though he was walking to the dressing room in shame. It was not quite shame, Meads said on TV in 2001. 'My first reaction was worse than that. I thought my whole career was over. I knew that there had been no other player sent off since Cyril Brownlie. But I never knew of any committee that would meet like they do these days. I thought I might be gone forever.'

The game ended soon after with the score unchanged. The tour ended a fortnight later, but the furore over the Meads incident carried on for years, and decades, and indeed into the new century and millennium.

Did Colin Meads deserve to be sent from the field on that murky day? I say, as firmly as I can, 'No!' A player lunging for the ball with a swinging leg might be careless, but being totally irresponsible he is not. Meads lashed out *for the ball* with his foot. Meads says his boot connected with the ball and drove it instantaneously into Chisholm's midriff. He said it at the time; he says it today. Chisholm knew that, too. The Scotsman stood up and straight away, in the tumult, made his way over to make a sympathetic 'it's OK' grab of Meads' arm in front of the referee. But Kelleher had in mind that his formal caution had been previously issued. He felt there was no other ruling possible than to send off the big man.

So he did. And the rugby world went crazy with debate. The headline writers reached for their strongest wording. The most famous player in the world had been sent from the field in disgrace!

However, I remember the words of Cliff Morgan working at the ground for BBC radio. Through a crackling radio report to New Zealand Morgan said, 'Not for me was it disgrace, for I saw, walking off the field today, with head bowed, the greatest player the game has ever seen.'

PROS AND CONS OF THE MEADS INCIDENT

From TERRY O'CONNOR

Despite the great shame of being sent from the field in a test match, there was general sympathy for Meads all around the rugby globe back in 1967.

LONDON.—Colin Meads has become the martyr of Rugby Union hypocrisy.

NOT that his sending off in the Scotland-New Zealand match was wrong according to the referee's interpretation of the laws, but at least 50 incidents in my experience have been far worse in watching 19 years and covering 250 Test matches.

Yet no player in touring overseas. This ma... any international during appear sad, but is true. these matches had been... According to the law...

General opinion backs Meads

According to the Wellington man in the street, Colin Meads did not deserve to be ordered off in the All Blacks' match with Scotland last Saturday.

A survey conducted by The Dominion last night indicates this.

The Dominion sought reactions to the ordering off after a film leading up to and showing the incident had been shown by WNTV1. Here are some of the reactions:

Mr. M. Law, insurance clerk: "In view of the way that international players approach rugby these days, the decision to order off Meads was rather harsh.

"But we must realise that the referee is always the sole judge. . . .

"Considering Meads' suspension—surely the humilia-

"If he wished to play the man, he could have sent him off on a stretcher.

"But he did not attempt to do it."

Mr. B. A. Heather, shipping clerk: "It's a bit sad, really, a great player like him being ordered off.

"HARSH"

ing technician: "TV showed only the part of the game in which Meads was ordered off, and not the events . . . earlier in the game.

"Presumably the referee and the disciplinary committee took everything into account.

"Meads' style of play was more vigorous than the

CABINET MINISTER ... CABLE TO COLIN MEADS

Special to "The Post" from T P McLean

CARDIFF, Dec 8.— The Minister of Internal Affairs in New Zealand (Mr Seath) has cabled Colin Meads: "There is tremendous good will for you here. Greatly regret uncalled for decision."

Mr Seath, incidentally, represents Mead's constituency. The former chairman of the New Zealand Rugby Council, Mr C S Hogg, considered the punishment to be "wholly undeserved."

Alec Septhon, of Yorkshire, and who played for the Istonians Club in Belfast, wrote: "My English wife has just been shouting at me and all other Irishmen in her rage against Mr Kelleher," and Mr Septhon went on to say that his wife considered all Irishmen to be "too impulsive."

Professor J D B Mitchell, of the department of constitution al law at the University of Edinburgh, sounded as brassed off as Mrs Septhon at the situation. He wrote: "I saw the match and consider it a most unjust decision."

They have come from far, they have come from near, the letters and cablegrams which all through this agonising week have assured the great All Black lock forward Colin Meads of the friendship and regard of friends, strangers and sympathisers all over the world.

you suspended for two games for what I thought was a complete accident. Although my opinion doesn't give you any real satisfaction, I am sure it is also the opinion of every player who has played against you and ever watched you play in the past.

"It has given me great pleasure to have known you, and I am sure you will go down in New Zealand Rugby history as their greatest forward.

Compare this with the letter of Master J P Harris, aged 9, who wrote "I am at King's School, Rochester, and we are doing a scrapbook about you. Please could you send me your autograph and picture?"

Compare this with the report of the celebrated French Rugby correspondent, Denis Lalanne, who told the readers of the Parisian sporting daily newspaper "L'Equipe": "No one can shame or soil the great name of Colin Meads. All the world's Rugby, embarrassed by the untimely deci-

sion of Mr Kelleher, was astonished at his presentation of excuses."

Many Offers

At the dance after the All Blacks' match against Monmouthshire at Newport last Wednesday, Colin Meads fell in with what appeared to be battalions of supporters of various clubs. To a man they offered the same message: "They've put you out for two tour matches," they said, their voices rising in excitement, "but that doesn't mean you can't play Rugby, does it? Now, look here, man. You play Rugby for us."

In short order, Meads offered a match with the E... end club on Thursday nig... match with Ebbw Vale o... day night, and a match Newport this Saturday noon.

One of the most pers... pleaders was the Lions'

forward of last year. Denzil Williams, who plays for Ebbw Vale.

"You'd enjoy yourself," he told Meads. "You really would."

"I'm sure I would," Meads answered, but . . .

Incidentally, Meads would be awarded the prize for the quote of the week. At breakfast last Wednesday morning after a good many of the party had had rather a heavy night to take away the sting of the adjudication committee's suspension of Meads for two matches, Kelvin Tremain, his roommate and great friend,

MEADS 'GENTLE GIANT

Wife: He's so humble

11. Who kicked Tiny White?

Jaap Bekker finally comes clean

It took 43 years for a notorious incident that took place in a most famous rugby test to be cleared up once and for all. From the incident one New Zealander carried physical pain that left his life altered forever while another man, a South African who had been involved, harboured an anguish that tormented him until he spoke out just before his death.

For the full story we must yet again cast our minds back to the circumstances of the 1956 tour of New Zealand by the Springboks. There are so many stories that still loom large from that team's visit. They were a squad full of strength, power and abrasive personality. They had a captain certainly, Basie Viviers, but by far the most powerful force in their team was their manager and coach, the great Dr Daniel (Danie) Craven.

He led a typical South African rugby team of the time. Brutal, grim, and sometimes devastatingly ruthless. Not that New Zealand's All Blacks were much different. The New Zealanders readied themselves for a conflict of the sternest rugby type. 'A state of mania' is how one writer described New Zealand as it stood guard, waiting for the arrival of the sporting enemy.

The Springboks had never lost a series to the All Blacks. In 1921, 1928, 1937 and 1949 the two had battled. The results were usually very close, but New Zealand had won just four of the 14 tests, and never a series.

In 1949 the Springboks, aided by having their own referees, sneaked home narrowly in each test to win the series 4–0. This rankled with New Zealand supporters. By 1956 the country was in a fervour for revenge. But any victories would not be achieved without a massive fight from the touring Springboks, fight being the operative word. So the scene was set.

From the first test match there were scuffles and scraps. At Carisbrook the All

Black strongman prop Mark Irwin broke several ribs and did not appear again in the series. Springbok winger Jan du Preez broke his leg and his tour ended. It required a good slice of luck for New Zealand to hold on to win 10–6, given the speed 'by which the forwards ran backwards at the scrum once the Springboks got stuck in' as one newspaper reported it.

South Africa levelled the series on a grey Wellington day, winning the second test 8–3. Some scratchy film of the match remains. It was shot from high on the Western embankment of Athletic Park, and even in the few moments that are left for us to scrutinise, squabbles can be seen breaking out. One of the first was between the New Zealand winger Morrie Dixon and his opposite Paul Johnstone, and there were more, especially in the front row. There Irwin's replacement, Frank McAtamney, can be seen to be having all sorts of problems with the bulky Springbok props Chris Koch and Jaap Bekker. The two Springboks were blocks of men with massive chests, necks and reputations. They were feared around the world for destroying opposition scrums. One report says the outcome of the Wellington test was decided by the strength of the early Springbok scrummaging.

The newsreel film shows McAtamney rearing up and referee Frank Parkinson struggling to gain a measure of control. Though some of the All Blacks described the game as the roughest they had ever played in, they were not blameless either. Somewhere in the first half New Zealand got their retaliation in first. Bekker, the strongman from a brilliantly talented sports family, staggered back at one point as though he had been well and truly dealt to. He stumbled about for the rest of the game.

He had been hammered. But by whom? Wellington's *Evening Post* published a dramatic dressing room photograph of Bekker looking dazed and stunned. It was said he was concussed. Terry McLean wrote that 'he was in a coma' and had to spend a night in hospital. He did not wake up until 3 am, when he asked what the final score had been.

In those days concussion did not require a stand-down period. Players could play again as soon as they liked. Bekker the battered did. He was back in the front row for the South Africans by the time the third test rolled around a fortnight later.

In the meantime the All Black selectors swung into action. The defeat had come about because South Africa were stronger in the forwards, and were winning the physical battles. 'Lose the fight, lose the game' became a rugby slogan of the time. New Zealand were deficient in other areas too — at halfback, fullback, and in goal kicking. The public, as well as the selectors, demanded changes be made.

There was a general call to discard McAtamney, who was considered too young to carry on with the battle against the feared Koch and Bekker. But who was there of equal strength to join prop Ian Clarke and square up against the power of the Springboks?

The selectors sent the former All Black prop Johnny Simpson to watch his former team-mate Kevin Skinner play in a Counties trial match. Skinner had not played for his country since the end of the 1953–54 New Zealand tour of Britain and France. He had been an Otago man all his rugby life but had moved to Waiuku, in the south Auckland region, to begin a new life in farming. He was welcomed by the local union but had been slow to get into his rugby that season.

It must have been a surprise for him to see Simpson. The two had been strongmen themselves on the beaten All Blacks tour of South Africa seven years earlier and understood only too well what the Springboks could do in a front row confrontation. Simpson, who had retired, told Skinner the All Black selectors had sent him to the trial to see if Skinner might be fit enough for the third test. It sounded like a call to serve 'Queen and Country'.

After the game when Simpson told Skinner that McAtamney had had his hand bitten in the second test by one of the Springboks, the hackles began to rise on the former amateur heavyweight boxing champion. He was persuaded to make himself available.

I was just a kid, but will never forget the radio crossover for the announcement of the third test match. We the nation, from little blokes like me through to the sage judges of rugby who you heard talking on the bus, or at the rugby, or in the streets, all wanted changes to the All Blacks. When the stentorian voice of Cuthbert Hogg, chairman of the New Zealand Rugby Union, began his radio announcement of the team with the words: 'Fullback . . . D . . . B . . . Clarke . . . Waikato!' the country gasped in satisfaction. The big booting kid from Mooloo-land was to make his test debut. He was just the man needed to land the crucial goals and be a stoic last line of defence. But there were still more surprises (and pleasures) in store.

From the desolation of the second test loss came seven changes and when 'K L Skinner — Counties' was the last name called there truly was a feeling of confidence restored. 'Now,' thought people, 'we can take on the Springboks in the front row.'

And so it proved. Skinner might have watched as Koch rushed clean through the first All Black lineout in the third test, but when the teams formed for the next lineout, he said, 'That'll be the last time you do that, Chris.' When Koch tried to do the same thing, he ran fair and square into a big Skinner right hand. The crowd at the ground roared in approval while the radio audience all over New Zealand gasped in contentment at the famous Winston McCarthy's commentary of New Zealand 'getting stuck into the Springboks at last'. Added to the work being done up front was young Don Clarke landing prodigious goal kicks from the back.

In the scrums it was no less fierce a battle. Of one of Koch's punches it was said: 'If it had landed his head would have been parted from his shoulders.' Skinner was in the thick of much of this.

In the years since he has told me several times he deplores the inference that there was a *lot* of fighting and that he was involved in all of it. Nonetheless, the legend now is strong and deep. And it says Kevin Skinner sorted out, or at the very least subdued

News Media Auckland

News Media Auckland

Former New Zealand heavyweight boxing champion Kevin Skinner (left) and Springbok strongman Jaap Bekker, who squared off in the famous series of 1956.

considerably, the two South African strongmen. They were stopped from making their charges through the lineouts and in the scrums. Skinner first 'quietened' Koch and then, in the second half, the New Zealander shifted to the loosehead side to relieve a struggling Ian Clarke. There, Skinner resumed a battle with Bekker that they had enjoyed in two provincial games in South Africa in 1949. Bekker, too, was 'quietened'. New Zealand won the torrid affair 17–10. Thus only one more victory was needed by the All Blacks for them to win their first test series against their bitterest rivals.

The Springboks were cut to the quick by the two losses out of three. It was said they were furious at how Skinner had intimidated and demoralised them at Christchurch. Intimidated? The word had never been heard before in South African rugby history. Certainly not in the many tales of the epic 1956 series. Until, that is, I was on a film trip to South Africa in 1999.

The purpose of the visit was to film for the *Legends of the All Blacks* TV series. Our production crew wished to seek out new information on the story of the rugby drama of so many years before. It was still a test series that caused considerable debate among those who had seen it.

We knew that Koch had passed away in 1986, and the hooker who had hung between the props, Bertus van der Merwe, had died in a car crash in 1974. That only left Bekker to seek out to obtain the South African view. We found him by phone and on a scorching afternoon we visited him in Glenstantsia, Pretoria.

Above: All Black lock Tiny White lies prone on the Eden Park turf after being kicked in the back by Jaap Bekker during the fourth of the 1956 series. Left: White is assisted from the field.

The passage of time had not sat well with the former strongman. He was 74 years old and clearly suffering from Parkinson's disease. He was still strong-looking and handsome with a full head of grey hair. Jaap told me he had suffered at various times in his life from depression. His home was small and well-ordered and there was a large opened bible on a stand in the hallway. Mrs Bekker prepared cool drinks for us as our cameraman made ready for an interview in the garden.

As we started to film, the hearts of our production crew sank when Jaap told us he doubted whether he could recall much of the tour. He had not thought about it for some time. Minutes later, though, he said some memories were very vivid. Later in the interview, that was to be made abundantly clear.

When I asked him about the first test he could only summarise that New Zealand deserved to win. He could not remember any more about the Carisbrook battle. We then moved our discussion to the second test in Wellington and I ventured that Jaap might remember more about that game. 'On the contrary,' said the South African, 'I only recall parts of the first half. I was unconscious for all of the second half and I only remember waking up in the hospital and a nurse telling me the score in the game and telling me to rest and be quiet.'

Bekker went on, saying the scrums had collapsed so often he felt he either lost consciousness by repeatedly having his head banged into the ground, or 'by someone kicking me from the second row of the All Black scrum.' He said he thought the someone might have been the 'All Black captain Bob Duff'. In fact, Duff was not captain in that game.

It was when our discussion, with the TV camera still rolling, reached the third test that memories from Bekker threw new angles onto the whole story of that larger-than-life series. He said he and Koch knew that when Skinner was brought in to the All Black team that things would be a whole lot tougher in the scrums and lineouts. And so it proved. Bekker said the punches and jabs from Kevin Skinner were 'demoralising to us right throughout'. It got to the point where the two strongmen started to concentrate more on Skinner than on the game.

Now Bekker warmed to his recall for our interview. The memories seemed to stir from deep within. Sitting in the shadows of his warm garden I could sense a rousing of remembrance.

He told us he and several of his team-mates approached Craven in his Auckland hotel room and told them of how the Springboks forward effort in the third test had fallen away with the arrival of Skinner into the New Zealand ranks. The word 'demoralised' was used to Craven to describe how the forwards had felt when Skinner began exerting his presence. Although Craven was not admired by many New Zealanders — after all, that winter he was the *enemy* — he was a man who had a true belief in the honour of rugby. Bekker told us that Craven did not approve of the demands he was hearing from his players that they be allowed to fight Skinner in a much sterner way in the final test. Craven said, 'No, definitely no.'

So, Bekker told me, the night before the fourth test he and Koch convened a meeting in their room where they and several other trustworthy Springboks decided to get Skinner in the game the following day. 'He had disorganised our test side, and we [decided] we must get hold of him, good and solid.'

The plan went horribly wrong. A strange look came over Bekker's eyes as the interview continued. He started to fidget about in his garden seat, looking more distressed. He carried on, though. 'We knew Kevin wore a white knee guard [bandage] on his right leg, but Tiny White always started a game with a similar knee guard. His was on his left leg. When the game was being played the next day there was a lineout and I thought I saw Skinner come down on his back. So, in keeping with our plan, I kicked him. But it wasn't Kevin, it was Tiny White. And he had to go off. I kicked the wrong one.'

Sitting with Bekker that day and having read and followed the tour of '56, with its widely publicised dramas, and having seen the pictures of the Tiny White injury incident on Eden Park, I was deeply shocked to hear Bekker say those words. White, we knew at the time, had been kicked so severely in the back that he feared at first that he had suffered a serious spinal injury. White's team-mates, including Skinner and Duff, had been so wild they had rushed in and a serious fight looked likely to break out. The crowd had seen something happen. They were incensed. Several policemen in uniform came down to the edge of the fray in case more violence broke out. It was a nasty scene. But the wrong man was writhing in agony.

Bekker added: 'I was sorry about it all; yes I kicked the wrong one. I never spoke to anybody about it till now. I have carried it here.' He touched his heart and choked back tears. It was a sad sight to see, an elderly man on the verge of crying while confessing to a rugby incident that had obviously burned up inside him for decades.

What the whole of New Zealand had previously believed had happened was that White had crashed to the ground from a lineout. Then, when the loose ruck around him moved away, White was seen lying in pain. Some of the crowd had seen what had happened and word had spread around the ground in a flash. White was assisted from the field and played only once again in his life before being forced to retire, such was his back pain. The injury that had caused such a shortened career resulted from a heinous foul.

> 'I was sorry about it all; yes I kicked the wrong one. I never spoke to anybody about it till now. I have carried it here.' He touched his heart and choked back tears.

For his part, Skinner was slightly sceptical when I brought back the Bekker video interview from Pretoria and played it to him in Auckland. 'Oh well, I am surprised to hear Jaap say that all these years later. I'm sad, but good on him for admitting it was him who put the boot in. I saw a boot go in. It was a big kick, not just a nudge, and it was with the toe of the boot. But a lot of stuff from that series [has been] exaggerated so often down the years, it has almost become the truth in some people's minds.'

When I spoke to White he was disappointed. 'The Springboks were such outstanding rugby players. They lowered their dignity if they planned such a thing. If you can sit down the night before a game and plan something completely unethical and outside the morals of amateur sport . . . well, no true sportsmen would do that.'

It was a series of great emotion all right. New Zealand won the Auckland game 11–5 and so beat South Africa for the first time in a series. The whole country

Author Keith Quinn with Jaap Bekker in 1999. It was during this interview that Quinn extracted the extraordinary confession from Bekker about the kicking of Tiny White.

rejoiced. Rugby was king; the All Blacks were heroes. But the questioning over some of the incidents in those games has lingered for decades. The first full live TV coverage of a rugby test was an England-Scotland game in 1938. Why was there no TV in New Zealand when we needed it?

On that quiet Pretoria afternoon to have seen the pain on the face of Jaap Bekker as he made a clean breast for us concerning the South Africans' secret plan was an indication of the anguish he had lived with for 43 years, not to mention the drama and national commotion that famous tour caused.

Footnote: Jaap Bekker stood at the gate of his home and graciously farewelled us that afternoon in 1999. He had been a generous host for the TV crew, and had also gone upstairs and lent to us films that he had shot on the tour with his private movie camera. They proved priceless in telling the story of 1956.

Jaap died a few months after our visit. He was unable to fulfil a desire he had expressed to us that he would one day return to holiday in New Zealand. He wished to include in his trip a visit to the homes of both Skinner and White. There he wished to apologise to them for the injuries and the destructive act he had planned so many years before. To their credit both Skinner and White said they would have welcomed their old foe.

12. Did Deans score?

The non-try which spawned a legend

If only there had been a video referee available at Cardiff Arms Park on December 16, 1905, a century of argument and discussion, claim and counter-claim would have been avoided. It was on that day that Dave Gallaher's 1905 Originals suffered the only defeat of their long and historic tour of Britain, France and North America. Wales beat the All Blacks 3–0, but the result of the match was clouded by a massive controversy. This erupted over the decision by referee John Dewar Dallas of Scotland not to award New Zealand centre Bob Deans a try that would have levelled the scores, with a Billy Wallace conversion attempt to follow.

It might seem heresy to say it, but in a way I'm glad the try was not awarded. That decision, and that result, has given Wales-New Zealand contests a much greater edge down the years. It has given old men, and young men too, something to discuss when their two teams have been preparing for another test match. Just as the infamous underarm incident in 1981 gave New Zealand cricket a huge shot in the arm with all the controversy it aroused, so the Deans 'try' turned out to have a positive spin-off for Welsh and New Zealand rugby.

When I first began touring Britain with All Black teams in the early 1970s, the issue was very much alive, the more so because Wales were a lot more competitive with the All Blacks back then than they have been in recent times.

When Joe Karam calmly kicked the All Blacks to a cliff-hanging 19–16 victory over Wales at the Arms Park in 1972, there was much gnashing of teeth in the Valleys, while New Zealand supporters felt the result went another step along the road of vindicating the 1905 team. Memories of the Deans incident were aroused again in 1978 when Andy Haden dived outrageously from a lineout, referee Roger Quittenton penalised Geoff Wheel for pushing Frank Oliver and replacement kicker Brian McKechnie coolly slotted the critical kick to get the All Blacks home 13–12.

The Deans incident is one of the great pieces of rugby folklore. Young New

Zealanders, in Britain for their mandatory OE, still duly troop to Cardiff Arms Park, walk down to the goal-line and have their photo taken at the spot where New Zealand was robbed all those years ago. Never mind that the field has been moved markedly since then, or that the entire stadium is so different these days. If you grow up in New Zealand, you know about rugby, and if you know about rugby, you know about how New Zealand was robbed that December day in 1905.

There have been various television and film re-enactments of the incident. I was involved in one myself. We filmed it at Athletic Park in 1980 and Winston McCarthy did the commentary. When the All Blacks play in Wales, the local newspapers produce supplements with stories about great New Zealand-Wales rugby moments. Swansea and Llanelli are mentioned in honour of the victories those clubs scored over New Zealand teams in 1935 and '72 respectively, and the 1935 and '54 Welsh test sides that beat the All Blacks. The story that often gets pride of place, though, is of the 1905 test when the Welsh side put the brilliant Colonials in their place, and then had to sit back and watch the New Zealanders cry 'Foul!'.

Down the years, young Welsh boys have been told the story of the 1905 test. I recall the brilliant Welsh flyhalf Cliff Morgan telling me once in that wonderful lilt of his: 'I was sat on my mother's knee from an early age and told that Deans did *not* score at Cardiff Arms Park in 1905.' Many thousands of other Welsh youngsters were no doubt told the story as part of their rugby education.

It was a different story in New Zealand, though. Billy Wallace, who before his death in 1972 was the oldest living All Black, was always adamant a grave injustice had been done, as I discovered a few years earlier. In 1967, when I was a trainee broadcaster, I went to a match at Athletic Park with Dave Henderson, a friend of mine. At the aftermatch function, we spotted Billy and went across to have a chat with him. We were only 21 and he was 88, but he talked to us for ages. Then it was time to go. He was living then with his daughter in Tawa, about 20 miles away, and we offered him a ride, which he gladly accepted. As we were driving through Wellington, he piped up: 'Boys, don't you think we should stop for a drink?' So we pulled up at the Grand Hotel.

Not surprisingly, our conversation soon turned to 1905. Though he'd been asked about the incident countless times, Billy was as passionate as ever when discussing it. He was emphatic that Deans had scored and that New Zealand had been robbed of at least a draw. I recall him using the condensation that had rubbed onto the table from under the beer glasses to sketch out for us where the key players were in the movement that led to Deans going over the line. It was a classic case of a legendary story being passed on.

Wallace always maintained that it was he who started the movement when he grabbed the ball following a lineout near his own 25 and went racing upfield. As he once wrote: 'Then I threw Bob Deans out a long pass which he took perfectly and raced ahead. Teddy Morgan, the Welsh winger, was coming across from the other

NZ Rugby Museum

The New Zealand team which was defeated by Wales in 1905. Bob Deans is third from left in the back row.

wing and Bob was becoming exhausted.

'Bob saw Teddy in time and altered his course to go straight ahead and just grounded the ball six inches from the line and about eight yards from the goal posts as Teddy dived at him and got him around the legs. But the try had been scored.'

Then, according to Wallace and other New Zealanders, Deans got up and a Welshman (halfback Dicky Owen is usually blamed) picked up the ball and replaced it about six inches in front of the line. When referee Dallas, dressed in his street clothes, arrived, they told him the ball had been grounded in front of the line. The New Zealanders protested vigorously at this, but Mr Dallas decreed no try had been scored.

It was ironic that Deans, at 21 the baby of the team, should be involved in the furore. He was one of the quietest and least controversial members of the team. He was a regular churchgoer and came from a wealthy Canterbury family. During the tour he made sure that some team members, who were struggling financially, had enough money to get through the trip comfortably. Whenever he attended church he would gather a group to go with him.

One time in Leicester, Billy Stead, the team vice-captain, stole his gold watch chain and sovereign case as a practical joke, and was then miffed when Deans said nothing. A few days later, Stead said: 'Bob, aren't you missing something?' Deans said his watch and chain and sovereign case had gone, but that he hadn't mentioned it because the only people who could have taken them were two housemaids, who, he said, had honest faces, and his team-mates, who would never do such a thing.

The 1905 Welsh team which squeaked to victory over New Zealand. Teddy Morgan is seated on the ground, at the left.

Another time, in Scotland, it was Deans who gathered £50 (of which he had donated £25) when he heard of the plight of a widow with a young family.

The team had a special fondness for Deans. 'His greatest possession,' said Wallace, 'was his nobility of character. He would never see a comrade stuck and his little acts of kindness were just as numerous as they were quiet and unassuming. There came a time, sad to say, when dear old Bob was called upon to lay aside those worldly goods, when that generous heart was stilled forever, when many comrades shed a tear around his open grave.' Deans died in 1908, aged just 24, a tremendous shock to his team-mates.

The 1905 All Blacks knew that if there was one player in their team who would never dream of falsely claiming a try, it was Deans. That heightened their indignation.

Deans himself later wrote, when filing a story for the *Press* from Swansea on December 20, 1905: 'Deans at last got over for New Zealand, but while lying over the line, was pulled back by the Welsh forwards and the referee, who was about 30 yards behind the play, gave it as no score.'

It can be seen that Deans' own account, that he was pulled back from the line, differs with that of Wallace, who says he got up and that the ball was then replaced.

There were similar discrepancies on the Welsh side. Teddy Morgan, like most of his team-mates, claimed Wales deserved to win the 1905 test, but when he signed a menu for Cliff Porter during the All Blacks' 1924 tour of Britain, he wrote on it: 'To Billy Wallace Carbine, from Teddy Morgan. Deans did score at Cardiff, 1905.'

Cliff Porter (left), captain of the mighty Invincibles, pictured with Teddy Morgan after the Swansea game in 1924.

Truthfully it doesn't really matter a jot now. But the episode has been consigned to sports folklore, like the debate over whether heavyweight boxing champ Jack Johnson lay down against Jess Willard, and about whose idea bodyline bowling in cricket really was.

Contemporary reports were many and varied. One press story credited Wallace with having scored. Some said Morgan tackled Deans, others that Rhys Gabe did. Some versions have it that Deans dotted down the ball and was pulled back; others that a Welsh played picked up the ball and replaced it in front of the line.

The language describing the incident was rather flowery. For instance, R.A. Buttery, the *Daily Mail* correspondent who wrote *Why the All Blacks Triumphed*, covered the affair: 'It was now that Wallace, chafing under the prolonged inaction which the Colonial three-quarter line had endured, rushed with desperation born of despair into the thick of the fray. Gathering the ball from an opponent's toe, he tore his way through every obstacle and in a trice was speeding down the field, with Deans on his flank and only two opponents to pass. It looked an absolutely certain try.

'Winfield, the Welsh fullback, went for Wallace a dozen yards from the line, but 'ere he could reach him the ball had been passed to Deans, racing down the touchline. He too was collared but not before he had grounded across the Welsh line, though the referee — whose decision is bound to be accepted in such matters — declared that he had been held up and ordered a scrum.'

What made the dispute so galling was that the New Zealanders lost their unbeaten tour record after so long, and to a team that had been eagerly awaiting them for months. 'Wait till you get to Wales!' was a cry the All Blacks heard often in the preceding months.

Really the New Zealand team which lined up to confront Wales at Cardiff Arms Park was a far cry from the side which 13 weeks earlier had begun the tour with runaway victories by 55–4, 41–9 and 41–0. Those were the carefree days of late summer, epitomised by Wallace at Camborne, playing at fullback in Gillett's hat.

But two or three matches a week, incessant travel, and injuries (no tour doctor or physio back then) wore down the New Zealanders. The All Blacks went into the Welsh test without three key players — Billy Cunningham, Billy Stead and George Smith — all injured.

After the match, Deans cabled the *Daily Mail* newspaper, writing: 'Grounded ball

NZ Rugby Museum

Bob Deans' famous cable which was sent to the *Daily Mail* after the All Blacks' controversial loss to Wales.

6 inches over line. Some of Welsh players admit try. Hunter and Glasgow can confirm was pulled back by Welshmen before Referee Arrived. Deans.'

Back home, where the tour created unprecedented interest, the defeat shocked rugby followers. Communication in 1905 was slow. The first word of a match played overnight came through on the early-morning cable and post offices throughout the country hoisted a notice, or board, bearing the result, which rugby enthusiasts would make the early morning trip to town to read.

Back home, where the tour created unprecedented interest, the defeat shocked rugby followers.

When the 3–0 result was posted the day after the Welsh test it was at first assumed New Zealand had won and a pall of gloom prevailed when it became clear the All Blacks had at last been beaten.

The *Press* captured the atmosphere on Monday, December 18: 'The *Rotomohana*, which arrived in Lyttelton yesterday from Wellington, brought many passengers, including several members of the Ministry, all of whom were naturally anxious to know the result of the match. The first news came from some men on the moles. When they shouted that Wales had won, there was a feeling of incredulity. "Oh, go on, you're having us on!" came the shout from the ship.

'Gradually the sad conviction of defeat sank into their souls, especially when they looked at Mr Seddon [the Prime Minister] and saw dejection written large on his usually radiant countenance. On arriving alongside the wharf, the news was confirmed and all the way up to town formed the sole topic of conversation on the train.'

Perhaps the final word should go to the referee himself. Mr Dallas, recounting the controversy, said: 'On the Monday morning I was astonished to read in the papers on my return to Edinburgh that Deans had scored a try I disallowed.

'When the ball went back on its way to Deans, I kept going hard ahead and when Deans was tackled, he grounded the ball six to twelve inches short of the goal-line. At that moment, he could neither pass nor play the ball and I blew my whistle shrill and loud. It is true that when I got to the spot to order a scrum, the ball was over the goal-line, but without hesitation I ordered a scrum at the place where the ball was grounded. I never blew my whistle at the spot. It had gone before. No try was scored by Deans.'

Cardiff was abuzz all night. The post office sent out 35,000 messages, compared with the usual Saturday's 800. Hotels and eating houses were swarming with people, all talking about the match, and the Deans incident.

The talk went on not just that evening, or that week, but for years and decades. A video referee would, indeed, have stamped out the controversy then and there. But just think of all the talk, the debates, that we'd have missed out on in the meantime.

Rugby's close call

Ninety years later, diehard rugby league fans are still chortling over the action of the Canterbury Rugby Union in 1912.

At a meeting of the Union that year, Mr S. Wilson suggested that the breakaway game of Northern Union (now known as rugby league) was a better game than rugby union. Mr Wilson felt Canterbury should adopt the new game and spoke with such persuasiveness that the meeting agreed to let the local clubs decide the matter.

So at the next Canterbury Rugby Union annual meeting, a vote was duly taken. Stunningly, the clubs supported the change to Northern Union rules, but as an amateur game, not professional.

The next step was to take the Canterbury plan to the New Zealand union. There, with support from Auckland, Hawke's Bay, Bush, Canterbury, South Canterbury, Otago and Southland, the remit was put to the general vote and narrowly defeated 34–28. The rugby union laws of the game remained.

Rugby union officials today who are derisory of league might do well to remember that if four voters had changed their mind back in 1912, their beloved game might have been swallowed up by rugby league.

13. Whistling up a storm

Questionable refereeing in Springbok–All Black rivalry

There's a saying I've heard many times. It goes something along the lines of: 'When you're here in South Africa, we cheat, and we beat you. When we're in New Zealand, you cheat, and you beat us.' There are variations, but that's the gist of it.

Until neutral referees became accepted as standard procedure for test rugby in the 1980s, the issue of home referees was a burning one. Touring teams invariably pointed at a local referee as one reason for a defeat. 'We're not saying he cheats, but . . .'

Nowhere has the subject of refereeing been more hotly debated than in the history of South Africa-New Zealand tests. We in New Zealand always talk about getting a poor deal from a succession of South African referees. What we sometimes overlook is that the feeling on the Springbok side is just as vehement the other way.

Let me make a brief journey through the decades of Springbok–All Black tests and you'll see what I mean. The first test between the countries was played at Carisbrook in 1921. The referee was Ted McKenzie, one of several brothers from a famous rugby family. McKenzie was a few years later to be one of the central figures in the infamous Battle of Solway (see page 156), but his appointment was greeted cheerfully enough on this occasion. It didn't take long for the first refereeing controversy. In the second half, a high kick by All Black first five-eighth Ces Badeley bobbled about behind the South African goal-line. McKenzie ruled that Moke Belliss had touched it first — a try for the All Blacks. The Springboks and many onlookers disagreed, feeling a South African defender had touched down the ball.

Not too much fuss was made of the incident, though. Eighty years ago, there was less of a spotlight on the referee. The media — and don't forget this pre-dated radio and TV — tended to go along with officialdom and it was regarded as not good form to be too critical of referees. Things have changed. For proof of that, just listen to Radio Sport's talkback callers after a big rugby match!

There is little evidence that Maurice Brownlie's men had too many problems with the referees in South Africa in 1928, at least none that they acknowledged publicly. Boet Neser officiated in all four tests and had a better understanding of the rules than many of the players, as was revealed during the first test at Durban when he penalised the All Blacks for a late tackle and awarded the kick where Bennie Osler's kick had landed. This rule was new to international rugby and caught most of the players unawares.

New Zealand's referees in 1937 didn't seem to cause too many problems for the Springboks, who were clearly the better team and won the series 2–1. The furore over refereeing really broke out in 1949, when Fred Allen's All Blacks lost all four tests in South Africa.

I have spoken to Fred and other '49ers many times about this tour, and they are in almost unanimous agreement that the standard of refereeing in the four tests was poor and that the decisions favoured the South Africans. The penalty count ratio for the series was 2:1 to South Africa and Springbok kicker Okey Geffin certainly made the All Blacks pay. Allen's team made a deliberate decision not to talk about the referees on their return.

'I gathered the players together on the ship coming home,' said Allen, 'and told them that I would prefer it if we didn't get home and start complaining about the referees. We'd lost the series and it would have looked like we were bad losers. With no TV, the New Zealand public didn't have much idea what had gone on, and it would have seemed like we were simply making excuses. I told the boys that if they had to blame anyone, they should blame me, because I was the captain. I was very proud of the way no one in the team really uttered a word about the referees for years and years.'

The first test, at Newlands, Cape Town, went to South Africa 15–11. Geffin's five penalty goals beat the All Blacks' two tries (one converted) and one penalty. Referee Eddie Hofmeyr awarded the penalties and Geffin kicked the goals, pulling the Springboks back from a 0–8 halftime deficit. This was to be the pattern for the series. There were many reasons for the All Blacks' whitewash — lack of a quality halfback, the absence of coach Vic Cavanagh, trouble with the scrum, the poor goal-kicking form of the otherwise magnificent Bob Scott. Difficulty adapting to, and even understanding, South African referees was another.

But, really, was this any different to what occurred in 1956? When we think back on that series now, we think of the might of Kevin Skinner, the kicking of Don Clarke, the Eden Park try of Peter Jones, and reflect on a tumultuous year of rugby. South Africans, on the other hand, gripe about the refereeing they encountered. After the first test, South African coach Danie Craven took complaints about the refereeing to the New Zealand union. The referees' attitude to the ruck was a major problem for the Springboks. Referee Bill Fright had a tough time controlling the two teams' forwards in the third test, when Skinner had been recalled to the All Blacks and dealt summarily with props Jaap Bekker and Chris Koch. The South African view was that Skinner was given too much latitude. 'They roughed us up and the referee saw nothing,' was how Springbok centre Wilf Rosenberg described the visitors' feelings.

There were further Springbok complaints. They felt Fright signalled one of Clarke's kicks at Christchurch as good when they believed it had missed. After all these years, legends grow. A story that has been printed since has it that when Fright raised his arm, Rosenberg said: 'That wasn't over, ref!' Fright is said to have replied, 'Shut your f—— mouth, sonny!' I doubt the veracity of this story, but it does indicate how hard done by the South Africans thought they were.

Referee Bill Fright, whom the 1956 Boks complained about long and loud.

There were more controversial decisions in 1960. The All Blacks believed they lost the fourth test because referee Ralph Burmeister (who often used to officiate wearing white sandshoes) refused to allow winger Frank McMullen a legitimate try. The game, to decide the series, had reached its critical final moments when McMullen, running hard for the corner, was tripped by Keith Oxlee's outstretched hand. Footage of the incident shows that McMullen fell short, but reached out and placed the ball over the line. Burmeister ruled that he had played the ball on the ground after a tackle and awarded a penalty to South Africa. It was a controversial decision to say the least, and the All Blacks were adamant they had been denied a series-levelling fourth test victory because of a refereeing error. Ironically, the scenario was to be repeated almost precisely in 1976.

When we recall the Springboks' 1965 tour of New Zealand, we think of a dominant All Black team going within a whisker of winning the series 4–0. Only a second-half lapse in the third test in Christchurch cost the All Blacks one test. The South Africans, though outclassed, still felt they had been harshly treated by the referees.

In the first test, at Athletic Park, Kel Tremain was awarded a try that even the New Zealand supporters felt was dubious, and in a 6–3 scoreline that was a decisive decision. In the third test, the South Africans trailed 16–5. There was a significant moment during the first half when referee Pat Murphy had to leave the field with injury and was replaced by touch judge Alan Taylor. The Springbok comeback coincided nicely with the exchange of referees. I have heard Colin Meads talk of that test and say, with a smile on his face, 'We were in trouble once we lost our referee.'

By 1976, with the tests being televised, there was much more focus on the job that

Welshman Clive Norling, who controlled the highly charged third test of 1981.

the referee was doing. For instance, in the third test referee Gert Bezuidenhout drew New Zealand wrath for overturning a penalty place-kick being taken by Sid Going. Bezuidenhout took the penalty off Going after the ball had fallen over three times before he could kick it. The rules stated that after 40 seconds, the clock was to be stopped. There was nothing about the penalty being reversed. The All Blacks felt they'd been hard done by. South Africans shrugged and thought: 'Fair enough.'

Bezuidenhout incited much more anger during the fourth test at Ellis Park when he twice penalised the South Africans for blatant fouls on Bruce Robertson. New Zealand fans, and the All Blacks themselves, were adamant both incidents, particularly the second, merited penalty tries. As mild a man as Tane Norton was so frustrated with the refereeing display of Bezuidenhout, which he believed had cost the All Blacks a deserved victory, that he had to be restrained in the players' tunnel afterwards.

The ironic twist to this series was that the New Zealand Rugby Union had been offered neutral referees and had declined the offer. Of course, they were not the people out on the field having to cope with a South African referee being placed under massive pressure from a home crowd. The All Blacks felt they really struggled to find a good referee that year. Ian Gourlay was their choice as referee in the first test, mainly because he had an English-sounding name. Gourlay had a mediocre test, and Bezuidenhout got the job after that.

By 1981 neutral referees had arrived, but that did not end the controversy, not by a long chalk. Welshman Clive Norling played a key role in the decisive third test, at Eden Park. It was a never to be forgotten test, what with the protesters, the Cessna plane, the flour bombs and all. It came down to injury time, with the score 22–22. After eight minutes, Norling awarded a free kick to New Zealand. He turned it into a penalty when, he said, the Springboks did not retreat 10 yards. Allan Hewson kicked a goal to win the series for New Zealand.

The Springboks are still complaining about Norling. With his tight shorts, sense of humour and rather showy mannerisms, Norling was a personality in his own right. The Springboks didn't mind that, but they still bitterly resent that he cost them at least a draw. I've spoken to Springboks who say they have studied the footage of those vital few moments at the end of the game. They say the Springboks were retreating and, in fact, did retire 10 yards before involving themselves in the play. They say Norling was determined the match would not end in a draw and that they were the victims.

The disgruntlement that Norling's refereeing caused in South Africa was matched five years later when Welshman Ken Rowlands refereed all four of the Cavaliers-South Africa matches. This wasn't an official test series, though it certainly seemed to be billed that way in South Africa. The Cavaliers had a tough schedule, with four tests on successive weekends, and the longer they were away, the clearer it became that they did not have the support of much of the New Zealand public. They seemed to feel in the end that only a series victory would justify the gamble they'd taken in making a rebel tour.

As has so often been the way in New Zealand-South African series, the score was 2–1 in favour of the home team going into the fourth and final test. The Cavaliers felt Rowlands' refereeing deteriorated the longer the series went. He slapped a 21–7 penalty count on the Cavaliers in that fourth international, at Ellis Park. Hika Reid, the Cavaliers hooker, shouldered the referee as they left the field. Jock Hobbs, Murray Mexted and Wayne Smith left the Welshman in no doubt that what they thought of him. Andy Dalton, the Cavaliers captain, whose jaw had been broken by a cowardly punch in the second tour game, questioned Rowlands' honesty at the after-match function.

The Cavaliers' complaints drew little sympathy from the South Africans. Ace goal kicker Naas Botha summed up their feelings when he said, 'Now you know how we felt in 1981.'

The Cavaliers tour signalled the last rugby contact between New Zealand and South Africa until 1992, by which time the apartheid laws had been repealed. Since then, the refereeing issue has not been the factor it once was.

There have still been headline-grabbing incidents, and there always will be. Irishman Brian Stirling penalised the Springboks repeatedly at Carisbrook in 1994. Two years later the South Africans felt they were victims of a harsh decision five minutes from fulltime at Christchurch when, while hard on attack and trailing by just one point, they were penalised for collapsing the scrum.

At Auckland in 1997, André Venter became the first Springbok to be sent from the field in a test. Welshman Derek Bevan sent him packing for stomping on Sean Fitzpatrick's head early in the second half. The following year, New Zealanders felt the All Blacks lost the test at Durban because Jonah Lomu was wrongly penalised for a late tackle on Stefan Terblanche just two minutes from fulltime.

What's interesting about these incidents through the 1990s was that in previous decades any of them could have been blown up into full-scale 'We wuz robbed!' controversies. But with neutral referees there is no chance for the visiting team to claim it is being cheated, or the referee is biased. The sting has finally been taken out of the argument.

14. Beaten by boys?

Swansea schoolboys help lower Black colours

'You can tell the people back home what you like, but just don't tell them the All Blacks were beaten today by a couple of schoolboys!' So said New Zealand captain Jack Manchester after his team had been humbled 11–3 by Swansea at the St Helens Ground in 1935.

The All Blacks — beaten by a couple of schoolboys! Could it be true? Well, the story has grown in the re-telling, but there was more than a grain of truth in what Manchester said. It happened like this . . .

Swansea, nicknamed the All Whites, were fairly inexperienced that year, especially at scrumhalf and flyhalf, so the selectors, thinking laterally, invited two

News Media Auckland

Jack Manchester.

cousins from Gowerton County School, Haydn Tanner and Willie Davies, to represent their city against Manchester's All Blacks.

The two teenagers, one aged 17 and the other 18, were unfazed by the challenge. They played with the absolute freedom of youthful spirit and mesmerised their illustrious opponents. Their combination was a vital factor in Swansea's shock win, the only victory the club has had over the All Blacks.

Davies went on to become a fine international player, but it was Tanner who had real star quality. He represented Wales from 1935–49 and was never dropped. Even in a country that has produced Dick Owen and Garth Edwards, many Welshman still swear there has never been a finer scrumhalf than Tanner.

15. A right royalties ruckus

All Blacks who were cooked by their books

The advent of professionalism in rugby in 1995 eliminated one of the game's great charades, the ubiquitous trust fund.

Rugby stars didn't generally write books before the 1960s. There were books by journalists and various almanacks, annuals and coaching manuals, but the era of the mass-marketed biography hadn't arrived. In the 1950s, Bob Scott and Ron Jarden wrote (or had ghost-written) biographies. But other big New Zealand names of that era, like Tiny White, Kevin Skinner, Fred Allen, Has Catley and Johnny Simpson, simply played out their careers, then retired.

Into the 1960s, George Nepia (belatedly), Peter Jones and Don Clarke were three big names who produced books. Still, there was no Kel Tremain book. Nothing from Wilson Whineray, Waka Nathan, Ken Gray or Des Connor. All would have been bestsellers.

By the 1970s, though, the sports book boom was under way, and in New Zealand, the sport to attract most attention was, naturally, rugby. It was *Colin Meads All Black*, by Alex Veysey, which set the pace — and still does. Including a few thousand overseas sales, the Meads book sold 61,000 copies, which beggars belief. It was brilliantly marketed, had the market virtually to itself, was the story of a genuine rugby legend, and was written with insight and humour by Veysey. In today's terms, Meads would pocket about $350,000 from such a sale, and even back in the early 1970s the proceeds were not inconsiderable.

What to do with the money? Ah, the trust fund. To a financial novice like me, it seemed the trust fund was a rather cunning way of retaining most of the proceeds from book sales without incurring the wrath of the amateur-minded rugby administrators of the time. Meads was certainly asked the question about what he was doing with the money (as he was a few years later when he began featuring in television advertisements).

Curiously, when Chris Laidlaw released *Mud In Your Eye* in 1973, he never had his

amateur status questioned. Yet *Mud In Your Eye* was a controversial and critical book that greatly displeased rugby officials of that era. 'I was overseas at the time,' says Laidlaw, 'so I don't recall that the professionalism thing was an issue. Most of the administrators were so outraged by the book that they just assumed I was automatically banned forever from anything to do with rugby! I don't think they thought to formalise the ban because they felt I was so far over the mark it was unnecessary!

'When I returned to New Zealand, I just carried on with my life and no one ever mentioned my amateur status to me.'

Through the 1970s and '80s, most big-name All Blacks who wrote books apparently channelled the profits into trust funds. There was a fair bit of nudge, nudge, wink, wink going on, and I don't feel the administrators of the time really minded, as long as it wasn't too blatant — a sort of 'Do what you want, but don't rub our noses in it' attitude.

But what about those rare few players who were determined to be utterly up-front? Three who come to mind are Graham Mourie, Stu Wilson and Andy Haden.

Mourie had *Graham Mourie Captain* published in 1982, announced he would be keeping the money he earned from the book, and was subsequently banned from rugby. Wilson's case shortly afterwards was even more startling.

Wilson and his fellow Wellington and All Black winger Bernie Fraser jointly had a biography written. Alex Veysey wrote *Ebony and Ivory* with wit and style. Wilson announced he would be keeping his share of the profits and was therefore also barred from rugby. Fraser went the trust fund way and continued his involvement with rugby, playing on long enough to be one of the rebel Cavaliers in 1986.

Haden, being Haden, tried another method when *Boots 'n all!* came out in 1983. He declared himself a writer and claimed that because writing was his occupation he was entitled to keep the money. What's more, despite gripes and groans at the Huddart Parker Building in Wellington, he won his case.

The ridiculous situation continued to exist for several more years. It led to Wilson coaching in Auckland under the name of Wilson Stuart, much to the amusement of many people, including various rugby officials. Mourie was John Hart's unofficial forwards coach with the Auckland team, but because he was one of those filthy professionals, this was not reported as such. In 1987 Mourie, still a professional, working for the West Nally public relations company, helped to organise the World Cup in New Zealand. He was largely responsible for the success of that tournament, but was still off-side with the game's crusty old law-makers.

The stigma of professionalism never seemed to worry Mourie or Wilson. As Mourie said when asked why he was breaching the game's laws and coaching his club team in Taranaki: 'It's a long way from Twickenham to the Opunake clubrooms.'

The whole issue is irrelevant now, of course. Rugby has embraced professionalism. The more professional, the better.

But the annual year-end stories that surfaced regularly about what so-and-so rugby star intended doing with the earnings from his book did serve to remind followers of the game here just how out of touch the law-makers were.

One match, three refs

We occasionally see a match in which a referee is injured and has to be replaced, usually by one of his touch judges. There was once a match in New Zealand in which three referees were used.

It was the Bush v Wanganui fixture played at Pahiatua in 1957. Roy Rice was the referee, but he was hurt when he crashed into a player scoring a try and was taken to the sideline for treatment. Up stepped touch judge Leith Parker, who happened to be president of the Bush union, to supervise the conversion attempt.

Obviously it wasn't satisfactory having Parker, with his vested interest in proceedings, continue to officiate, and when it became clear that Rice would be unable to continue, a third referee, Wray Hewitt, controlled the rest of the game, Parker returning to the touchline.

Bush were unfazed by the revolving referee situation and won the match 20–16.

16. Telegram of shame

South African racism, 1920s style

The history of South Africa–New Zealand rugby relations has been a long and dramatic one. The two countries, bound by a mutual passion for rugby, have trod a tortured path, mainly as a result of South Africa's vile apartheid laws. The white South Africans' respect, or lack of it, for their black, Coloured and Indian countrymen has always been an issue, and through the years it became increasingly thorny.

In the face of all the much-publicised disputes down the years, it is easy to overlook the first time the South Africans' inherent racism was brought into sharp focus for New Zealanders. It occurred in 1921, when Theo Pienaar led the first Springbok team to tour New Zealand. It was an outstanding touring team, and included such famous rugby figures as fullback Gerhard Morkel, winger Attie van Heerden, and forwards Boy Morkel, Frank Mellish and Phil Mostert. Two of the pack, Royal Morkel and Baby Michau, weighed more than 17 stone (108kg), which was huge for the time.

The team eventually split the three-test series 1–1 with one draw and that set the

> Bad enough having play team officially designated NZ Natives but spectacle thousands Europeans frantically cheering on band of coloured men to defeat members of own race was too much for Springboks, who frankly disgusted.

Above: The 1921 Springboks receive the haka prior to their match against New Zealand Maori at Napier. Below: The Maori team which lost narrowly 8-9 to the Boks.

tone for some tough, uncompromising contests in the decades ahead. Unfortunately another tone was also set in 1921. New Zealanders got an early insight into the ugly side of the white South African mentality.

The Springboks' 17th match was against the New Zealand Maori team at Napier. The visitors won a tight and physical contest 9–8, but the result was overshadowed by what happened afterwards.

A local Postal and Telegraph worker was so horrified by the contents of a report by South African reporter Charles Blackett that he leaked it to the *Napier Daily Telegraph*, and its publication caused a storm throughout New Zealand.

Blackett's report said in part (bear in mind it was written in the shortened telegraph style of the time with many words left out): 'Most unfortunate match ever played. Only result great pressure being brought to bear on Bennett induced them to meet Maoris, who assisted largely entertainment Springboks. Bad enough having play team officially designated NZ Natives but spectacle thousands

Europeans frantically cheering on band of coloured men to defeat members of own race was too much for Springboks, who frankly disgusted. That was not the worst. The crowd was most unsportsmanlike experienced on tour, especially section who lost all control of their feelings. When not booing referee, they indulged in sarcastic remarks at his expense. On many occasions, Africans were hurt. Crowd, without waiting for possibility of immediate recovery, shouted "Take him off, take him off". Their faithful coloured allies proved loyal to New Zealand for in addition to serious injury to Kruger's leg, Van Heerden had to stay off field for 15 minutes. Others limping badly. Maoris flung their weight about regardless of niceties of the game.'

Blackett's report was incorrect in parts. For instance the local team was in fact the New Zealand Maori XV. And he claimed he had been quoted out of context. But what he wrote seemed indefensible to New Zealanders.

The reaction of the South African team manager, Harold Bennett, was interesting. He distanced himself from the report, but had no problem with the many remarks made to or about the Maori players by Springboks during the match, though these comments, often racist or superior in nature, angered locals.

There were many repercussions from the leaked report, which led to the sacking of the postal worker. The Hawke's Bay union was so incensed by Blackett's writing that it fired off a broadside at Bennett: 'Whoever was responsible for the telegram does not know or understand how highly the Maori race is regarded by his Pakeha fellow citizens. Trust your contact with Maori race will have shown you that they are worthy of the position of equality assigned to them and should not be looked upon as nothing better than a kaffir.'

The wounds from this match took a long time to heal. On Bennett's recommendation, the next Springbok team to tour New Zealand, in 1937, did not have a match scheduled against a New Zealand Maori XV and the fixture did not resume until 1956.

17. Rain, hail or war . . .

Our game stops for nothing

It should not have been a surprise that the game of rugby hardly blinked in 2001 in the face of the stark headlines of war when United States forces responded to terrorist attacks on New York and Washington. That the sport continued all over the world, including tours by almost all the major rugby nations, was merely a repeat of what had gone on before in rugby's long history. The game has always gone on, no matter what. In fact, in the 19th century, it was the services that kick-started New Zealand rugby, providing the organisation and players for many of New Zealand's earliest matches.

Way back in 1870 sailors from HMS *Rosario* played a bastardised version of rugby against teams from Auckland and Wellington. The Auckland match, played at the Mount Albert Barracks, led to the formation of the Auckland club, which in 1873 adopted the rules of rugby. In 1874, a team from HMS *Blanche* met Nelson, losing two goals to nil.

During the New Zealand Wars of the 1870s, rugby teams comprising members of the military and police force played against the Wellington club in 1871 and Wanganui two years later. To see how pivotal this was to the development of New Zealand rugby, we can note that one player in the Armed Constabulary team was Thomas Eyton, who in 1888–89 was one of the shakers and movers behind the famous Natives team.

New Zealand rugby continued throughout the major wars of the 20th century. The Boer War in South Africa from 1899–1902 attracted such players as Dave Gallaher (later to captain the Originals), Bill Hardham and Bunny Abbott.

Even the Boer War could not stop rugby. A halt to hostilities was called in April 1902 to permit a game to be played between opposing forces. The original letter, signed on behalf of General S.G. Maritz of the Transvaal Scouting Corps and addressed to a Major Edwards, was written in High Dutch. The English translation of one of the most remarkable pieces of correspondence in rugby history reads:

The Honourable Major Edwards,
   O'Kiep.

Dear Sir,

   I wish to inform you that I have agreed to a rugby match taking place between you and us. I, from my side, will agree to a cease-fire tomorrow afternoon from 12 o'clock until sunset, the time and venue of the match to be arranged by you in consultation with Messers. Roberts and Van Rooyen who I am sending to you.

I have the honour etc.,
   p.p. S. G. Maritz,
      First General
         Transvaal Scouting Corps.

Concordia, April 28, 1902.

Closer to home, look at the 1914 All Blacks on their tour of Australia. In his book *Gold and Black*, which summarises a history of rugby encounters between New Zealand and Australia, author Spiro Zavos writes of the New Zealand match against a New South Wales selection (called Metropolitan Union) on August 5, 1914. Some time after the game had started, news reached Sydney by telegraph from London that the British government had joined with France and 'war accordingly had been declared on Germany'.

   Two boys climbed a ladder and spelt out the words 'War Declared' on the Sydney Cricket Ground scoreboard. The game did not stop, though presumably the news was whispered around the ground and conveyed to the players. The All Blacks went on to win (the score, yes it is important to record, was 11–6) and the tour finished two weeks later.

   In the *Official History of the New Zealand Rugby Football Union* the summary of the 1914 season notes that 'the outbreak of hostilities occurred at such time as to allow no interruption of the season's programme'. In fact, a Ranfurly Shield match was played in New Plymouth on the same day as the outbreak of war (Taranaki defended successfully against Horowhenua, winning 14–3). A minister of religion, the Reverend W.B. Scott, controlled the game.

   It has to be said that so great was the response to serve in the war by young New Zealand men that rugby almost faded out in the years 1915–18. But not quite.

   The annual North-South fixture was suspended, as were Ranfurly Shield challenges. Matches for that famous trophy resumed in 1919; thus Wellington, who had beaten Taranaki in the last challenge of 1914, had held the Shield for four seasons unbeaten!

During overseas wartime action, many thousands of New Zealanders lost their lives. Seven of them had been All Blacks, including Dave Gallaher. Most units possessed a rugby team and football action involving New Zealanders was played in France, Britain, Egypt and the Palestine.

NZ Rugby Museum

In 1918–19, before coming home at war's end, the leading New Zealand rugby-playing soldiers formed two teams, one touring in Britain and the other in France. When King George V announced he was putting up a trophy for all nations' service teams to play for before demobilisation, the two New Zealand sides played off in a trial game for a best team selection. The New Zealand Divisional team (which had toured France)

Dave Gallaher, who was killed in action during World War II.

beat the New Zealand United Kingdom XV and from that the New Zealand Army team to play for the King's Cup was formed. New Zealand won the tournament, beating the Mother Country XV 9–3 in the final at Twickenham.

On the way home by ship, the team was engaged in a controversy, which has never been truly explained. Included in the New Zealand team was an outstanding forward, Sergeant Arthur Wilson of Wellington. He had been an All Black from 1908–14 (and was on the field in Sydney the day war broke out). But Wilson was of Anglo-West Indian parentage and was dark-skinned. Therefore, in the first incident of the 'colour bar' being invoked in rugby, Ranji Wilson (he was nicknamed after the great Indian cricketer Jam Sahib Ranjitsinhji, who played for England) was not permitted to play when the Army team stopped on the way home in South Africa. In Cape Town, Wilson could not even leave the ship. The Army team stayed for 15 games over two months, but Wilson sailed on for home.

The Second World War in 1939 was greeted with equal 'indifference' by rugby in New Zealand. Rugby did not stop immediately just because there had been the official announcement of hostilities declared. The finest Fijian rugby team of all time just happened to be touring New Zealand in 1939.

The day New Zealand's government announced they were declaring war on Germany, Fiji took on Auckland at Eden Park. The touring team beat New Zealand's top provincial side 17–11. Nowhere in the records of the Auckland Rugby Union is it recorded that the mood of the occasion was affected in any way by pessimism of impending war. Rather, the occasion was celebrated by 17,000 people turning up to watch! The Fiji team played four more matches before heading home. From their eight-match tour, they remained the only unbeaten overseas national team to tour New Zealand until Tonga undertook a four-match unbeaten tour in 1994.

As a sidelight, the Fijians were playing in their first season wearing boots. Previously all matches at home had been played in bare feet. And the Fijians were the last team in world rugby to favour the 2-3-2 scrum formation, with an extra roving player standing off all set scrums. They changed part-way through the tour to the now standard 3-4-1 formation.

In September 1939, both the Australian rugby team and the New Zealand rugby league team had to abort tours of Britain. The Wallabies arrived in England the day before war was declared. The Kiwis had played just two matches. However, the first major New Zealand rugby casualty of wartime was the cancellation of the 1940 All Black tour of South Africa. Trials were held in Wellington in 1939 and more were scheduled for 1940, but the latter series was cancelled.

Throughout the war, whenever rugby was talked by New Zealand soldiers, there was speculation as to who might have made the touring team to South Africa. In his book *Haka! The All Blacks Story*, Winston McCarthy speculated with some authority on the touring team's possible lineup. Winston was on strong personal terms with the sole All Black selector, Ted McKenzie of Wairarapa. But McKenzie only let slip information that Tom Morrison of South Canterbury (later Chairman of the New Zealand union) was in the team, and also that he would nominate Charlie Saxton (then of Southland) as the tour captain.

The New Zealand government did encourage rugby to be played at club and representative level during the war. But budgets had been slashed and some provinces found it hard to travel any distance for games. Nevertheless 72 games of first-class status were played in 1940; 58 in 1941; 56 in 1942; 42 in 1943; 48 in 1944; 63 in 1945. Many of those games involved teams from all three Services. Ranfurly Shield matches were suspended, as, initially, was the inter-island fixture. However, the New Zealand union decided that, as there were significant numbers of top players being held back in New Zealand for defensive purposes, should the Japanese attack, the inter-island match would resume in 1943.

Rugby goal posts sprang up all over the war zones as soon as New Zealand teams pitched camp, wherever they were. The standard of play was high with all the players being so fit. In North Africa, the 2nd NZ Expeditionary Force Division Commander, General Bernard Freyberg, encouraged rugby as a diversion from the rigours of battle. The General even donated a cup for competition between the various units.

Later the wartime rugby competition was expanded to include some famous matches against Army teams from Australia, Britain and South Africa. In a western desert location in Egypt, the first of these was played. At a place called Baggush, the NZEF met the South African Armoured Forces. The playing surface was sand and anti-aircraft defences surrounded the field. This famous match, under a blazing sun, was won by New Zealand 8–0.

In fact, dramatic matches in colourful locations were played right through the war years; in Egypt first, then in support of morale for the Italian campaign. Such was the enthusiasm of the soldiers to play and such was the confidence shown by General Freyberg that the war would be won soon, he ordered trials to be held to find the best New Zealand players in Europe. He wanted them formed into a team to tour Britain after the war.

Not everything went to plan, of course. It took two years for the NZEF team to be finalised and when it was, the captain was the team's only pre-war All Black, Charlie Saxton.

The Army team of the Expeditionary Force was quickly nicknamed the Kiwis and their tour was a huge hit with the greatly relieved, and at peace, British sports public.

News Media Auckland

Kiwis captain, Major Charlie Saxton.

News Media Auckland

Members of the Kiwis perform a haka for the Lord Mayor of London during their famous tour of the United Kingdom, France and Germany in 1945-46.

RUGBY INTERNATIONAL

• • •

ENGLAND

VERSUS

NEW ZEALAND

TWICKENHAM,

SATURDAY, NOV. 24th, 1945

KICK-OFF 2.30

SOUVENIR

• **PROGRAMME** •

RUGBY FOOTBALL UNION, TWICKENHAM

ENGLAND XV v NEW ZEALAND ARMY

SATURDAY, 24th NOVEMBER, 1945.   Kick off 2.30 p.m.

IN AID OF SERVICES' CHARITIES

WEST

Upper Stand

ENTRANCE   ROW   SEAT

L   **L**   133

Should the match be postponed and eventually played, no money will be returned, but this ticket will be available for the later date.

As every reasonable precaution has been taken for the safety of spectators, the Rugby Football Union disclaims responsibility for injury or damage to the holder of this ticket, either from accident or otherwise.

Price 10/- (including admission to Ground)

F. Cooper

Engineer-Commander, R.N., Secretary, R.F.U.

The 1945 programme (left) called it England v New Zealand, while the match ticket correctly spelt out the fact it was New Zealand Army v England XV.

Massive crowds turned up for every game and the rugby was open and thrilling at all times. The Kiwis met Wales, England, Scotland and France (twice) in international matches and lost just two of their 33 games. As their presence effectively re-started rugby in Britain after the war, the team is most fondly remembered to this day.

New Zealand continued to spread the rugby gospel through its servicemen even after the Second World War. Perhaps the best examples were the New Zealand J Force and K Force teams that played many matches in Japan in the late 1940s and early '50s. The J Forces, which included nearly 5000 New Zealand troops taking part in the occupation of Japan immediately after the end of the Second World War, boasted some fine players, including several All Blacks. There were three New Zealand battalions in Japan and they played among themselves for the Freyberg Cup, which was brought over from Europe, where it had been contested by New Zealand servicemen.

Tiny White, the outstanding All Black lock, was one of the J Force soldiers. He told me: 'Each battalion built its own rugby field, usually near an air strip, and put up goal posts. It's what New Zealand servicemen have always done all over the world. The Freyberg Cup matches were very keenly fought. Each battalion had its home ground and a lot of thought and effort went into the inter-battalion matches. From memory the 27th battalion ended up with the Freyberg Cup when the occupation finished.

'As well as the Freyberg Cup matches, we New Zealanders were also involved in the Duntroon Cup tournament. This cup was donated by the Chief of the British Commonwealth Forces, and was played for by teams representing the New Zealand, Australian and Combined British Forces. New Zealand won that one, too. It was a long time ago and it's hard to recall all the names, but our team had several All Blacks, including Tiny Hill and Ray Bell, and also Pat Ryan, another very well-known player.'

New Zealand J Forces, who were stationed in southern Japan, played matches through much of the country, and several times drew large crowds to games in Tokyo. There the rugby was often played at the stadium built for the 1940 Olympics (which because of the outbreak of war were not held).

Within a few years, New Zealand servicemen were back in that part of the world, this time as part of K Force, fighting the North Koreans in the Korean War. From scanning through old programmes, it seems to me that the New Zealand K Force combinations were not as strong as those in the J Force had been, though teams boasted a smattering of provincial representatives and plenty of senior club players. Again, there were some torrid matches played, with national pride on the line.

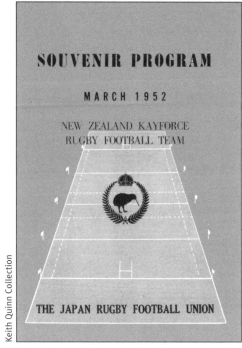

I have no doubt that the rugby played by the J and K Forces did much to popularise rugby in Japan.

A game of four quarters

The expression 'a game of two halves' is one of the great rugby clichés. Well, how about 'a game of four quarters'? It happened once, and in a test match, too.*

New Zealand and Australia clashed at Athletic Park, Wellington, on September 6, 1913. Surprisingly, the weather for the big game was terrible — driving rain, wind and bitter cold. Referee Len Simpson, a local official in charge of his first international, felt the conditions would be such a pivotal factor in the match that he decided to split the game into four quarters, each of 20 minutes with sides swapping ends after each break. His plan couldn't stop New Zealand dominating the match and they won 30–5.

To the best of my knowledge, Mr Simpson's novel idea has not been copied in any test, but it did not seem to hinder his career as a referee. He continued to be a respected referee and in 1924–25 accompanied the Invincibles through Britain and France, as their touch judge.

*Some games in the Super Six in the early 1990s, just before the introduction of the Super 12 were, in effect, played in quarters.

18. Hell for leather
Big Don and the case of the exploding boot

News Media Auckland

Big Don Clarke and those big boots.

Wilson Whineray tells a story about one of the most amusing sights he saw on a rugby field. It happened during the All Black tour of South Africa in 1960.

'Now Don Clarke was a giant figure in our team,' says Whineray. 'His massive kicking intimidated opposition and was a real match-winner. There was always a lot of fuss about Don's boots. They were precious to us.

'We got to the ground before one test and Don opened his gear bag in the dressing room and said with horror, "I've left my boots at the hotel." This was a tragedy. Someone was dispatched to race back to fetch them, but in the meantime the game had to begin.

'What was Don to do? It so happened that Kel Tremain always carried a second pair of boots. It was a superstition of his. He didn't intend using them, so it didn't matter what sort of condition they were in, as long as he had a second pair in his bag.

'He pulled out his second pair. They were dirty, old, worn, with the stitching ripped. He said, "Here, Camel, you can use these if you like."

'So Don pulled on Kel's second pair and out onto the field we trotted. We hadn't been going more than a few minutes when we were given a penalty, just inside Don's range. He placed the ball, took his full run-up and really launched into his kick. As he kicked the ball, there was a sort of explosion. The ball went one way and pieces of the boot flew in all directions. Kel's ancient boot hadn't been able to withstand Don's kicking power and had disintegrated. We nearly fell over laughing. It remains one of the funniest sights I've ever seen on a rugby paddock.'

19. Battle of the Bridge
The wildest NPC final of all

It was always going to be odds-on that tempers would flare during the 1994 Auckland–North Harbour NPC first division final. North Harbour had played outstandingly to beat Auckland in the preliminary round of the competition. They felt they were no longer the poor relations of Auckland rugby. In fact, players such as Eric Rush, Frank Bunce, Ant Strachan and others regarded themselves as having been not wanted by Auckland. They had a point to prove.

Auckland had not had a great NPC and had had to beat Otago away to even make the final. They found some form in their 33–16 semi-final win, but still North Harbour, impressive 59–27 victors over Canterbury in the other semi, fancied their chances and weren't afraid to say so.

An Auckland civil war loomed.

The North Harbour union approached the final very aggressively. For a start, it wouldn't concede the home advantage, even though that meant the match would be played at Onewa Domain, with a capacity of about 12,000, instead of the larger, more suitable Eden Park. Remember this was in the pre-Albany Stadium days. During the build-up week, North Harbour's union and its sponsors aggressively marketed the game, erecting provocative billboards all over the city. Local radio stations got into the act.

By the time the final got underway, things seemed set to explode, and so they did. It was an abrasive, ugly match, during which senior players, many of them All Blacks, allowed their emotions to get the better of them. Rugby played a secondary role to brawling, punching and other unsavoury incidents.

Robin Brooke and Eric Rush were sent from the field by referee Colin Hawke, who would have been justified in claiming double pay for his work that day. Rush had smashed his fellow All Black Zinzan Brooke. Brooke was eventually banned for one month, Rush for one week. In addition, no fewer than five other players were cited

Eric Rush follows the play after being ordered from the field by Colin Hawke.

and had to appear before the judicial committee. The five, Aucklanders Zinzan Brooke and Richard Fromont, and Harbour's Blair Larsen, Mark Weedon and Graham Dowd, could easily have been joined by others.

Auckland battled to a 10–0 lead at halftime, but the gap was closed to 10–9 by three Warren Burton penalties. Sean Fitzpatrick and replacement Jason Chandler then scored tries that sealed the game, despite Walter Little's late try for North Harbour. When we think back on this match, which has since become known as the Battle of the Bridge, the over-riding memory is not of Auckland's 22–16 win, or the tremendous work of Auckland's forwards, especially front-rowers Olo Brown, Sean Fitzpatrick and Kevin Nepia.

No, the picture which comes to mind is of injured Auckland flanker Mark Carter leaving the field covered in blood. Carter, in fact, went into the match carrying an injury that had required stitches, but somehow the sight of him covered in blood seemed to epitomise a match that brought no glory to the NPC.

20. And in the red corner(s)

Canterbury versus the Lions, 1971

Back in 1971, they were a hard lot, those Cantabs. Blokes like Grizz and Hoppy, Jake and Tane. Not to mention them 'other fullers' like Scaly and Fungus in the backs. Even their nicknames made them sound tough.

Canterbury were a team that used to like to dish it out hard and heavy and go hang anyone who got in their way. So the day John Dawes' flash-Harry British Isles touring team came to town, Canterbury had a rugby side that was not at all impressed by the visitors' unbeaten and imposing record against the provinces. It wasn't difficult to imagine Wyllie, Hopkinson, Burns, Norton, Davis, McCormick and co meeting and uttering words to the effect of: 'Stuff these jokers. Who do they think they are?'

Well, that's my take on the build-up to the match that took place at Lancaster Park on June 19, 1971. The Lions had looked sharp in their eight matches in New Zealand by the time they arrived on a brisk Christchurch afternoon to play Canterbury. They had been in the country six weeks and already among their scalps were Waikato, Wellington and Otago, plus the New Zealand Maoris. Mind you, Canterbury were also unbeaten in their four matches to that point. They were the best team in New Zealand, no doubt about it.

The only common opponent the British and the Cantabs had had was Wellington. The Lions had humbled the boys from the capital 47–9 (nine tries to none) and Canterbury had followed a week later, beating Wellington 16–6 (four tries to none). Wellington's defence was like a sieve in those days!

So Canterbury and the Lions shaped up across the kick-off line. A record crowd of 53,000 was present. These days many more will tell you they were there and that they heard every crunch and crash that followed in 80 minutes of turbulent drama. The referee was a real good bloke, a gentle doctor. 'Humph' we called him — Humphrey Rainey, of Wellington. What unfolded on his day of personal rugby destiny haunted him for years. In fact, he wrote a book designed

Lions prop Sandy Carmichael is on the ground clutching his head, while Canterbury prop Alister Hopkinson (right) looks like he might have just seen some off-the-ball action during the infamous 1971 match at Lancaster Park.

to get off his chest what happened in this one game.

Both teams went at it from the first scrum. In those days (and even sometimes today) you used to hear commentators say, 'No quarter was given and none asked for.' Well, this was such a game. Right from the start punches were thrown between the two front rows. Alister Hopkinson, in particular, stood his ground in the Canterbury front row, declining to take the boring-in work of his opposite Sandy Carmichael, of Scotland. More punches followed in the second scrum, and then the third . . . and so on. The fighting then moved into the open.

Irish loose forward Fergus Slattery was just getting up off the deck at one point when someone clouted him around the head and down he went. He wore a brace on his teeth for the rest of the tour.

Another time, the other Lions prop, Ray McLoughlin, punched Alex Wyllie and broke his thumb. The mayhem went on . . . and on . . . and on. Eventually Dr Rainey called out the two captains, John Dawes and Ian Penrose. They stood there while the ref gave them a right dressing down. But those were the days of no touch-judge help for the man in charge, and no video evidence, either. Rainey would have had to have eyes in the back of his head, and in his ears, to catch and act on all of the biff-o and kicking going on. He decided to throw the responsibility back on the two distinguished captains.

Sadly for Rainey, a version of that midfield conversation appeared in New Zealand's *Rugby News* a few days later. It was included in a story written by the English writer John Reason. The story said: 'At one stage Dr Rainey called the captains together and as good as told them that he was opting out of his job.' Reason claimed the Doc then told the game's leaders, 'From now on I'm going to follow the ball and if anything else goes on it's up to you two to sort it out.'

According to Rainey, that quote, incorrect in every way, gravely influenced his refereeing future. In his book *Referee Referee Referee*, Rainey

Les Bloxham

Dr Rainey implores for help from the captains.

claims what he actually said to the captains was: 'It's hard enough trying to follow the ball here, and at the same time control the players in the mood they're in.' He then 'asked for the help of the two captains in controlling their teams'. To me, that's surely a fair enough request.

The problem was that Reason's *Rugby News* quote, which was surprisingly omitted from his tour summary book, was first published only days after the game. It stuck like mud on a blanket on Rainey's reputation. Rainey, who was hoping to get a test match appointment on that tour, was advised by rugby officials to make no public utterance. His strong response in print did not surface until his book came out in 1982. He abhors the fact that the Reason quote was given so much authority at the time and now stands in many people's eyes as the truth of what happened.

Irish loose forward Fergus Slattery was just getting up off the deck at one point when someone clouted him around the head and down he went.

What Humphrey Rainey asked of the two captains was good sense. What else could he do? He might have called off the game, I suppose, or at least sent someone off. He insists that though he dished out warnings, he never saw anything that warranted a dismissal. And you can't have refs sending off players for things they think might have happened.

Whatever was said, and I side with the Rainey version, the teams were in no mind to accede to the other in terms of decency and ra-ra fair play. Rainey carried on and whistled the game as best he could, while the players continued to rail and glare at each other. It was a most unpleasant game, a disgrace in fact. Hardly anyone remembers the final score. (I'm not going to record it here. No one was much interested in it on the day. Why should they be now?)

At the end, the scrapping was still going on ('snarling and snitching', was how Rainey colourfully described it) and McCormick was seen taking on two Lions players, John Bevan and Mike Hipwell, when the whistle blew for fulltime. The teams then filed off the field to count their wounded. Though they were definitely not innocents in what had gone on, the Lions acted with umbrage and headed north to Blenheim for their next fixture as soon as they could.

In the newspaper reporting that followed over the next 48 hours each team blamed the other. Grim front-page newspaper photos showed some of the results of what had gone on. Bruising and puffy eyes of the British players burst out at the nation. Three members of the Lions team had to return home with injuries.

Dr Rainey never received another appointment of similar significance.

I was a youngster working for New Zealand Broadcasting at the time. The way the highlights were edited for Monday night's showing on nationwide TV also caused a stink. You see, the producers cut out all the knuckle bits for some reason. I cannot recall if there was a directive; I do not think so. Maybe on thinking about it, the punching and kicking and elbowing might have happened too far away from the ball to have been captured on video by the modest composition of only three cameras which covered rugby in those days. And 1971 was well before any isolated TV replay systems had come to our shores. To many people, though, the video coverage was also a disgrace and was seen by some as a kind of cover up.

One more thing should be remembered when recalling that squalid affair. A curious attitude to fighting in rugby prevailed in the 1960s and '70s, and not just in New Zealand. In many ways it was akin to the honour and glory that men gave to fighting in old wars. I can recall reading about the way laurels of admiration were heaped on the soldiers who marched off never to return. There was a similar attitude in rugby. There was honour in fighting.

So while everyone loudly and publicly abhorred what had gone on concerning the rugby warfare that day at Lancaster Park in 1971, pssst . . . in the name of honour and glory they also all wanted to see all the juicy bits again on replay, eh!

21. Angel of no mercy
The sending home of Keith Murdoch

I have met Keith Murdoch only once, but wouldn't mind a dollar for every time I have heard his name mentioned. Murdoch played just three tests, yet remains one of the most-discussed All Blacks in history. Shortly before Ian Kirkpatrick's 1972–73 All Blacks set out on their long tour of North America, Britain and France, I was walking through downtown Auckland with Bill McCarthy when we came across Murdoch, who was busy attending to all those last-minute details players have to get through before they depart — passport photos, documentation, shopping . . .

Bill introduced me to Murdoch and we had a short, amicable chat. He seemed rather reserved, but certainly friendly, and was clearly looking forward to the tour. Who would have guessed what effect the tour would have on his life?

Murdoch had been overseas once before with the All Blacks, to South Africa in 1970 under Brian Lochore. He was regarded as an outstanding prop, one of whose major assets was his immense strength. But in South Africa he'd been troubled by injury and played just the last test. Suffering from a rumbling appendix, he played that match in extreme pain, and went straight to hospital afterwards. Those who were there talk of his courage and ability to withstand pain.

In 1971 Murdoch was selected to play against the British Lions in two tests, but was forced out through injury on each occasion. So even though he'd been playing rep rugby since his debut for Otago in 1964, and had had stints for Hawke's Bay and Auckland, he had not had the international experience you would have expected for a player of his ability. He had played in eight games on the New Zealand team's 1972 internal tour and in the third test against Australia that year, but the trip to the northern hemisphere was his chance to cement his place as a great All Black.

What do we know of the 29-year-old Murdoch who set out on that tour? According to anecdotal evidence, which, of course, often grows in the telling, he was involved quite often in fights and brawls, though not usually of his making, and he

Coach Bob Duff, skipper Ian Kirkpatrick and the man himself, Keith Murdoch.

liked to have a drink, or sometimes more than one drink. He was rather shy, but was definitely not inclined to take a backward step when confronted.

In the three decades since that tempestuous Northern Hemisphere tour, hundreds of thousands of words have been devoted to Murdoch. I don't propose to recount blow by blow the incident that led to him being the first All Black to be sent home during a tour. But in a book outlining the outrageous moments in New Zealand rugby history, the Murdoch affair stands out.

The tour had been stuttering along. The British media had reported the All Blacks rather aggressively and the visitors, after a couple of big wins in North America, had played 10 matches in Britain, losing two of them, to Llanelli and North-Western Counties. The first test was against Wales at Cardiff on December 2. It was a tough match. New Zealand led 13–3 at halftime and held on to take the game 19–16. Murdoch scored New Zealand's only try, after a bullocking run along the touchline.

So it was a victory over the old enemy. The All Blacks were in good spirits that evening as they celebrated at the Angel Hotel in Cardiff, none more so than Murdoch, one of the outstanding figures in the match.

Late that evening there was an incident involving Murdoch and a security guard, Peter Grant, at the hotel. Some New Zealanders there claim Murdoch was the victim of an overly aggressive guard looking for trouble. The guard claimed a tanked-up Murdoch attacked him. Trying to thread together various strands of the story, as they have emerged down the years, it seems the All Blacks had celebrated until after midnight at their hotel and had then gone back to various rooms to continue drinking and partying. At about 1am, Murdoch, feeling peckish, had made his way

Security guard Peter Grant sporting the impressive 'shiner' Murdoch delivered him.

to the hotel kitchen to find something to eat. There he was confronted by Grant.

What happened next? Did Grant hit him? Did he hit Grant? Were there merely some angry words spoken? Did All Black team manager Ernie Todd inflame an already tense situation when he arrived on the scene? Did Murdoch lose control totally and become engaged in an all-out brawl? Had there been another incident involving Murdoch earlier in the evening? All these versions, and more, have surfaced in the years since.

Whatever really happened, the result was catastrophic for Murdoch, the team and the All Blacks' reputation. Murdoch was sent home.

There remain several disconcerting factors about the whole business. Perhaps the worst is that the player himself was never given the chance to explain his side of events. He was tried, convicted and sentenced without the benefit of a defence.

Having said that, there may have been sound reasons why Todd elected to send Murdoch home. It is inarguable that there had been other incidents during the tour, beginning with Murdoch's rowdy behaviour on the flight from Auckland to Honolulu. Todd was unable to quieten Murdoch down on that flight, despite complaints from other passengers.

There were other incidents, involving water bombs, some damage to hotels, a threat to throw a piano out of a hotel window, assaults on journalists. Manager Todd had been forced to pay for damage to a Belfast hotel; police were called after an incident in Swansea. Not everything centred around Murdoch, but he was a leading figure in many of the scrapes. While Murdoch was generally on the quiet side and a very loyal team man, he became over-exuberant, even unruly, when he had been drinking. To the British media, he was simply a 'wild man'.

It seems, from discussing the tour since with players, that Todd had become extremely irritated at times with Murdoch. The manager began to show increasing signs of stress. An aggressive British media, looking to turn any incidents into headlines, didn't help his predicament. Witnesses talk of Todd telling off Murdoch during the tour, and even threatening to send him home.

Then came the Angel Hotel incident.

Seen with the benefit of hindsight, the punishment was a nonsense, if it was merely for the altercation with the security guard. In 1979, Brian Ford was charged and convicted of assault and the incident hardly even made the headlines. In 1989, two All Blacks, Joe Stanley and Andy Earl, were actually jailed while assault charges against them were investigated, but continued their tour without a hitch.

But perhaps Todd felt he had no alternative, that the seriousness and regularity of incidents involving Murdoch had become unacceptable.

Murdoch's banishment has always rankled with Ian Kirkpatrick. 'Looking back, I'd do a few things differently on that tour, but not too many,' he told me. 'The one thing I'd definitely want to change would be my handling of the Keith Murdoch incident. That's always raised my hackles, Keith being sent home. The way it was done was shocking. They tried to send him home before we understood what was going on, so that by the time we became aware, it was a fait accompli.

'He was off at quarter to seven in the morning. If I'd expected it, or if I'd had some time to think about it, I'd have said, "If he goes, we all go." But Keith just popped his head in and said, "Hooray fellas, I'm off."

'It was a situation none of us had experienced before. I felt, and still feel, that the Home Unions wanted to get him home. I don't know why. It had nothing to do with them. Ernie Todd, our manager, had a lot of pressure on him after that. I felt he was not

Ernie Todd, the much-maligned manager of the 1972-73 All Blacks.

handling the manager's job very well. I had no idea he was sick. If he'd told me, that would have explained a lot and I could have helped. None of us knew he was sick, except Graham Short, our baggage-master. He told me a few years later that he'd known.'

Todd was to die of cancer in 1974 without revealing publicly in any detail what went on in those hectic hours before Murdoch was sent packing. In a press conference at Birmingham, he said: 'I acted, so I thought, for the benefit both of the player himself and also of the team as a whole. It was not an easy decision to make, but was one of the managerial responsibilities one must face up to. Team discipline is of paramount importance in any large group subjected to the pressures of a rugby tour of this size. A decision like this requires a lot of consideration and every point of view must be thought about.'

In April, 1973, Todd addressed the New Zealand Rugby Union in the Wellington Town Hall and said: 'There were insinuations that outside influences were brought to bear on me at the time of the dismissal, but this was not so. It was my decision and my decision alone. It was an experience that I hope I never have to live through again. But if I was faced with the exact same set of circumstances, I would make exactly the same decision.'

It is not easy to piece together what happened on the Sunday after the Saturday night fracas with the security guard (bearing in mind Murdoch was told early on Monday morning that he was going home). What we do know is that the All Black management spoke to Murdoch and with local officials. Murdoch was given a don't-do-it-again-or-you're-in-trouble message and everyone thought the affair was closed. He was selected to play in the next tour match. It does seem that four Home Unions

Peter Bush

Stern-faced Keith Murdoch makes his way through Euston Station after being banished from the All Blacks' tour.

committee chairman, Englishman John Tallent, who visited the Angel Hotel on the Sunday morning, was most unimpressed with Murdoch's behaviour. He denied he demanded Murdoch be sent home.

Todd said he had come under pressure from the Home Unions, though the final decision was his. This ties in with what New Zealand union chairman of the time, Jack Sullivan, said. Sullivan and Todd had some long discussions through that Sunday night before Todd resolved that the player must go. There will always be different versions to this story, but I was intrigued to read Ron Palenski's take in *Our National Game*. Palenski, one of New Zealand's best sports writers, is not a man to rush into print without ascertaining the facts. He wrote: '. . . The four Home Unions committee decided to get into the act and after a series of phone calls to and from the chairman of the New Zealand union in Wellington, Jack Sullivan, it became apparent that the rest of the tour was in jeopardy. Their chairman of the committee at the time was John Tallent, a man with a long and usually warm relationship with New Zealand rugby.

'What was actually said in the phone calls (made without Todd's knowledge) has not been preserved but the direct result was that Sullivan phoned Todd. These days, such a call would be recorded at one end or the other; although the technology certainly existed then, it would probably never have occurred to Todd or Sullivan. Both men had known each other a long time, since their pre-war playing days. Had the All Blacks gone to South Africa in 1940, they would surely have been team-mates. They were administrators together and friends, each of them with a deep commitment to rugby.

'Sullivan told Todd to send Murdoch home on the next flight. Todd didn't argue, but did ask Sullivan if he was sure. Sullivan affirmed he was. Sullivan consulted no one before the decision and after it, and while he may have discussed it with some of his closest colleagues and may even have told the whole council about it, silence descended.'

The All Blacks were dumbfounded when they learned what was happening to their team-mate.

Joe Karam was just 20 on the tour, but he's never been a person to blindly accept authority decisions — witness his tireless work on behalf of David Bain, a person he is adamant has been convicted and jailed for murders he did not commit.

'I felt very sorry for Kirky over the Murdoch business,' says Karam. 'He was very worried in Cardiff. They had a meeting on Sunday and discussed the whole thing. Eventually Kirky came out. I'll never forget how pleased he was. He and Sid [Going, the vice-captain] stuck by Keith absolutely and Kirky said it would be okay, that Keith would be staying.

'On the Sunday we had a few beers in the morning and then hopped on the train at lunchtime. Keith appeared and played his portable stereo. He served drinks at the bar and was in a buoyant mood. As far as the team was concerned, it was all resolved.

'Kirky never became involved again on the Sunday night in Birmingham. He found out Keith was being sent home with the rest of us on the Monday morning, and he was blown apart by that. He'd been told by his manager that Keith would be staying. The New Zealand union had told Ernie Todd to do what he thought was best. The next thing Kirky knew, Murdoch was on his way home.

'By the time Kirky and the rest of us found out, Keith had his bags packed. He had tears in his eyes and a taxi whisked him away. To us, it seemed like a Home Unions conspiracy to beat us.'

Murdoch made his way to Heathrow Airport, still wearing his All Black blazer, but with the identifying silver fern removed. New Zealand photographer Peter Bush followed Keith to the airport and took some photos of the grim-faced prop, images that have been reproduced many times over the years.

> 'By the time Kirky and the rest of us found out, Keith had his bags packed. He had tears in his eyes and a taxi whisked him away. To us, it seemed like a Home Unions conspiracy to beat us.'

Murdoch got as far as Singapore on the way home, then hopped off the plane. He headed for the Australian outback, and that's where he has lived since. There have been occasional reports of him returning home to visit his mother and friends, including former team-mates such as Colin Meads and Graham Whiting, a publican in Taranaki, but he has shied away totally from the media.

In 1974, the intrepid Terry McLean located him in north-west Australia, but was met by an aggressive Murdoch who sent him on his way quick smart, threatening to rub his face into a puddle of oil.

In 1990, Margot McRae, when making *Mud and Glory*, tracked him down in North Queensland, where they filmed him, now bushy-bearded, smiling and looking happy and content, but there was no interview. Murdoch has received book offers, with plenty of money as a carrot, but has generally not even bothered to reply. He was invited to attend the New Zealand Rugby Union centenary celebrations in 1992, all expenses paid, but declined. He has not taken part in any All Black team reunions.

I thought I was onto a Murdoch story scoop in 1978 when covering the All Black tour. I was in the Royal Hotel in Cardiff where Graham Mourie's team were staying after the test when I saw a security guard in the foyer who seemed to very closely resemble Peter Grant. As I had never seen Grant, I wasn't sure, but thought that I might be onto a good story if I could interview the same guard six years after the 1972 incident.

I knew Peter Bush was 150 metres up the road at the Angel Hotel, so I ran up the street and alerted Bushy (complete with mandatory cameras). We ran back down to the Royal, hoping for a story and a photo. Unfortunately the man had disappeared and none of the other security people could tell us who he was or where he had gone. They played dumb. So we'll never know, but I reckon I had spotted Peter Grant.

And that's how it was with the Keith Murdoch stories — constantly chasing shadows — until this last year or so when the former All Black once again hit the headlines.

He has been one of the central figures in the inquiry into the murder of 20-year-old Aborigine Christopher Limerick in the Northern Territory town of Tennant Creek. Limerick had apparently burgled Murdoch's lodgings more than once, and the New Zealander had caught him. There was an altercation. Three weeks later, Limerick's body was found at the Nobles Nob opencast gold mine, just out of town.

Murdoch, always of itinerant persuasion, had left Tennant Creek by then, and was sought to appear at Limerick's inquest. It took the police a considerable time to find him in the vast expanses of the Northern Territory outback. He duly appeared at the inquest, though he added little to what was already known.

Reporters, sensing a story, made a beeline for the tiny township. They learned snippets about Murdoch's life over the past two decades . . . how he worked as an odd jobs man, how he liked to drink beer but did not do so to excess very often, how he was generally popular and was described as a 'gentle giant', how he tended to suddenly pack up and move on.

But at the end of it all, they never did get an in-depth interview with Murdoch. His lifestyle, and his involvement with Limerick's death, remained as shrouded in secrecy and speculation as the events on that December night at the Angel Hotel in Cardiff in 1972.

I guess Keith Murdoch is destined always to be one of the mystery figures of New Zealand sport.

22. Enter Hollywood Haden
Big Andy's infamous dive

Life around Andy Haden has never been dull. During his playing days, the big Aucklander was always looking for an edge, on the field and off. Consequently he was lively company and tended to have a different take on most issues.

He was always a somewhat controversial character. Whether it was pushing for more match tickets for players, seeking money for the players' tour fund, debating the toss with sponsors or potential sponsors, stating that his occupation was a writer, or a rugby player, or negotiating contracts, he was seldom far from the news.

It was typical of Haden that he should be brought to appear before the Rugby Union to answer charges of professionalism, then, within a few years, be employed by the same Union to market the game. Haden has continued to be an outspoken character. He questioned Todd Blackadder's worth as an All Black when it wasn't fashionable to do so, and was roundly condemned for doing so, yet time proved him right. He backed John Hart before, during and after Hart's reign as All Black coach, and didn't care what the rest of the country thought of him.

But of all the various Haden capers, the one he is most remembered for is the infamous lineout dive at Cardiff Arms Park in 1978. With time almost up, and the All Blacks trailing 10–12, a lineout was formed near the Welsh 22. As the ball was thrown in, Haden fell monstrously from the lineout. A split-second later referee Roger Quittenton blew his whistle and penalised Wales.

Adding insult to gathering Welsh injury, Brian McKechnie, on the field as substitute for the injured Clive Currie, coolly stepped up and kicked the match-winning penalty. It transpired that Quittenton had in fact penalised Geoff Wheel for putting his hand on Frank Oliver's shoulder, but such information did little to appease the Welsh rugby fans, who were emphatic they had been cheated out of a much-deserved and long-awaited victory over the old enemy.

I've spoken to some of the principals from that incident and it is interesting to

Referee Roger Quittenton (left) and Geoff Wheel, the man he claims he penalised for jumping off Frank Oliver's shoulder in the All Blacks–Wales test of 1978.

hear their views with the benefit of nearly a quarter of a century of hindsight:

Andy Haden: 'During training, one of the boys had mentioned a match between Taranaki and King Country when Ian Eliason dived out of the lineouts three or four times against Colin Meads and got a penalty each time. With a minute to go in the test the next day, those are the sorts of things that flash into your mind if you are fresh and thinking quickly.

'I thought about what Eliason had done. It doesn't actually say in the rules that it's cheating, but it was certainly a variation in tactics. Given the same circumstances, even with the maturity of the past 20-odd years, I would do it again, unfortunately, because it's the way I think. You do what you can within the rules to win. I didn't want to go back to my dressing shed and sit there and say to myself that there was something else I could have done to win the test.

'There was an injury to Doug Bruce and a collection of players gathered. I said to [Graham] Mourie that I was going to dive and he knew what I meant straight away. Then I went back and told Frank [Oliver]. When the lineout took place, I heard the referee's whistle before the ball had left the hand of the thrower. He can say what he likes, but I'm sure he was attracted by the noise that went on at the same time [as Haden and Oliver dived from the lineout]. Had the lineout proceeded without us diving, I have no doubt there would have been no penalty.'

Andy Dalton: 'I couldn't believe what happened. I threw in the ball and suddenly both Andy and Frank just flew out of the lineout. It all happened so quickly, I didn't see much of it. We got the penalty. Everyone talks about Andy, but Frank's not a

Never far away from controversy, Andy Haden (left) gets a congratulatory slap on the back from All Black team-mate Gary Seear after the Welsh test of 1978.

very good actor! I suppose Andy has to live with what he did. There is talk that it was discussed before the game, but I wasn't aware of it and was as surprised as the Welsh team and the referee to see these guys flying out of the lineout. It set a precedent I wouldn't like to see followed. I'd be a lot happier not having to win games like that.'

Graham Mourie (smiling): 'We believed Andy had an inner ear infection and had lost his balance! On reflection, maybe Andy wouldn't do it again, and as a team we wouldn't want him to, but these days the ethics of the game have become a greater consideration.'

Brian McKechnie: 'After the game, I was taken into a room for an interview. That's when I saw what had actually happened at the lineout incident. I don't think they got a word out of me at the interview because I was so stunned at what had taken place out there.'

23. When selectors get the squash

The dumping of J.J. Stewart

It is expected that an All Black selector or coach will have an inner ruthless personality streak when it comes to picking his players for any upcoming test or tour. The selector/coach has to have that slightly mean touch. There is no place in his world for sentiment or favouritism before the announcement is made of the 15 players for the test — and the reserves as well.

But what would happen it the boot was on the other foot? What if the All Black players had the chance to consider the form of their coach? And perhaps drop him from their team plans if necessary?

It did happen, you know. And on a deeply serious All Black tour of South Africa as well.

The sport in question was not rugby, though.

On the 1976 All Black tour of South Africa, the game of squash became very popular as a pastime for the players. Between games and training sessions, in the team's downtime, a number of them enjoyed stern contests against each other. As the tour unfolded, the players noted that their popular team coach John (J.J.) Stewart was also a keen squash player. J.J. was soon involved in any number of games against his players. And he had his share of wins along the way.

Then someone in the large South African and New Zealand press corps following the tour had the bright idea that the media should assemble a team and challenge the best players among the All Blacks. Soon it was agreed that six media should play the best six All Black squash players in a 'test' match. The prize would be nothing more or less than drinks paid for the other team.

To find the media team of six was easy. There were only six men who claimed they were players of any ability. They were automatic choices.

For the All Blacks it was different. They had any number of contenders who had been playing regularly and were keen to make the final cut. To find their final six meant they assembled a small selection panel. Then much bantering and bargaining began among the players as they sought to influence the selectors and make the final 'test' side.

But Mr Stewart had no part in negotiations. In fact, it was leaked that he was slightly miffed when his ability as a judge of sport was ignored. He was overlooked as one of the selectors. Then, a more major bombshell: the coach discovered he had been dropped. And the dumping ignominy came from his own players!

The whole episode, drawn out over several days, made for a lot of fun for everyone involved in a long 24-match tour. The Chief All Black Squash Selector (self-appointed I seem to remember) was Canterbury prop Kerry Tanner. He announced to anyone who cared to listen (probably at one of his famous five

J.J. Stewart . . . dumped.

o'clock drinkies sessions) that 'He [Stewart] has just not come up to scratch lately . . . I had no option but to drop him'.

For his part, Stewart spoke out strongly about his non-selection: 'Tanner has told me there is nothing personal in it, but I think he should stick to picking his nose.'

It was a moment in All Black history, I guess — the day they gave their coach some of his own medicine.

For the record the squash test was a lively affair, held one afternoon at the Orange Free State University complex. The All Blacks beat the Media 4–2.

Much money, and drinks, changed hands afterwards.

And how did the All Black coach cope with his non-selection? The story made the South African newspapers bit by bit in the days leading up to the big 'test'. One report sums up his reaction well.

'I suppose I'll get over it,' said the popular J.J. 'A few gins will help.'

24. No Fletcher, no tour

All Black strike avoided

In the modern world of professional rugby, there will perhaps come a day when the leading players of New Zealand, maybe even the All Blacks, will go on strike over working and pay conditions. I mean, near the end of 2001 England's professional soccer players went within a whisker of striking as they sought a bigger slice of the revenue from television coverage of their games. It is part and parcel of the employer-employee struggle in every other part of the workplace, so why not rugby?

If it does happen, it will not be a famous first. There was a time when solidarity and unity among the All Blacks won out in a personal dispute after the team threatened to go on strike.

It happened in 1920. The situation concerned a tough Auckland forward named Charlie Fletcher, who was a top player immediately after First World War and was a certain choice for the first post-war tour by the All Blacks.

The destination was Australia, but before the team departed by ship there were to be a couple of warm-up games, in Auckland and in Palmerston North. To give as many of the tourists as possible a run before departure, Fletcher was assigned to play for his home province, Auckland, against his All Black colleagues.

Sadly, during the game he broke an ankle and his hopes of touring were dashed. Though his leg was heavily plastered, he was permitted to travel to the second home game, against a combined Manawatu-Horowhenua-Wanganui XV. The All Blacks duly won by 39–0. Fletcher then figured his time with the All Blacks would be over and prepared for the train trip home.

But several senior All Blacks then spoke to their tour management. Led by Moke Belliss, who had been a first-class player since 1914, the players told New Zealand rugby officials: 'We want Charlie on tour with us.' It was a direct request, stated firmly and with steely resolve. The players felt sorry for Fletcher, and they

Charlie Fletcher.

Even though there was no way he would be able to play, the players wanted him along as company. In fact, the players were emphatic: 'No Fletcher, no tour.'

liked him immensely. Even though there was no way he would be able to play, the players wanted him along as company. In fact, the players were emphatic: 'No Fletcher, no tour.'

There was a standoff.

Eventually middle ground was found. The Rugby Union said that if before departure Fletcher could actually walk without help to the ship in Wellington he could go on the tour. So the rest of the team stood back and Fletcher made his march up the gangplank. With the aid of his walking stick he hobbled up the wooden walkway. He made it onto the ship and effectively booked his ticket.

Fletcher therefore went on the full tour of Australia, a tour that lasted three weeks, and watched all seven games from the sidelines. In their official publication *The History of New Zealand Rugby Football 1870–1945* the Rugby Union list Fletcher as a member of the team, as do the authors of *The Encyclopedia of New Zealand Rugby*. Essentially, though, he became an All Black only because of the threat of strike action by his team-mates.

Charles Fletcher did eventually play for the All Blacks. He appeared the following season against New South Wales in Christchurch in 1921 and in the famous drawn third test against the Springboks in Wellington a fortnight later.

25. Sacking the skippers
A long line of deposed All Black captains

By 2001, the All Blacks had had three captains — Taine Randell, Todd Blackadder and Anton Oliver — in as many years. This was an unusual turnover, because when we think of good All Black eras, we think also of captains who led New Zealand teams for years, men like Wilson Whineray (1958–65), Brian Lochore (1966–70), Graham Mourie (1976–83), Wayne Shelford (1987–90) and Sean Fitzpatrick (1992–97).

Yet, despite these periods of harmony, the captaincy issue has often been a thorny one.

Dave Gallaher led the famous 1905 Originals in an outstanding manner, yet it was midfield back Jimmy Hunter who captained the side for their preliminary tour of Australia, and again in 1907–08. It required a vote on the ship going to Britain before Gallaher felt his captaincy was secure.

In 1921 centre George Aitken captained New Zealand for the first two tests against the Springboks, but was dropped from the side for the decider, at Wellington, and halfback Teddy Roberts was promoted in his place. This caused an outcry at the time.

When we think of the 1924–25 Invincibles, we think of a well-organised side functioning smoothly, but there were many issues swirling about over the team leadership. Ces Badeley, the Auckland five-eighth, had captained the All Blacks in 1924 in Australia, but when the team set sail for England, his job went to Wellington loose forward Cliff Porter. It is hard to discover exactly why the popular Badeley was demoted, unless there were concerns about a knee injury he was carrying. Porter himself had trouble with the captaincy during the tour. He was injured early on and Canterbury flyer Jim Parker took his place in the test team. Even when Porter was restored to full fitness he could not displace Parker from the test line-up, so it was Jock Richardson who captained the Invincibles in the tests in Britain.

Ron King captained the All Blacks in the torrid series against the1937 Springboks, but even though he held his test position, he lost the test captaincy to centre Brushy Mitchell when New Zealand toured Australia the following year. In the third test in

News Media Auckland

Fred Allen (right) sensationally dropped himself for the third and fourth tests of the 1949 series against South Africa. At left is coach Alex McDonald.

Australia, when Mitchell was out with injury, the captaincy went not to King, or to another former All Black captain Jack Griffiths, or to brilliant halfback Charlie Saxton, but to flanker Rod McKenzie.

After the war Fred Allen led the All Blacks between 1946 and 1949, but, always the pragmatist, dropped himself after two tests in South Africa in 1949. Fred explained to me: 'I'd done all I could do and we weren't winning, so I thought it might be time to try someone else.' It was a decision that spoke volumes for Allen's fairness and willingness to put the team first, but on reflection it was probably wrong, even though Ron Elvidge was a good replacement captain. Allen was a very fine five-eighth, not an area in which the 1949 side was particularly strong, and some of Fred's team-mates that year have told me he was very much missed when he dropped himself.

All Black captains came and went over the next few seasons, but few were treated as brutally as halfback Pat Vincent, who led the All Blacks in the first two tests of the dramatic 1956 series against the Springboks. Before the third test, the All Black selectors rang the changes. Those most talked about now were the inclusion of young fullback Don Clarke, and experienced prop Kevin Skinner. Often overlooked is the fact that the All Black captain was dropped from the side, Ponty Reid taking his place.

Fred Allen had another interesting captaincy decision to make in 1966, with Wilson Whineray having retired. He had several experienced and capable provincial captains in his All Black side, Kel Tremain, Colin Meads, Ken Gray and Chris Laidlaw among them. But Allen liked the look of Brian Lochore, a quiet farmer from the Wairarapa, and elevated him. It was a decision that could have split the team, but the senior players got in behind Lochore, who grew into a fine All Black captain.

Few All Black captains have been treated as cruelly as was Ian Kirkpatrick in 1974. The popular Kirky was standing in the function room at Athletic Park when he heard, along with a room packed with rugby people, that he had lost his job as All Black captain. To his credit, Kirkpatrick immediately congratulated his successor, Andy Leslie, and offered him unwavering support over the next couple of seasons. It wasn't the last time Kirkpatrick suffered at the hands of unfeeling selectors. In 1977, he was dropped from the test side, a shock decision that seems scarcely credible in hindsight. How did he find out? Not by way of a quiet phone call from coach Jack Gleeson, or the Rugby Union chairman. No, Kirky was hopping onto the Poverty Bay team bus when he heard the All Black team had been announced, and could tell, from the reaction of his provincial team-mates, that he had not made it. Such a great and loyal player deserved better treatment.

I could say the same of Gary Whetton in 1992. Whetton was the Aucklander who was promoted to the test captaincy when hugely popular Wayne Shelford was dropped in 1990 (see *Bring Back Buck*, p. 47).

The Shelford decision created a furore, but at least Shelford did get the courtesy of some prior warning, though he remains unhappy at the way the decision to axe him was reached.

Whetton received no such courtesy from new coach Laurie Mains. After leading the All Blacks through the 1991 World Cup campaign, Whetton (along with his brother Alan) was not required to even take part in the 1992 All Black trials. He had effectively gone from being the best lock in New Zealand, to not even in the top half-dozen. Mains intended naming Mike Brewer as captain, but when Brewer was injured, he went instead for Sean Fitzpatrick.

He never contacted Whetton to explain his omission from the trials, a lack of courtesy and feeling that I thought reflected very poorly on the new coach. Mains' attitude was: 'I never

News Media Auckland

Gary Whetton, who was dumped from the All Blacks by Laurie Mains in 1992.

chose Whetton. He was not one of my players, so I owed him no loyalty.' But I thought it was one of those occasions when a little human decency was called for. Whetton, an All Black for 12 seasons, deserved better.

The same could have been said of new coach John Mitchell when he dropped All Black stalwarts Jeff Wilson, Christian Cullen and Taine Randell in 2001. Mitchell adopted the Mains line — they were not his players; he had not picked them previously. This rather ignored the All Black history and tradition that he was so keen to invoke.

In 1999, John Hart got himself into a tangle over his captain. Taine Randell had led the All Blacks through the spectacularly unsuccessful 1998 season and most felt it was time for a new captain in 1999 in the build-up to the World Cup. Hart's problem was that the choices were not vast, especially as it was imperative his captain be assured of a place in the team. Jeff Wilson and Anton Oliver were mooted, but neither seemed keen on the job. Robin Brooke was a leading candidate for a time, but at a critical moment his Auckland Blues team's Super 12 campaign was derailed and Brooke suddenly did not look All Black leadership material. So Randell kept the job, though he never seemed entirely happy with it and it appeared to me he did not always enjoy the full support of every team member.

When Wayne Smith was promoted to All Black coach in 2000, he turned to his trusted Canterbury captain Todd Blackadder, a decision the whole country seemed to agree with. Blackadder led the All Blacks throughout 2000, and there seemed general agreement that he was the man for the job. That made the reaction in 2001 all the more remarkable. Blackadder lost not only the captaincy, but also his place in the All Blacks, yet there was hardly a word spoken on his behalf.

Apparently he was the obvious choice to lead the All Blacks in 2000, and was also just as obviously going to get the axe in 2001. It was an illogical reaction from the rugby public. But then, down the years, there have been lots of issues about the All Black captaincy that have been hard to fathom.

Footnote: Mind you, who are we as a rugby nation to worry over captaincy? When Neil Back took over the England leadership in November 2001 he became England's 14th captain in 14 seasons!

News Media Auckland

Canterbury's Todd Blackadder, who led the All Blacks for just one year.

26. To our eternal shame . . .
South Africa and the Maori debate

It was the tour of the rebel Cavaliers team in 1986 that finally spelt the end of New Zealand's rugby relations with South Africa, at least until that country's abhorrent apartheid laws were dismantled. What is sometimes overlooked, or ignored, is that opposition to rugby contact with South Africa had been building for decades.

The first inkling of what was to follow came when Ranji Wilson, a member of the 1919 touring New Zealand Army team, was not permitted to join his team-mates in South Africa. Wilson, of Anglo-West Indian parentage, was forced to remain on the team's ship when it berthed in South Africa. While the rest of the New Zealanders played 15 matches over the next two months, Wilson had to sail home, an early victim of South African racism.

Despite the Ranji Wilson incident, it was a leaked press report of Charles Blackett, the South African journalist, which really opened New Zealanders' eyes to how racist white South Africans were. I have dealt with the Blackett incident elsewhere in this book, but one sentence from his match report of the 1921 New Zealand Maori v South Africa game bears repeating. Blackett wrote: 'Bad enough having to play team officially designated New Zealand natives but spectacle thousands Europeans frantically cheering on band of coloured men to defeat members of own race was too much for Springboks who frankly disgusted.'

It became clear then to the New Zealand Rugby Union, and to New Zealand rugby followers, that they had little comprehension of the superior attitude white South Africans had to their black, coloured and Indian compatriots.

The repercussions were varied and far-reaching. When the All Blacks toured South Africa under Maurice Brownlie in 1928, no Maori players were included. This was a decision made by the New Zealand union out of respect to their hosts. Thus the All Blacks lacked legendary fullback George Nepia and that fine halfback, Jimmy Mill, two players who might have swung a drawn series New Zealand's way.

Vince Bevan . . . overlooked.

South Africa toured New Zealand in 1937. Like the 1921 team, their tour party did not include any non-whites. Further, there was no game scheduled against the New Zealand Maori team.

In 1949, Fred Allen took the All Blacks to South Africa, and had to suffer through a 4–0 series defeat. Again no dark-skinned players were included, and again it was a decision taken unilaterally by the New Zealand union. Any protests were muted, partly because the outstanding Maori player of the day, centre Johnny Smith, said he agreed with the decision. Another player to be omitted was future Cabinet Minister Ben Couch, who ironically when in government argued in favour of continuing contact with South Africa.

Halfback Vince Bevan, who would have been a godsend to the '49ers, was also overlooked. This was a strange one. Allen recalls: 'We'd have dearly loved to have had Vince. He was an extra good halfback, but he was ruled out after Winston McCarthy blew his cover in Newcastle, New South Wales, in 1947. Winston mentioned several times during his broadcast that day that we were fielding an all-Maori backline for the first time. Most people didn't know until then that Vince was a Maori because he didn't look like a Maori. But after that there was a big outcry in South Africa and he was barred from being selected in 1949.

'In those days they wouldn't allow us to take over any dark-skinned players. It was a real tragedy for us because with Vince we might have won. The irony was that Maori people didn't feel Vince had enough Maori blood in him to play for the New Zealand Maori team!'

Though the South African invitation for the tour was not qualified, the New Zealand union's council issued this statement in 1948, the same year as the first Afrikaner-dominated Nationalist Government in South Africa was selected and the racism was formalised and legalised: 'In view of the domestic policy of South Africa, the council of the NZRFU reaffirms its previous decision made both this year and prior to the 1928 tour that as much as it is regretted, players to be selected to tour South Africa cannot be other than wholly European. This is in accordance with the policy of the Maori Advisory Board, which adds it is its wish not to interfere with the government decrees of another country.'

It was about this time that voices of protest began to be heard. Brigadier General Sir Howard Kippenberger, the renowned soldier and historian, spoke of having had Maori soldiers under his command for two years. 'In that time they had 1500 casualties . . . I'm not going to acquiesce to any damned Afrikaner saying they can't go.' In other words, if the Maori people are good enough to fight for New Zealand, they are good enough to play rugby for the country. It was Kippenberger who led what is believed to be the first anti-racism, anti-tour march, down the streets of Wellington in 1949.

South Africa toured New Zealand in 1956 and for the first time in 35 years, a New Zealand Maori team played the Springboks. But according to Maori team members, they were given such a stern lecture before the game about the importance of maintaining discipline and not offending the visitors that they turned on a totally sterile display and were heavily beaten.

Nothing much seemed to have altered in 1960, when the All Blacks again toured South Africa, but the winds of change were in the air. Before Wilson Whineray took his team away, there were some large protests in Wellington. Noticeable among the

Brigadier General Sir Howard Kippenberger.

protesters was George Nepia, who said: 'I marched for the concept of South Africans accepting us, Maori and Pakeha, as one people.' Nepia was joined by hundreds of others, white and Maori, with many churchmen and Maori elders prominent.

New Zealand's first anti-apartheid group was formed — the Citizens' All Black Tour Association. It opposed rugby links under the slogan of 'No Maoris, no tour'. A petition was presented to the New Zealand government calling for the 1960 tour to be abandoned, and the fact that it was signed by 162,000 indicated the strength of feeling was growing. Adding impetus to the protesters' pleas was the news that came back from South Africa of the Sharpesville massacre. On March 21, 1960 police broke up a peaceful protest by killing some of the protesters.

Noted cleric Allan Pyatt wrote in *Sports Digest* in 1960: 'It was even worse that the discriminating decision was made by New Zealanders rather than South Africans. I imagine that had this Rugby Union decision not have been made, the team would have been selected on merit and availability . . . Guarantees should then have been sought from the South African board about equality at hotels and on transport. If these could not have been given, then a further decision would have been necessary. But at least this thing would have been done by the South African board and not by the New Zealand union against its own players. What really is disturbing is that this thing was done by New Zealanders against New Zealanders, within New Zealand.'

Touring team manager Tom Pearce attempted to explain that the decision was made by the Rugby Union 'only from the love of the Maoris . . . these gentle people'. The Rugby Union stated: 'To include Maoris would be to expose them to intolerable indignity.' Such sentiments were beginning to wear thin.

The pressure was building, and strangely the next step came from South Africa. The first Maori people to officially go to South Africa as rugby representatives were Ralph Love and Pat Walsh, who were invited to attend the South African Rugby Board's 75th anniversary celebrations in 1964. They were so well received that it became clear Maori players in an All Black team would receive a similarly enthusiastic greeting.

This caused problems for the South African government. While Danie Craven, in New Zealand with the 1965 Springboks, was talking about a time when black and white-skinned players could tour South Africa in one team, South African Prime Minister Hendrik Verwoerd announced his government was totally committed to separate development.

In 1967 New Zealand was invited to tour South Africa 'under the old terms'. This was no longer acceptable, and the tour fell through, a hastily arranged tour of Britain and France taking place instead.

By 1970, South Africa was facing increasing sports isolation and desperately needed an All Black tour, even if the team included Maori and Pacific Island players. This time the invitation had no caveats. New Zealand Deputy Prime Minister Jack Marshall met South African Prime Minister Johannes Vorster in Pretoria and was told the New Zealand union was free to choose whichever players it wanted for the next tour of South Africa. Maori players would be acceptable, he apparently said, provided there weren't too many, they should not be too 'black' and there should be no violent controversy on their selection. The invitation, when it arrived, was for a 'representative' team.

But by now the protest movement was not simply calling for players of all colours to be permitted to tour South Africa. It was calling for no more tours of the country until the apartheid laws were repealed.

Brian Lochore eventually led a team that included 'dark-skinned' players Sid Going, Bryan Williams, Buff Milner and Blair Furlong. These four players were granted 'honorary white' status, which seems doubly insulting. Not only was their presence legitimised in the eyes of the hosts by calling them whites, as if they weren't good enough in their own right, but it is doubtful if New Zealanders would have wanted to be whites in that South African regime, encompassing as it did the racist laws of the apartheid system. Williams was the sensation of the tour and even now it is doubtful if any winger has played better than he did that year. He was the Jonah Lomu of his generation. I have spoken to him since about this issue. While some feel Williams showed a support of the racist government by touring, he feels that he achieved a lot of good by going there, showing that the ability of a player did not depend on the colour of his skin, and giving the non-white people of South Africa something to cheer for.

Still South Africa held fast to its apartheid laws. The anti-apartheid movement gathered force throughout the world and was particularly well organised in New Zealand. A planned 1973 tour by the Springboks was cancelled at Prime Minister Norm

Kirk's request, after Kirk had been told that the police could not guarantee law and order. Kirk no doubt had in mind the fact that the 1974 Commonwealth Games were to be held in Christchurch and was not keen to run the risk of a boycott.

The All Blacks toured South Africa in 1976, though. To travel there, they had to take a circuitous route through Europe to Johannesburg to overcome trade union and official protests along the way. The tour followed closely on the horror of the Soweto incident when on June 16 that year, 176 protesters who wanted school subjects taught in English, not Afrikaans, died as a result of police gunfire in the township of Soweto, on the outskirts of Johannesburg.

By this time New Zealand had a new government, and National Party leader and Prime Minister Rob Muldoon did not have the same inclination to intervene. This was not a happy time for New Zealand

News Media Auckland

Buff Milner . . . granted 'honorary white' status in 1970.

sport. To those of us who travelled to South Africa that year, it was eye-opening stuff. I recoiled at the way blacks were treated and could see why someone like Chris Laidlaw had so turned on South Africa after touring there in 1970.

For New Zealand sport, 1976 was a low year. New Zealand's continuing friendly rugby relations with South Africa meant we were perceived by most of the world as South Africa's ally and it required only a small leap for some to believe New Zealanders therefore supported apartheid. There was a massive boycott at the 1976 Olympics because of New Zealand's presence, most of the black African and Caribbean nations walking out. In all, 28 countries boycotted the Olympics and New Zealand's international reputation was undoubtedly tarnished.

Unbelievable as it now seems, the National Government permitted the 1981 Springbok tour to proceed. Prime Minister Muldoon said many times he wished it wouldn't, but that he was powerless to intervene. I don't believe this. Muldoon was seldom powerless in any situation and my opinion was that, with an election looming, it suited him politically to permit the tour.

The Springboks arrived in New Zealand from the United States, having been forced to avoid Australia, where local authorities refused to provide transit facilities for the team.

It was a bitter, divisive tour, during which two matches were abandoned and the rest took place in front of barbed wire fences in increasingly acrimonious circumstances. The tour split not just the country, but even families. The Rugby Union councillors believed they were there simply to act in the best interests of rugby and that that could be best achieved by permitting the tour. The South African party included two non-whites, one a player and one an official, but was still very much a white team.

Through the 1980s, South Africa became increasingly isolated in terms of sport. Soon the main international sport in the country took place in the guise of rebel tours, rugby and cricket.

Astoundingly, the New Zealand union still decided, though not unanimously, to proceed with the scheduled 1985 tour of South Africa. By now anti-apartheid protesters were extremely vocal and growing in numbers all the time. It seemed a head in the sand attitude by the union.

The Prime Minister by now was David Lange. He implored the union to rethink the issue, but the decision remained the same. Yet the tour did not proceed. Six days before the players were due to leave, it all fell through.

Two Auckland club rugby members, Paddy Finnigan and Phil Recordon, issued proceedings claiming the Rugby Union was not fostering rugby by its decision to tour. It seemed at first glance a rather eccentric piece of legal action. The claims were rejected, but that decision was overturned in the Court of Appeal. The case was sent to the High Court.

Then with the players literally packing their bags, Justice Casey began hearing the substantive action. Two days later the plaintiffs applied for an interim injunction because it was clear the case would not be completed before the All Blacks were due to leave. On Saturday, July 13, Justice Casey granted the injunction, which in effect scuppered the tour.

The players were dumbfounded and there was serious talk of a tour anyway, a few weeks later. This fell through. Out of that resentment, disappointment and anger, plans for the rebel tour the following year were hatched. This tour, by a team that became known as the Cavaliers, proved to be the final nail in the coffin of rugby relations with South Africa.

Few wanted the tour to go ahead. The Rugby Union, feeling deceived, did not, and neither did the anti-apartheid movement. On their return, the players were suspended for two test matches. It was now clear South Africa was a no-go area for New Zealand rugby, and this remained the case until Nelson Mandela was finally released and the apartheid laws were repealed in 1992.

When people today talk of the anti-apartheid movement and the Halt All Racist Tours (HART) group, their minds go back to the 1970s and '80s. John Minto, Rob Muldoon, Tom Newnham, the Gleneagles Agreement, the Cavaliers, Ces Blazey, Danie Craven . . . they are the prime focus.

But this is a story that had its roots decades earlier. Charles Blackett unintentionally played his part. So did Ranji Wilson, Jimmy Mill, Johnny Smith, Vince Bevan, Howard Kippenberger, George Nepia and many others.

27. Hyped up and hypothermic

The hurricane test of '61

The test between New Zealand and France in Wellington in 1961 was one of the most remarkable ever played. It will never be forgotten by those who were at Athletic Park that day. I was 14 years old at the time, lived just along the road in Berhampore, and couldn't wait for the game. I'll never forget it, either, but not for the reasons you might think. The test was played in hurricane conditions. Looking back, it is hard to believe it was not postponed.

The only rugby match I have seen played in conditions which even approach Wellington's that day was the 1989 All Blacks-Llanelli encounter at Stradey Park. Llanelli officials had built a temporary stand beside the main stand, but the gale force winds made it too dangerous to use this facility, and the hardy souls who turned up that day were squashed onto the terraces where they had to endure hurricane winds and heavy rain. Roads around Stradey Park were closed and it was really amazing that the game was played. In the circumstances, it was impossible to play constructive rugby, and the All Blacks were happy to win 11–0 to maintain their unbeaten streak.

But back to Wellington, 1961. As I say, I was desperately keen on rugby. I'd been a ball boy at Athletic Park two years earlier when the All Blacks had beaten the Lions. I loved listening to Winston McCarthy's wonderful commentaries, I devoured every morsel about rugby in the newspapers and on radio, and I had looked forward to the French test for weeks, probably months.

It was traditional in those days for the really keen rugby fans, and I mean the super-keen ones, to queue up outside the ground the night before. They'd sleep outside the gates and so be in the best position to get good seats the next day once the tickets were issued. It might seem bizarre now to think of parents letting their

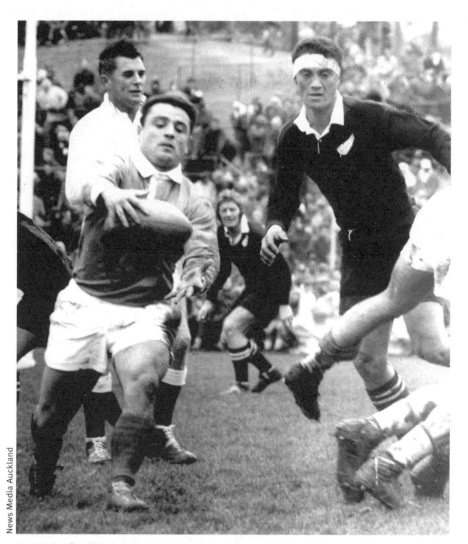

**French halfback Pierre Lacroix kicks from a scrum during the famous 'Hurricane Test'
at Athletic Park in 1961. The All Black pictured here is Victor Yates.**

youngsters sleep outside in the middle of winter just to get a better seat at a rugby
ground, but there was nothing extraordinary about it 40 years ago.

So on the evening of August 4, 1961, a group of us, school and rugby mates, duly
set up camp outside the Athletic Park gates. We were armed with the usual
accoutrements — sleeping bags, blankets, thermos flasks and the like. We had each
other for company. There was a big rugby test the next day (a rarity back then). These
were exciting times.

But there was one problem. That evening, a southerly gale blew up in Wellington.
Not just any gale, but a once-in-a-decade gale. It got stronger during the night and by

the early hours of the morning it was bitterly cold. In addition, there was driving rain all night. We boys liked to be right by the gate so we would have the pick of the very best seating once inside the ground the next day, but the conditions were so extreme that night that we talked it over and decided that we would all retire to the relative shelter of a fence about 50 yards away. We reasoned that if we were all there, then no one would be at an unfair advantage when it came to seat choice on test day.

The night seemed interminable. I know now that the weather was so bad that the liner *Canberra*, on its maiden voyage, was prevented from berthing at Wellington. I know that the New Zealand Rugby Union went within a whisker of postponing the game. I know that hardly anyone, even Wellingtonians used to a bit of a breeze, were willing to brave the towering Millard Stand, which had just been opened, to watch the test.

These things I know now. Back then, I knew only that there was a test to be played, but that I was incredibly cold and wet through. I felt ill. So did my mates. By early morning, we had to give up. We had been licked by the weather. I trooped off home shivering and shaking. I couldn't feel my hands, or my feet, or my legs. I was aching with cold.

In these enlightened times people would say I was suffering from hypothermia. In 1961, I knew only that I was frozen stiff. I got home, and was placed in the tender care of my mother, who gradually nursed me back to life.

As for the test? Well, I didn't get to watch it. I was still trying to thaw out. I was lying in bed, along the road from Athletic Park, when it was played.

Rugby historians will tell you it was an amazing match, totally dominated by the weather. They talk about the tries scored by French winger Jean Dupuy and New Zealand flanker Kel Tremain, and of the miraculous conversion by Don Clarke when he aimed for the corner flag and had the wind sweep the ball between the posts. They talk of French kicker Pierre Albaladejo kicking from his own 25 and seeing the ball blown back to his own in-goal area. Film of the test shows the goal posts swaying all over the place in the face of 80 mph-plus winds.

Yes, there are these and other enduring images from that game. But not for me. By mid-afternoon on August 5, 1961 I didn't care about the All Blacks or rugby. It hasn't happened to me often, but on that day, I was truly beaten by Wellington's weather.

A real poser

Here is a question, slightly outrageous, but certainly one for New Zealand rugby supporters to consider: who are the only set of brothers to both score tries in a test match on Eden Park — and on the same day?

The answer — the Iro Brothers, Tony and Kevin, in the 1988 rugby league World Cup final.

28. Authors who packed a punch

Controversial moments in rugby publishing

The two most sensational New Zealand rugby books, of the hundreds published over the past 125 years, have in my opinion been Chris Laidlaw's *Mud In Your Eye* and Michael Laws' *Gladiator*, the Norm Hewitt story.

Laidlaw's book, published in 1973, and the Hewitt biography, published in late 2001, rose well above the normal mundane and often bland rugby books that we see year after year in New Zealand.

Even three decades later, *Mud In Your Eye* stands up well. In the introduction, Laidlaw said: 'Perhaps the most persuasive reason for writing a book about rugby is simply because under rugby law, it isn't permitted. On all fronts, players are sworn to silence. After an international tour, they are "bound" to remain mute for two years. Such a ruling is nonsensical and a reflection of the rugby community's fear of exposure or embarrassment.'

Laidlaw wrote his book in a rather humorous vein, sometimes poking fun at well-known rugby figures, or at the rugby establishment, but often softening his criticism with wit. Nevertheless, he opened up the All Blacks, writing about issues such as groupies, which had never been

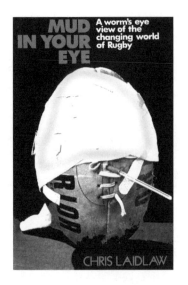

Chris Laidlaw's *Mud In Your Eye* stands up well after almost 30 years.

publicised previously. He mocked the rugby establishment, and it seems the establishment was even more affronted that a player would not only dare criticise, but do so in a mocking manner.

The halfback got serious when he discussed the South African issue. He'd toured there in 1970 as a player and now he came down vehemently anti-South Africa, or at least vehemently anti-apartheid. Rugby people of course categorised him as wanting his cake and eating it. It was a simplistic answer, but one that was thrown at Laidlaw for many years.

Laidlaw also pointed out some of the fringe benefits that All Blacks enjoy, such as benevolence by the Customs Department when the team returned from distant shores. This last revelation apparently caused All Black teams headaches as, stung by the adverse publicity, Customs became far more vigilant when they spotted All Black sides arriving from overseas. At least that was the urban legend passed on by future All Blacks.

In my travels with many teams from 1974 to 2001 I never saw too many problems for the All Blacks, not that they were openly abusing the Customs. But boy, on some of those shopping trips in Singapore in the late 1970s and early '80s, the New Zealand Army corps stationed there helped many players to heaps of electronic bargains which no doubt livened up their return.

Laidlaw even took shots at icons such as captain Wilson Whineray and coach Fred Allen.

Not surprisingly, the book was a sensation. Exact sales figures are hard to get, but it was released in several editions, and was published in Britain and New Zealand. Thousands of copies went to South Africa and many more to Australia. 'I think it sold something like 45,000 in Britain and about 40,000 elsewhere,' says Laidlaw, 'though I don't know if I ever got a final sales figure.

'When it was published it did provoke a lot of talk. I was overseas at that time, so missed some of the reaction back in New Zealand, though it filtered through to me. There were rumblings, though a lot of the All Blacks didn't give a damn. I think Wilson and Fred were a bit wounded, but they are both big men, big enough to take some criticism for what it was, then move on. I have remained friends with both of them. I was just pointing out areas where they might not have done their job the way I would have liked; I wasn't saying they were bad people. The book caused a bigger fuss in Britain.'

Laidlaw says he is pleased he did the book. It was certainly a more upfront and honest book than that written by most famous All Blacks. It was apparently selling like hot cakes in South Africa, until the authorities got wind of its contents, and then it was withdrawn.

Considering it wasn't mass-marketed, as are today's big-name biographies, its sales were astonishing, reflecting the content of the book. Laidlaw, a Rhodes Scholar, wrote his own book. He has always been an eloquent speaker and these days is a prolific columnist.

MICHAEL LAWS

GLADIATOR
The Norm Hewitt Story

Compulsory reading ... one of the best sports books you'll ever read. COLIN MEADS

Norm Hewitt's *Gladiator* . . . one of the most sensational rugby books ever published in New Zealand.

Hewitt clearly does not possess Laidlaw's skill in putting words together, and it was a good decision to link up with Laws, who writes well. Where Hewitt surpassed even Laidlaw was his willingness to expose himself.

In *Gladiator* he spoke of his problems at Te Aute College, mentioning bullying, drug-taking and making a vague reference to sexual molestation. He talked about his tough life at home, where violence was an issue, and then went on to catalogue the major controversies in his life, and when they are tallied up, there are quite a few, including:

* The Roger Randle affair, when on a Hurricanes trip to South Africa, Randle was accused of rape and other Wellington players were involved in the incident.

* The incident at Queenstown in 1999 when Hewitt got so drunk he put his arm through a plate glass window and ended up slumped in the gutter wondering if he was about to die. This led to a public apology (which Hewitt now seems to feel was a sham) and hard-man Hewitt crying on television.

* A story about two strippers turning up at Hewitt's house to visit him and some other rugby players. One of the strippers eventually filed assault charges.

There are many other similarly salacious stories, but that gets the idea across.

In addition, Hewitt fires some broadsides at many well-known rugby identities. Chief among these are John Hart, Sean Fitzpatrick and Graham Mourie.

Hart, Hewitt seems to feel, was officious and involved himself unnecessarily in his players' lives. Fitzpatrick was the No 1 All Black hooker virtually throughout Hewitt's international career, forcing Norm to spend a record amount of time on the reserves bench. Hewitt felt Fitzpatrick played when injured and didn't like being sledged by him on the field. Mourie was a 'follower' as a coach.

It's interesting that all three people dared to cross Hewitt.

Hart told him repeatedly he had a drinking problem that he needed to attend to. He was right — Hewitt is now a confessed alcoholic. As for the racist slur, this is laughable. Hart discovered and mentored Samoan Michael Jones, whom he called the greatest player he had ever seen and had a Maori, Taine Randell, as his captain. And he was very close to many Pacific Island and Maori players. Mourie dropped Hewitt from the captaincy of the Hurricanes. Of the thousands of rugby players I've

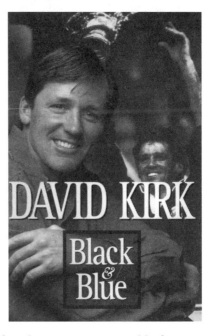

Black and Blue . . . David's Kirk's biography, which told of the World Cup-winning halfback's problems with the Cavaliers.

known, few were as original, individual and independent as Mourie (see *Rugby Under Siege*, p142). It is difficult to see him as a follower.

My feeling on reading Hewitt's book is that while this might be big Norm's view of things, it is not always the truth. Rather it is Hewitt's truth.

Regardless, I found it an absorbing and compelling book. I picked it up one evening and didn't put it down until I'd finished reading it, at 2am. I can't say that's happened with many New Zealand rugby books.

Others? Well, there have been surprisingly few that remain memorable for their content.

Andy Haden took some hefty swipes at rugby officialdom in his *Boots 'n all* (published in 1983). David Kirk wrote well about the problems he encountered with the returning Cavaliers players when he produced *Black and Blue* (1997). John Kirwan spoke honestly about his battles with depression in *Running on Instinct* (1992) and Josh Kronfeld had some swipes at Hart and others in *On the Loose* (1999). These are among the few rugby books that gave readers a genuine and previously unreported insight into at least one aspect of an All Black's life.

Kronfeld took an incredible risk with the timing of the conclusion and release of his book. Presumably the bulk of the writing (done excellently, by the way, by Brian Turner) was finished and typeset for release just as Kronfeld set off with Hart and Taine Randell before the 1999 World Cup in Britain. Kronfeld was critical of both Hart and Randell.

If perchance New Zealand had won the Cup, Kronfeld and his publishers might have been left looking rather foolish with stacks and stacks of a needlessly critical book on their hands. Or did King Josh have an innate sense that there would be doom and gloom at the Cup?

Many other rugby books have been exceedingly well written. For instance, it would be hard to imagine better writing than Alex Veysey managed in *Ebony and Ivory* (1984), the story of Bernie Fraser and Stu Wilson. Terry McLean ghost-wrote the story of one of our most famous fullbacks in *I George Nepia* (1963) and did an outstanding job. In late 2001 the great McLean, aged 88, after a request from Britain, was updating the Nepia story for a re-release.

Graham Mourie Captain (1982) was another book I enjoyed for its intelligence and original thinking.

But for every book like this, there have been dozens of innocuous, forgettable biographies, in which a famous name and a good photo adorn the cover and the next 200 pages trawl over well-worked tours and matches with perhaps a sentence or two of controversy to produce an eye-catching headline.

That's what made Laidlaw's *Mud In Your Eye* such a pioneering book. It broke the mould and was the first instance of an All Black stepping out of line. Hewitt's book, whether you believe all he has to say, and whether you end up liking him or not, is similarly upfront and outspoken, and he deserves credit for that.

Hey, that's not Jonesy's jersey

Famous All Black flanker Michael Jones (right) was only a reserve for the third test against South Africa at Eden Park in 1994. Shortly after halftime in a dramatic and closely fought match, Jones was called to replace the injured Blair Larsen.

News Media Auckland

In those days it was standard procedure that test jerseys were numbered from 1 to 22. Yet when Jones made his run on, he was wearing jersey 23. How did that happen (I hear you ask breathlessly)?

Well, it was because in his haste exiting the team's hotel on Auckland's North Shore to head to the game, Jones left his jersey — number 22 — in his room. When he discovered the omission, it was too late for him to retrieve it. Therefore he ducked into the 'extras' pile in the team's gear bag. There he uplifted the next number in the jersey sequence to wear.

If that was no big deal, at least it was a point of trivia. There was one other curious aspect to Jones' appearance that day. When he ran across from the substitutes bench, the other forwards were forming a lineout. Jones joined in and checked who he would be marking. He noted he would be up against the Springbok captain, François Pienaar. Therefore the likeable New Zealander confirmed his always impeccable manners by leaning over and shaking the hand of the somewhat startled South African.

What a nice, but sometimes forgetful, man that Michael Jones was!

29. Sink or swim

The wettest test of all

I have commentated on rugby matches that have been played in all sorts of weather, from the gale force winds of Llanelli in 1989, to the heat of the 1998 Commonwealth Games sevens tournament in Kuala Lumpur.

But possibly the most bizarre conditions of any match I've covered occurred on June 14, 1975 when New Zealand and Scotland faced each other at Eden Park. In the early hours of the Saturday morning it began bucketing down in Auckland and torrential rain continued right up till kick-off time. Nearly 10cm of rain fell that day, most of it before mid-afternoon.

Remember, these were in the days before rugby fields were upgraded with modern drainage facilities and by kick-off time, at 2.30 pm, there was an astonishing amount of water on Eden Park. The in-goal areas and the corners looked like swimming pools and the rest of the park was hardly any better.

It was such uninviting weather that though Eden Park was sold out, only 45,000 people turned up to watch. If the Scots hadn't been booked to fly home immediately afterwards, the match would surely have been postponed a day.

New Zealand dominated the game and scored four tries on their way to a 24–0 victory, a fantastic score in the circumstances. There were genuine concerns that day that a player might drown. I could envisage a player falling to the ground face down and having other players pile on top of him. The man at the bottom would have had his head well under water — a dangerous situation.

Aspects of the match were farcical. The deep water obliterated much of the touchlines and goal-lines. A ball would be kicked ahead, and then would come to a dead stop as it hit the water. Players therefore tended to overrun the ball as they chased it.

Before the match a large group of firemen pumped water away from the field, but it seemed to hardly make any difference. It was so wet that planks had to be supplied

News Media Auckland

Aquatic action from the All Blacks–Scotland test match at Eden Park in 1975.

to help those who had tickets in the covered stand reach their seats.

Some snapshots of the match linger . . . Scotland fullback Bruce Hay breaking his arm only a quarter of an hour into his debut; Bryan Williams splashing his way across the line for one of his two tries; Sid Going's dominance in the unusual conditions; both teams' reluctance to kick for goal (13 penalties were awarded, but no attempts at goal were made), Joe Karam lifting four consecutive conversions out of the water and over the bar.

Veteran writer (and former Welsh international) Vivian Jenkins covered the match for the *Sunday Times* and wrote that 'it was as foul a day as one could possibly conceive'. He said: 'Only in New Zealand could so many apparent lunatics have put in an appearance, in spite of everything.'

Nevile Lodge's take on the wet test.

30. 'Ears to you, Fitzy

Johan le Roux chews out the skipper

In my time as a commentator, working alongside expert former All Black co-broadcasters like Grant Fox, Wayne Graham, Grahame Thorne, Earle Kirton and Jock Hobbs has always been a delight. I learned a lot from them. In fact, I would often come home and grump to my wife that while I fancied myself as a rugby know-all 'those buggers keep showing me up with all the extra things that they can see'.

In retrospect, that is a good thing. Any sports broadcaster needs to keep learning. There was one time, though, when John Hart alerted me — and the rest of the world — to an incident which no one except him saw in the instant it happened.

I use the Hart eye sharpness as a simple intro to a story that truly outraged New Zealand rugby in its time and eventually enabled the game to rid itself of a thug.

It was at the second test in 1994, when Athletic Park hosted the Springboks and the All Blacks. At one point in a rugged, brutal test, there was a forward rush during which the two packs tumbled together. All Black captain and hooker Sean Fitzpatrick disappeared under a pile of bodies.

Somehow from 100 metres away, John Hart saw something in the ruck that caught his eye. Into the microphone he immediately bellowed: 'Fitzpatrick is complaining he's had his ear bitten!' I couldn't believe it. I looked at Hart. I had seen nothing.

But Hart was right. Fitzy emerged holding his ear, with blood clearly seen on his hands. He complained bitterly to the referee.

Author Keith Quinn with his trusty comments man, John Hart.

Fitzy, meet Johan. The notorious ear-biting incident of 1994.

What we all could see soon enough, via the TV replay, was that the biter was the Springbok with the reputation for being a hard man, prop Johan le Roux. He was chastised by the referee, but little else happened.

Immediately after the game, Fitzpatrick tried to put a dampener on the incident. Using the old adage that what happens on the field stays on the field, Fitzpatrick stipulated that he would not be interviewed live if any reference was made to the trickle of blood coming out of his ear. That was the man's style — he always elected to keep incidents on the field, and nowhere else.

Johan le Roux was something else. He later wrote a book, the contents of which were based almost totally on the Wellington incident. That is confirmed with the book's title — *Biting Back*. It was not a big seller in New Zealand.

In the book he tries to justify his actions that day at Athletic Park. To my mind he fails miserably. He also tries to rubbish the style of play of Fitzpatrick. Although he offers certain comments about the robustness and aggression of Fitzpatrick that have some justification (such as, 'To this day Fitzpatrick has been put forward as a lilywhite angel . . . In fact he masterminded the art of intimidation . . . the man is a menace on the field.') le Roux's attempts to justify his biting were extremely feeble.

He bit an opponent on the rugby field. Say it slowly and the horror stays on your palate like the worst taste of unpleasantness. Le Roux went totally beyond the bounds of rugby's unwritten contract where eyes, ears, teeth and testicles are never touched in any game, for whatever reason.

The media scrum of flashing cameras and bulbs which were there when le Roux entered the judiciary hearing two days later should have told him that he had committed a heinous foul, one of the worst in rugby's history. But though he apologised, he did not take the 19-month sentence well and the tone of his book is far from that of remorse and humiliation.

I write from a New Zealand standpoint, so there is undoubtedly a bias, but it must be said that rugby worldwide was better off once le Roux was prevented from appearing in any more in major games.

Ocker soccer stopper

Ouch! Do New Zealanders really need reminding of yet more outrageous behaviour by Australians in their manner of celebrating a test victory over the All Blacks?

Take this example of two lower grade soccer teams in Sydney on the afternoon of August 5, 2000. They were involved in a vigorous game, but at a loud call from the sideline the two teams raced to huddle around a transistor radio which was held by a watching spectator. The reason for this bizarre behaviour is not so strange as would first seem. The person holding the radio had been shouting out progress scores to the soccer teams from the Bledisloe Cup rugby match being played at the same time across the Tasman Sea in Wellington.

This was the game that was heading towards its climax at Wellington's Stadium in much the same nail-biting fashion as the first Cup game that season had gone down at Stadium Australia just weeks before. New Zealand had won the Sydney thriller 39–35. Three weeks had passed and now all of Australia hung on for a better result from the Wellington re-match.

At a certain incident late in the Wellington game, as heard on ABC's radio broadcast, the person at the soccer game who had been monitoring the score called out: 'It's a penalty to Australia! In the last minute of the game! If it goes over we win!!'

The soccer teams instantly ran to the radio and clustered near the crackling commentary. At that moment in Wellington, John Eales, the Australian captain, lined up a last-minute penalty shot at goal. New Zealand were leading 23–21.

On the wind-swept field in Sydney the soccer players listened in silence and at the sound of 'It's a goal!' from the commentator in Wellington, the soccer players danced with glee. With whoops of celebration the two teams high-fived with each other — Australia had won! Then, after the grins had died away, the two teams sagely resumed their lower grade soccer match against each other.

Speaking as a New Zealander, doesn't that sort of story want to make you spit sparks!

31. No Vic, no victory
49ers dealt dud hand by union

Vic Cavanagh is often described as the best rugby coach never to coach the All Blacks. How he came to be overlooked for the job when the All Black team travelled to South Africa in 1949 remains one of the great mysteries of New Zealand rugby.

Cavanagh, born in Dunedin in 1909, came from a rugby family. His father, also Vic, represented Otago at rugby in 1899 and coached the University and Southern clubs, and Otago. He was a national selector in 1913 and the Otago Rugby Union president in 1922.

Vic junior was a product of Otago Boys High School. He made the first XV in 1926 and by 1931 was appearing as a wing forward for the Southern club and Otago. But his great skill was as a coach. He had good communication skills, understood rugby intimately and developed in his teams a rucking style that made them a formidable challenge for any opposition.

The 1949 All Blacks paid dearly for that New Zealand Rugby Union blunder.

Cavanagh was the Otago selector-coach from 1946–49 and was the mastermind of the great Otago Ranfurly Shield team of that era. Otago repulsed 17 Shield challengers and in 1949 there were 11 Otago players in the All Black team chosen for South Africa. It seemed a racing certainty that Cavanagh would be asked to be coach — or in the term of the day, assistant manager — of the touring side, but that appointment, which seemed so logical to everyone else in New Zealand, was never made.

Instead Jim Parker, a 1924 All Black, went as manager and Alex McDonald, an All Black way back in 1905, was appointed coach. Fred Allen, who captained the 1949 All

Blacks, has often spoken to me about what a tragedy it was that Cavanagh was not sent to South Africa.

'In my playing days, the management, and particularly the coaches, were too old. They were fine gentlemen, but didn't know very much about coaching. Before the team for South Africa was named, I was called over to the centre of Athletic Park, very muddy it was, and asked who should be coach. Naturally I said Vic Cavanagh, because he's one of the greatest coaches who never coached an All Black side.

'They said they couldn't name Cavanagh because he wouldn't get on with the Auckland players, which was nonsense. At that stage there were nearly a dozen Otago players and eight or nine Aucklanders. Alex McDonald was going to go as manager, but then Jim Parker

Vic Cavanagh . . . a great talent ignored.

decided he wanted to go, so he went as manager and Alex as coach. Vic Cavanagh, a great character who knew rugby like the back of his hand, was left behind.'

The 1949 All Blacks paid dearly for that New Zealand Rugby Union blunder. 'Alex was 66 years of age on that trip and sick for a lot of the time,' says Allen. 'The high altitude and heat made it difficult for him. Things were different to what he knew. The grounds were rock hard, and there were lots of injuries. The travel was enormous — at one stage we spent 10 days out of 13 on a train, playing two games in between. We had the odd hard case who took on old Alex a bit, but generally his health wasn't up to it. He was interested in coming home and in the days of flying, he might have. But he struggled on. You could actually see him going downhill. Having said all that, I was very fond of Alex McDonald and Jim Parker. It's just that they weren't the right people for the job in South Africa.

'All these years later, I still say that if we'd had Vic Cavanagh with us, with his knowledge of rugby, especially forward play, we might easily have won a test series that we lost 4–0.'

Cavanagh was perhaps the greatest in a line of outstanding Otago coaches who have had a massive influence on New Zealand rugby over the past century. Jimmy Duncan was the coach of the 1905 Originals. Others in the royal line were Cavanagh, Charlie Saxton, Eric Watson and Laurie Mains. The influence spread even wider because Fred Allen, who is arguably the finest of all New Zealand rugby coaches, says that the two people who most influenced him were Cavanagh and Saxton.

32. Rugby under siege

Graham Mourie and the 1981 Springbok tour

My admiration for Graham Mourie was already very high even before 1981. I'd watched Mourie grow as a person and a rugby player through the 1970s and been impressed with the quality he brought to everything he did.

Mourie was never a conformist. He thought about things, then did what he thought was right, regardless of how his actions might be perceived by others. He was an outstanding All Black flanker and an even better captain. In terms of great openside loose forwards, he might be in the top half-dozen in All Black history, and we have had some fine ones. But among captains, there are some who would put him right at the top. He is certainly in my top three.

Mourie's team-mates knew that their captain was the fittest player on the field, that he was willing to sacrifice his body for the team. They could see his ability to remain cool and unflustered under pressure. Off the field, they saw how Mourie carried himself. On tour he was interested in the history of places the team visited. He was more rounded than most rugby players.

When his teams had a rare loss, such as to Munster in 1978, Mourie took such reverses with good grace, even humour.

He was able to take good teams and make them great, the mark of an exceptional leader. There was no better example of this than the 1978 team that toured Britain and eventually completed the first All Black Grand Slam. Mourie's team that year had some excellent players, but there have been more talented All Black sides. Somehow Mourie and coach Jack Gleeson devised tactics and game plans that got the best out of the team. In the end, the All Blacks beat all the Home Nations, sometimes in the last minute or two, when the pressure was really on.

So it can be seen from all this that I held the All Black captain in high esteem. But my admiration for him rose immensely when he announced that he would not be available to play against the Springboks in 1981. This was a massively significant act for the incumbent All Black captain.

On a rugby level, he was surrendering his place in the New Zealand team. And even if he regained a test spot in subsequent years, would the rugby establishment want him as captain again? On a personal level, Mourie knew that he ran the risk of being branded a traitor by a rugby-mad country. He risked the scorn of a nation, and for that he earned my absolute respect.

News Media Auckland

Graham Mourie . . . decision not to play was about being true to his 'inner being'.

With the wisdom of hindsight and the safety of two decades we can look back upon that turbulent year and say Mourie was right. He saw that the Rugby Union was harming the game by inviting the Springboks. He saw the country would be thrown into chaos if the South Africans toured. And he felt that it was morally wrong to play against a team that represented a racist regime. These things we see clearly now. Back in 1981, with claims and threats flying about the country, it was nowhere near as easy to think with clarity and logic.

Mourie's decision to not play against the Springboks did not endear him to some of his All Black team-mates. Years later I detected that a few had not totally forgiven him. Mark Shaw, for one, has spoken of his admiration for Mourie as a player, but could never understand how he could turn his back on his team.

'The decision not to play against South Africa that year was a part of a commitment I made that I would be true to my own personality and inner being,' Mourie explained. 'It's part of whether you sell out in life and become more concerned with just taking everything.' The decision not to play was made only after deep thought. In his autobiography, Mourie revealed that a few years earlier, he might have made a different decision. And if the All Blacks had been touring South Africa in 1981, he would have seriously considered going.

Mourie says he got strong support for his stand. He says 98 per cent of the mail he received was positive. And in the rugby community, while many of his friends and team-mates didn't agree with him, they had enough respect for his integrity and intelligence to let him go his own way.

Eventually a few other high-profile players joined Mourie. Among them were Bruce Robertson and Gary Seear. The Springbok tour placed all of us in a dilemma. I had been to South Africa and seen the problems there. I hated what South Africa stood for at that time.

What would I do? I decided I would not squander my career, but would make my own protest in my own way. So I commentated on the Springbok matches, but refused to do any other work on the tour, such as covering news stories.

It was the strangest season in New Zealand rugby history. There were ugly scenes all around the country. Families, even All Blacks' families, were split. Allan Hewson was the All Black fullback and his wife Pauline was one of the tour protesters. This scenario was repeated all around the country.

I discussed the pros and cons of the tour with hundreds of people that year. Wilson Whineray probably summed up how I felt when he said: 'It was a difficult time. I had friends on both sides of the fence. They all believed they were right and there was a certain logic in what they all said.' I never did find out what Wilson himself thought. Another whose personal views remained unclear was Ces Blazey, the chairman of the New Zealand Rugby Union. He was the spokesman for the union, but refused to give a personal opinion on the merits of the tour.

Let's not beat about the bush. The Springbok team was racially chosen, as it had always been. There was one coloured player, Errol Tobias, and one non-white official. Perhaps they were there on merit, but it was hard not to think they were token gestures.

The pro-tour brigade felt that sport and politics should not mix. Further, many felt that South Africa was the old rugby enemy and that to beat them would make it all worthwhile. The anti-tour protesters were appalled at the apartheid laws in South Africa, and felt that by inviting the Springboks to tour, New Zealand was giving tacit approval to such a regime. I must add that, as the tour progressed, and civil unrest increased, I did feel that some of the protesters and demonstrators were turning up because there was the chance of a stoush with the police, rather than for any moral considerations. But these people remained in a minority; most protesters were there because of a strongly held belief that the tour should not proceed.

Prime Minister Rob Muldoon, who could make most things happen when he wanted, permitted the tour to go ahead. He said he wished it wouldn't, but that he was powerless to stop it. I don't believe that. It suited him politically to get the rugby people — heartland New Zealand — on

Errol Tobias was the only coloured player among the 1981 Springboks.

News Media Auckland

side with an election looming later that year.

So the tour proceeded. It began on July 22 when the Springboks beat Poverty Bay 24–6 in Gisborne. That was the first of 14 matches that took place in unprecedented circumstances in this country. It was rugby behind barbed wire. There was a rugby battle on the field and another battle off the field, often in the streets outside the park as police and demonstrators locked horns.

I got used to being accompanied by security staff. On test days, Grahame Thorne and I would be escorted to the venue with military precision. It made work very unenjoyable and I wondered if this was what rugby had come to.

The tour stuttered along, the rugby gradually being pushed into the background as there was more and more talk about batons and barbed wire, the Red Squad and demonstrators. Ces Blazey and John Minto were discussed as much or more than rival test captains Andy Dalton and Wynand Claassen.

> **I got used to being accompanied by security staff. On test days, Grahame Thorne and I would be escorted to the venue**

Two games were abandoned. The second scheduled fixture, at Hamilton's Rugby Park, was called off when demonstrators could not be cleared from the field. There was a seething anger that day among the rugby spectators packed into the ground. It was a victory for the anti-tour people.

A month later the match against South Canterbury was called off when police said they could not guarantee security at the ground. Another victory for the demonstrators.

But, between times, there was some rugby played. Players slept at the grounds, or they travelled there many hours before kick-off. It was surreal.

As for the test series, New Zealand won the first, at Christchurch, 14–9, then lost the second 24–12, at Wellington.

Everything built to a head on September 12, 1981, when the last match of the tour, the third and deciding test, took place at Eden Park. What an occasion this was. There were thousands upon thousands of protesters. Eden Park was crammed with rugby followers. The police planned and practised their tactics.

The game itself was a thriller, probably the most dramatic of any I've commentated. In front of 49,000 spectators, New Zealand charged to a 16–3 lead at halftime and seemed secure, if that is the right word to describe the frenzied atmosphere that day.

Above: Police stand guard after Taranaki — minus Graham Mourie — played the Springboks in 1981. Opposite: Graham Mourie down on the farm.

But this was no ordinary rugby match. A Cessna plane circled repeatedly over Eden Park, making dangerously low sweeps of the ground. We all feared a disaster was imminent. Imagine if the plane had ploughed into a grandstand. Was this what rugby had come to? The plane dropped leaflets and flour bombs onto the field until, by the end, white splodges pock-marked Eden Park.

Protesters lit flares on the field and early in the second half there was a considerable delay while they were removed. Later in the half, New Zealand prop Gary Knight was hit by a flour bomb and dropped to the ground. This led to the comical remark by Welsh referee Clive Norling, who said as he stood over the fallen Knight: 'For goodness sake, don't use water. He'll turn to paste and we'll never be able to move him.'

The game stuttered along, with seemingly as much time used in stoppages as in play. The Springboks fought back. Captain Claassen explained to me many years later that his team felt better going into the second half because 'we were playing with the aeroplane at our backs'. It had been a constant source of concern to all the players, but especially to those looking at it as it came speeding towards them. Looking at film of the game now, you can see that in the faces of some of the All Blacks in the second half. They are clearly seen to be looking with eyes upwards instead of concentrating with heads down.

Referee Norling would call a lineout, look at the sky and say, 'Duck, duck, boys — here it comes again.'

The amazing thing is that with this going on, the rugby was good and South Africa gradually closed the gap. Winger Ray Mordt scored three tries and crack goal-

The third test of the 1981 series will forever be known as the 'flour bomb' test.

kicker Naas Botha landed two conversions and three penalties. The scores were 22–22 when normal time expired.

But this was no normal game. Everyone knew there would be substantial injury time, but how much? Eight minutes into injury time, the All Blacks were awarded a free kick that was turned into a penalty because the Springboks had not retired 10 metres. The ball was outside their 22 near the right side of the field, so the left-footed Allan Hewson stepped forward. If the ball had been on the other side of the field, the right-footed Doug Rollerson would have been given the kick.

Hewson didn't seem especially nervous as he lined up the most important attempt of his career and he kicked it straight and true. 'It had to go over, it had to,' he said later. It did and the New Zealand fullback thrust his arms in the air in triumph.

The South Africans still claim they were robbed. Claassen says New Zealand dominated the first test, South Africa the second. In the third, New Zealand won the first half and South Africa the second. 'A draw in the third test and in the series would have been a fair result,' said Claassen. 'That's how it should have been. The referee felt he had to make a decision that would decide the outcome of the series.'

Naas Botha said to me in Pretoria a few years ago: 'It has gone down as the flour bomb test and for the Clive Norling penalty. That's sad because we had a long, hard tour and it all came down to flour bombs and a referee. Both teams deserved better.' I must say I don't necessarily agree with Naas' assessment.

So the Springboks returned home and the curtain came down on a tumultuous time in New Zealand rugby, and in the development of our nation. There weren't many winners that year. It took rugby some years to recover from the stench and taint of what went on in 1981.

But one person who did emerge with reputation enhanced, at least in my view, was Graham Mourie. In the years after his playing days he was a sports promoter for a while, playing a major role in making the 1987 rugby World Cup a logistical success. It was again typical of the man, though, that he watched the All Blacks win their World Cup final on Eden Park against France from down behind the goal posts

The protest scenes of 1981 are etched deeply into our consciousness.

wearing working clothes in which to shift advertising hoardings so as to make the TV coverage a viable success. Not for him a seat in the stand wearing a flash businessman's blazer and tie.

Later still, he returned to farming in Opunake, preferring the quiet of the country and family life to the bustle of the city. By the end of the millennium he had moved with the tides to become a professional rugby coach. These days there are a number of New Zealanders who deride him for his expertise. Are their views a hangover from his stand during the Springbok tour of 1981? Maybe, maybe not.

I believe those people tend to starkly judge his ability on the previous week's results of his Hurricanes or Wellington representative team. Solid judges of Mourie should always weigh up that he is more than just a coach. He certainly did not deserve the cruel taunts sent his way by former All Black Norm Hewitt in his book towards the end of 2001.

These days Mourie remains a thoughtful and still private person. He remains different from the average New Zealand rugby bloke. Today when I think of his contribution to New Zealand rugby I consider the fact that he was one of our finest loose forwards, and a great captain. I also cannot help but throw in the memory that he chose to be nowhere near Eden Park that fateful day in September 1981.

He risked everything for a principle, preferring to be working quietly on his farm in Opunake. It was a good day to be nowhere near a rugby field. To my mind, his decision not only did him no harm, but increased his stature.

33. Fullback sent to Coventry

Kit Fawcett's great gaffe of '76

The record books don't do justice to Christopher Louis Fawcett, known to all in rugby as Kit. Fawcett played 13 matches for the All Blacks, all in 1976, and appeared in two tests on the New Zealand tour of South Africa. His first-class career stretched only from 1975 to 1978. He played his last game of rep rugby when he was just 23.

It all sounds fairly mundane, but cold statistics don't reveal the warm, witty character that was Fawcett. He was one of the friendliest All Blacks I've encountered. His treatment on the 1976 tour was shocking and in a way it was no surprise that following that experience he was lost to rugby soon afterwards.

I caught up with him a couple of years ago while researching *Legends of the All Blacks* and am pleased to report that these days he is a prosperous businessman living in Hamilton. One of his successful schemes was to buy the accommodation blocks that were used for the 1990 Auckland Commonwealth Games, and transport them to Hamilton, where they were set up as student accommodation for the University of Waikato.

Fawcett will go down in All Black history as the man who announced at the start of that 1976 tour of South Africa that the All Blacks would score more off the field than on. In fact, the story is largely a myth, as he explained to me:

'We arrived in Johannesburg after a long flight that involved us going from New Zealand to Europe and then down to South Africa. We were dealing with autograph hunters and the media. Then I met a woman reporter named Viv Prince from the *Johannesburg Woman's Weekly*. She asked me if I had a minute to answer a few questions. I said, "Fine."

'Then she asked me about my attitude towards socialising on the tour. She said

Kit Fawcett (wearing sun glasses) 'on safari' in 1976. Next to Fawcett (with camera) is All Black captain Andy Leslie and, in front, Joe Morgan.

that when the 1974 Lions were in South Africa they had a trophy for the most scoring off the field. I said, "Well, I'm only 21. I haven't really got a preference in terms of different types of women. It's a bit like a cheeseboard at the end of the meal. It's optional if you order it, though you know it's available."

'I was trying to be diplomatic. Then she asked me who were the romantics in the team. I had a little bit of a think and said all the guys would be romantic if they met the right women at the right place and the right time, meaning it was a very personal thing. Then she asked me how I was going to go. I said, "Well, I'm a fullback and I hope to score more on the field than off."

'I was rooming with Laurie Mains when the paper came out the next day. It was all over the front page — "All Blacks hope to score more off the field than on, says 21-year-old Kit Fawcett, who likes blondes, brunettes and redheads and wants them all to come to the hotel."

'Laurie told me I was in the shit. I hoped it wouldn't get back to New Zealand, but the same day about 250,000 *New Zealand Herald*s went out with the same story in it. I went down to breakfast and couldn't figure out why nobody was sitting with me.

But what had happened was that all the wives had rung overnight and asked what was going on over there.

'The quote was turned around, but she was obviously looking for a story. And it was a bloody good story because it went around the world and probably ruined my career. But what can you do? Do you hold up the white flag and say, "This ain't fair"? You have to take it on the chin and get on with life.

'To give credit to Andy Leslie, he did come and sit with me and say, "Bad luck, Kit." He explained about the wives being upset and so forth. I had only been trying to do a little PR, but I had no idea of the consequences. She wanted a story and marketed it all around the world.

'Viv Prince turned up on the last week of the tour and wanted to do another interview about how I'd got on, which I thought was quite cheeky of her. She knocked on the hotel door and said, "Hi, Kit. I'm back. I want to do an article on how your tour's been."

'I said to her very politely that she'd probably caused enough problems and could she just leave this one. She agreed, but some of the other press saw her at my door and wrote a little story about her returning. You just couldn't get away from the press.'

Fawcett was an approachable and rather innocent person. He was picked for an All Black trial in 1974, when he was just 18, and had me in stitches when he told me about how he turned up:

'I had been in Dunedin, but had not played for Otago, so didn't have a uniform. My air tickets arrived by mail, and I turned up at the hotel. They said, "Who are you?" They asked me where my blazer was. I was wearing a bright red pair of striped leather shoes, a pink pair of trousers and quite a bright shirt. I think I was wearing a cap, and of course I had long hair. They didn't know if I was an artist or what, but they certainly got a shock when I turned up.'

It was interesting talking to Fawcett about those now dimming days in South Africa. He said he and Mains were opposites in every way, and that Mains was resentful because Fawcett's presence shoved him into the background. Fawcett told me that in hindsight he felt the selectors didn't do a good job of picking the right fullbacks in 1976. He felt Greg Rowlands should have been the No 1 and he should have been his understudy.

I'd agree with Kit on that, and I feel sorry for what happened to him during the tour. I'm pleased that he seems to have emerged unscathed, the same colourful, affable personality as before, and a successful businessman at that.

●

34. Shutting up the know-alls

World Cup trivia is always a winner

Having been involved in rugby reporting for quite a few years, with the travel that has entailed, I have noticed there are certain types of people who cannot resist approaching and asking broadcasters, reporters or writers to answer questions that irk them.

I suppose the rugby reporter is an obvious target. After all, the reporter is on radio, TV or in the press several times a week expounding a degree of knowledge. Generally, those in the reporting business do not mind such questions or intrusions as most of the enquirers are courteous and civil. However, since 1995 I have noticed trends among the questioners and the questions they ask.

There now seem to be two types of people making enquiries. Most people earnestly want an answer and hope the reporter can provide it. But there is a second type, much more dangerous. These people already know the answer to their question and want to see whether the so-called hotshot reporter does, too.

These people can be slightly tiresome. But not to worry — there are ways that crafty reporters and broadcasters have learned to fight back. I use an old Jewish method. In no way do I want to diminish an age-old Jewish technique, but I always answer a question with another question!

The easiest way to catch out a New Zealand rugby know-all is to ask them questions about the scoring sequences, structure and composition of the four defeats by the All Blacks during the 1991, 1995 and 1999 World Cup tournaments.

It is uncanny. The average New Zealand rugby bloke knows plenty about all manner of games down the years, and can provide statistics for anyone who wants to hear them. But those four World Cup matches that the All Blacks lost in the 1990s are games the average Joe-know-all rugby New Zealand bloke does not want to know anything about.

Yes, it's Nelson Mandela with victorious Springbok skipper François Pienaar after the 1995 World Cup final. The real test of rugby knowledge, though, is in accurately recalling the game statistics.

Deeply learned though questioners might be, they never want to know about the time Australia beat New Zealand in Dublin the semi-final of 1991; nor do they crave questions about the final against South Africa in 1995; certainly there is no desire to relive any issues of the French victory over the All Blacks at Twickenham in 1999 or the subsequent defeat by South Africa in the third place play-off at Cardiff.

Rather, when those games are mentioned, these knowledgeable people will often quickly move on to the next time the All Blacks beat that particular country and refer to some sort of revenge having taken place over that World Cup enemy (which, of course, is nonsense, for the Cup wins will stand in the record books for all time).

But still, that is the way New Zealanders are. It is as if the All Black supporters of that time have mentally blacked-out all remembrance of the above four defeats.

That's sad because one of those games stands out as one of the most amazing ever played. Strangely, it is the one in which New Zealand were highest placed and in which they gave one of their bravest performances. We are talking here about the 1995 final against the Springboks in Johannesburg.

New Zealanders should have proud memories of that tough, tense match, especially as it was played under such intense pressure. The mighty Springboks, hosting the World Cup in Nelson Mandela's new 'Rainbow Nation', were against the old enemy, New Zealand, who had played the most attractive football of the tournament. And while the South Africans battled to overcome huge nationalistic expectations of a home victory, the All Blacks struggled to overcome illness within their team.

About 62,000 excited people were packed into Ellis Park and watched enthralled as the battle raged for two hours. No tries were scored, nor did many seem likely. The defence was magnificent. The only scoring came from a few penalties and a couple of dropped goals landed by flyhalves Andrew Mehrtens (New Zealand) and Joel Stransky (South Africa).

Finally fulltime was reached . . . 80 minutes of unrelenting test rugby. And the score at full-time Mr Know-All? Well, you tell me. And who had led at halftime? Ah, the hesitation. I'm not surprised. The memories of New Zealand's rugby fans are selective and picky. They want to recall and relive only those games where their famous team has tasted glory.

So you try it folks. Next time a deeply proficient rugby scholar, at a party or pub, wants to dispute your knowledge of All Black rugby history, dig into your memories of just four games and at least you will certainly hold your own.

Try questions like these:
• Who refereed the game at Dublin in 1991 when the All Blacks lost to Australia?
• Come to think of it, what was the final score that day?
• Who was New Zealand's fullback that day?
• In the 1995 semi-final, what was the score after 80 minutes?
• How many points did New Zealand score in extra time?
• Amid all the fuss about food poisoning, how many players were actually substituted by New Zealand that day?
• In the 1999 semi-final at Twickenham, what was the biggest points margin New Zealand led France by?
• Who scored New Zealand's three tries that day?
• Where was the third place play-off staged?
• How many tries did New Zealand score against South Africa in that play-off game in 1999?

35. Battle of Solway Park
The daddy of all Ranfurly Shield matches

The Ranfurly Shield has produced some chilling and thrilling matches since challenge matches began way back in 1904. We'll all have our favourites. Last-minute drop kicks to salvage a draw, stirring comebacks, huge upsets. In terms of drama and controversy it would be hard to go past the 1927 encounter between holders Wairarapa and challengers Hawke's Bay, a match that has become known as the Battle of Solway.

First, a little background. Hawke's Bay had a wonderful Shield team during the 1920s, with such illustrious All Blacks as George Nepia, Maurice and Cyril Brownlie, Lui Paewai, Bert Cooke, Bull Irvine and assorted others. Gradually the great Shield team, coached by the famous Norm McKenzie, wore down and on June 3, 1927, Wairarapa upset the Bay 15–11 to end a five-year reign during which they had withstood 25 challenges.

By this time, the Bay were missing some of their giant figures. Cooke, always a wanderlust character, had moved to Masterton and Irvine, too, had gone south to the Wairarapa. Nepia was no longer playing for Hawke's Bay.

Still, it was a big upset and it stunned rugby followers in the Bay. By chance the two provinces had a return match scheduled for five weeks later and, after some discussion, Hawke's Bay decided to challenge for the Shield. Coach Norm McKenzie took his players into a three-day training camp and the whole province was galvanised. It was a rugby mission.

Hawke's Bay's stocks were boosted by the return of New Zealand Maori captain and inside back Wattie Barclay and they travelled to Solway Showgrounds in Masterton full of hope. Backing them were nearly 3000 Bay supporters who journeyed south, an amazing occurrence in days when cars were a rarity. The Showgrounds were built to house 5000 spectators. There were 10,000 there that day.

Adding a certain edge to proceedings was the fact that McKenzie's brother, Ted, coached Wairarapa and a third brother, Bert, was the referee.

The match was a vicious, spiteful affair in which two players, Maurice Brownlie and Quentin Donald, Invincibles All Black team-mates, were ordered from the field after a scuffle. The crowd encroached onto the field, reducing its width appreciably. At one stage some spectators rushed to support one player, Hawke's Bay's Jack Blake, whom they thought was being choked by another, Jim Donald, the Wairarapa captain!

The scores were level at 5–5 at halftime and the game continued to degenerate into a series of brawls, 'a slaughterhouse rules display', one critic called it. Even with 14 players each, the teams seemed as intent on fighting as playing rugby.

News Media Auckland

The Ranfurly Shield remains a prized trophy in New Zealand rugby.

Eventually Hawke's Bay, playing aggressive, forward-dominated rugby, won 21–10 and their fans headed home satisfied. But Wairarapa had another trick up their sleeve.

A New Zealand Rugby Union member (some say it was the chairman, Stan Dean) suggested to a Wairarapa official that they lodge a protest against the presence of Barclay. Barclay had been shuttling back and forth between Auckland and Hawke's Bay and there was some doubt about whether he fulfilled eligibility requirements.

Wairarapa duly protested. This was a little rich, considering the sides had met beforehand to thrash out any eligibility problems and at that point Barclay was cleared to play.

At any rate, the protest went to the New Zealand Rugby Union, which a fortnight later awarded the match to Wairarapa. Hawke's Bay appealed unsuccessfully and threatened to take the matter to the Supreme Court if they did not get satisfaction. In the meantime, they refused to hand over the Ranfurly Shield.

Before the appeal could be heard, Wairarapa had lost the shield to Manawhenua. While those in the Bay continued to follow the creed that possession is nine-tenths of the law, Manawhenua could celebrate their victory, but not physically display the spoils of their win.

Six weeks after the Solway game the New Zealand union's appeals committee heard the Hawke's Bay case and ruled in favour of Wairarapa. The Hawke's Bay union

Norm McKenzie (left) working with renowned rugby historian Arthur Carman during recording sessions which provided material for *On With the Game*, his 1960s book of rugby reminiscences. The Battle of Solway features prominently in the book.

huffed and puffed a bit more, then quietly announced it would not be taking the matter further.

Finally, late in the season, a leading Hawke's Bay player, fullback G. Yates of Napier, mentioned he was leaving Napier to holiday in Auckland. He was deputed to take the Shield to Palmerston North, where he handed it over to officials of the Manawhenua union.

There was a footnote to this bizarre encounter. Donald was duly cleared of any breach when an inquiry was held by the Wairarapa union. Referee Bert McKenzie talked of a 'whitewashing'. The next evening, Hawke's Bay exonerated Maurice Brownlie of any misconduct charge. Again the player received no penalty, it being deemed that the referee's action had been unwarranted.

McKenzie not surprisingly took exception to these decisions. He resigned his position as secretary of the Wairarapa Referees Association. Referees associations up and down the country backed McKenzie, and so did the New Zealand Rugby Referees Association, which added further that in future referees might consider seeking legal recourse in such situations. The New Zealand union received a stinging letter from the Referees Association, reminding them of their obligations to support their referees.

●

36. Boozing brings banishment

The tragic story of Ron Rangi

Back in the three seasons 1964–66, Ron Rangi was the first choice centre three-quarter for the All Blacks. He was a thrustful, urgent, bursting runner, very hard to stop when in possession of the ball and tough to get past on defence. All Black coach Fred Allen loved Ron and stood by him, bringing the lad from obscurity as an Air Force cadet, then through the Ponsonby club and Auckland rep teams, to national recognition.

But in the days of a news media that was vastly different to what it is in today's competitive age, Rangi had a problem away from the field of play. It was a problem that was never reported.

After being raised as a quiet lad from a decent home there was no explanation of how Rangi later in his life developed a huge appetite for alcohol. Especially beer.

To put it mildly Ron's appetite for the brown stuff became legendary around Auckland rugby. Anyone close to the game, sooner or later, would have seen him at one of his drinking sessions. Rangi was a loyal and popular bloke and was seen in a lot of rugby clubs and hotel establishments. Many a time he was far from his best when finally persuaded to head home.

Rangi had one of those throats that are unusual to some people, so we are told. These people are so structured physically that they can cope with the contents of a bottle of beer being poured straight past the mouth and directly into the gullet. Rangi could do that and often did so with a great flourish. When I lived in Auckland, I often saw Ron pick up a glass or quart bottle of beer and with a twinkle in his eye as he looked at that day's circle of friends, the amber liquid would disappear in a flash.

As an example of his love for a beer or three, Rangi once led the way in a three or four-day drinking spree. His beloved Ponsonby club, in those days of staunch rugby

News Media Auckland

Ron Rangi was handed playing bans by both the Auckland and New Zealand unions.

union amateurism, used to hold a regular fund-raising raffle where hundreds of dollars worth of beer and spirits were offered as a prize. Or the winner could take the monetary equivalent. In my time of taking tickets in that raffle, Rangi was the only winner who actually took home the cartons and boxes of liquid product. The others always took the cash equivalent.

The time when Ron won, the party at a popular flat in Dominion Road remains a classic memory for those who were there. The boxes of Ron's winnings were stacked on top of each other in the middle of the living room floor and the party raged on around the pile, which slowly dwindled.

The way the All Black schedule worked out in the three years Rangi was in the test team meant that he never went overseas with the team. All of his tests were at home. Nothing should be read into this. That fine Wellington fullback, Mick Williment, played through the same period and, like Rangi, never represented New Zealand offshore.

Rangi played 10 tests, Williment nine. In 1964, Australia toured New Zealand, in 1965 it was South Africa who came and in 1966 it was the British Lions. Rangi bested all of his markers in those keenly fought series. He racked up his tests in a consecutive sequence and, approaching 25 years of age, looked set to play for years. A tour of South Africa by the All Blacks was set down for 1967. Ron set his sights on that.

But after three years as a first-choice test player, his All Black career came to a jolting halt. And it was because of a scandal that the media of the time failed to adequately report. Even today, more than 30 years later, parts of the story are still cloaked in hearsay and non-speak.

What we do know is that Rangi was banned over an incident that occurred after a serious session of drinking. On September 6, 1966 Rangi was one day away from joining his All Black team-mates for the fourth and final test against the British Lions. Along with some friends, he decided to make the one-hour journey south to Papakura to watch the last midweek game of the Lions' tour, at Massey Park. This turned out to be a narrow 13–9 win over Counties-Thames Valley.

Before, and perhaps during, the game, Rangi, it is said, consumed enough alcohol to be not in his most sober state when he entered the game's aftermatch function at the Papakura Military Camp. There the partying by Rangi and friends continued.

It was, by all accounts, an enjoyable affair, especially as the drinks were free and everything was turned on in a stylish way. That was probably because many of the New Zealand Rugby Football Union's top brass were there being entertained by the army base commander.

At one point Rangi approached a table laden with drink. The allegation, though it has never been confirmed in public, is that he picked up a bottle of spirits and made to conceal it under his jacket. No one noticed him, except the base commander's wife.

She spoke to Rangi, pointing out that she had seen him place the bottle under his jacket. Ron turned and told her in short, sharp Anglo-Saxon terms where to go. The exact wording of his reply isn't known. Perhaps it is better that way.

The repercussions for Rangi were to be disastrous for his rugby career. By the next day, the big bosses of rugby in Rangi's world had moved quickly to reprimand him. He was sharply rebuked by the Chairman of the New Zealand Union, Tom Morrison, and also by Auckland RFU chairman Ron Burk.

In a curiosity, given events that were to follow, the censure was not so severe as to cause Rangi to be banned from playing for the All Blacks three days later. He played his usual forceful game as New Zealand swept the test series 4–0, winning that final match 24–11.

Within days the Auckland Rugby Union's committee had met again and after further consideration, suspended Rangi from all further games that season. In fact, that turned out to be just two fixtures, but it was a ban nevertheless.

That was not the end of the matter, either. When the 1967 season rolled around Rangi played again for Auckland, having served out 'time'. It was reported at the time that his form was not what it had been previously. The All Black selectors, however, passed over Rangi for the only home test that year, against Australia (the 75th Jubilee match) in Wellington. Some said the young Hawke's Bay challenger Bill Davis had overtaken Rangi.

Rangi broke down in tears when he heard of the ruling and was almost inconsolable. 'Why,' he asked of one reporter, 'do I have to accept a second punishment? It's a knockout blow.'

A couple of days before the test team's announcement, in early August of 1967, following a meeting of its council in Dunedin, the New Zealand Rugby Union dropped its own piano on Rangi. Out of the blue they issued an edict banning Rangi from international rugby for that season. The reason was for his role in the incident with the commander's wife nearly a year earlier.

Rangi broke down in tears when he heard of the ruling and was almost inconsolable. 'Why,' he asked of one reporter, 'do I have to accept a second punishment? It's a knockout blow.'

To this day there remain many other unanswered questions over the incident and the manner in which it was handled by the New Zealand union. Why, for instance, was Rangi not permitted any representation at the Dunedin council meeting? We know that 10 months after his alleged misdemeanour the committee hearing was held behind closed doors. That colourful rugby personality of the time, Auckland's Tom Pearce, a life member of the New Zealand union, was not even allowed to put a case for Rangi to his former council colleagues. Instead, all Pearce could do was dispatch a letter couched in the strongest words of protest.

It condemned the secretive actions of the New Zealand Rugby Union, which had allowed Rangi to play on at a representative level for the early part of 1967. Pearce also pointed out that if the NZRFU had felt so strongly over what Rangi had allegedly done at Papakura, he would have been banned from playing in the final test against the Lions. Pearce concluded his inimitable tirade of protest with these words: 'This player has been tried and convicted without an adequate hearing. [To pass sentence on him] 10 months after the incident is completely indefensible. I

Former NZRFU Chairman Tom Morrison, who sharply rebuked Rangi for his conduct.

cannot condemn such action too strongly. I suggest you take steps to rectify the wrong done to the player in the interests of the game. . . . It is part of the Rugby Union's function at all times to act as protection of the players. Therefore it should have acted at the time, not 10 months later.'

In essence the judgement destroyed the self-assurance of a person like Rangi. He accepted his wrongdoing and sometimes would talk to close friends about it, but he could never accept the harshness of the double penalty. He played a few more games for Auckland in 1968, and club rugby for a few years after that, but never again did he approach the kind of form that would enable him to push for All Black status.

His problem with alcohol increased and he became a sad figure in his years after his active rugby days. It was rumoured around Auckland that he never worked because he lived off 'Maori land cheques'. This was never confirmed. He did keep his loyal friends, but even their support couldn't keep him away from endless hours in the pubs around town.

He died, a sad and heavily overweight figure, in 1988, aged only 47.

37. 50-year sentence
All Black who paid the ultimate price

We must hope that never again will an All Black be treated with the indifference verging on contempt that Graham Duncan McMillan Gilbert was subjected to at the end of his rugby union playing days. The New Zealand public loved Mike Gilbert to bits when he was the star fullback in the 1935–36 All Black touring team.

Gilbert gave his guts on that tour to Britain, playing 27 of the team's 30 games and topping the points scoring. He also trialled for the All Blacks in two other seasons, 1934 and 1937. But when he made the dreaded switch to rugby league in 1938 on a four-year contract with England club Bradford Northern, the New Zealand rugby community, led by their administrative bosses, coldly turned their backs on their hero.

That's how it was in those days. If you played rugby union back then, you were almost not allowed to even think of the term 'rugby league'. New Zealand rugby was still smarting over the departure of so many union players 30 years before, in 1908, when the All Golds team was formed. In Gilbert's case, the harsh and spiteful treatment that he suffered for changing to rugby league lasted for nearly 50 years after his playing days in both codes ended.

The Gilbert timeline from adulation to scorn reads something like this:

1935–36 — chosen as the much-admired All Black fullback for the British tour. Like George Nepia of the previous All Blacks in Britain, in 1924–25, he dominated appearances as the only fullback chosen in the touring squad.

1937 — was a trialist again for the All Blacks. Gilbert was named reserve for the third test in Auckland, but was unable to travel north because of an injury suffered in a club match on the West Coast.

1938 — on the advice of fellow former West Coaster and All Black Eddie Holder, he signed for Bradford Northern on a four-year league contract.

1939 — after only two seasons, the outbreak of war interrupted his rugby league career and he returned to New Zealand to work in national domestic service, in the

'What are you doing here, Gilbert?' barked the official. 'You're not wanted here.'

NZ Rugby Museum

Mike Gilbert . . . shockingly treated.

vital Post and Telegraph Department. The installation of phone lines was important work, of course, and deemed highly significant to New Zealand's war effort.

1942 — went to Athletic Park in Wellington one day to see 1935 All Black team-mate Doug Dalton, who was playing in a services game. Gilbert was ordered out from under the grandstand by a local rugby official. 'What are you doing here, Gilbert?' barked the official. 'You're not wanted here.' Apparently having played league tainted Mike. Dalton was deeply upset and the two had to arrange to meet outside the grandstand to have their chat.

1943 — Gilbert was asked by a Canterbury sub-union to play in a couple of local games. Reinstatement from league was considered a formality during war years as the New Zealand union had graciously (my term) granted an amnesty (their term) for rugby league players, who could return to union in the war, if they liked. However, the letter from Gilbert's sub-union was not considered by the New Zealand union, who deemed that the application should have come more properly from his former West Coast union!

1946 — because of the red tape over the proper application channels, Gilbert was denied reinstatement to rugby union. Others, including George Nepia, Eddie Holder and Dave Solomon, who had all played league before the war, were allowed back into rugby union circles. Nepia went on to enjoy a glittering and deserved lifetime of recognition for his All Black exploits. Gilbert was ignored for most of his life.

1967 — even at the New Zealand rugby Union's 75th Jubilee celebrations in Wellington, Gilbert was snubbed. Every living All Black was invited to participate in a memorable parade around the ground on test day at Athletic Park, and there was a formal dinner afterwards. Mike recalls that his friend Sol Heperi (a former New Zealand Maori player and grandfather of current sevens star Karl Te Nana) took it upon himself to break the news that he had heard Mike would not be getting an invitation to the celebrations.

1995 — finally, at the age of 84, Mike Gilbert was reinstated to his first sports love, rugby union, from which he had departed during those tough financial years of the 1930s. The year 1995 had no special significance (unless it was for being the 60th anniversary of Gilbert's sole All Black tour). By then Mike was living quietly in Trentham in Wellington's Upper Hutt Valley. He had been wheelchair and housebound for much of his later years, having lost a leg to gangrene.

The ignorance with which Gilbert was treated remains one of the Rugby Union's great shames. By 2001 Mike had grown to be the second-oldest living All Black, aged more than 90. He remained a man of fierce and proud opinion. In his wheelchair and armchair years he discovered radio talkback as a way to expound his views on life. 'Mike of Trentham' featured regularly on all manner of subjects on all the local radio stations for many years.

The passage of time has somewhat muted Gilbert's disappointment, when he talks about his treatment by the Rugby Union. But he does remain annoyed about one matter in particular. 'Why has the 1935–36 All Black team not been given its rightful recognition in our country?'

To me, it is a fair question. History has treated Jack Manchester's tourists poorly. Maybe the three losses on tour out of 30 games does not sit well in comparison to the one loss suffered by the 1905–06 team and the unbeaten record of the 1924–25 Invincibles. Gilbert maintains that the 1935 team was 'up there with them as a team'.

He says: 'Unlike the earlier tours to Britain, we played many more combined counties and services combinations and we faced the best players on three or four

occasions. That made it hard for us, but we battled through. We lost only once in our first 25 games and we split our test matches 2–2. We suffered badly because we lost 13–0 to England in the last test before we headed home.'

When I have called on Mike or spoken to him on the phone his memories of the tour are detailed and loving. If the Rugby Union knew how much he cared about the team and his mates who went with him, they would have made him the Chairman of the Maintenance of its Memory. Instead they rubbished him.

'We were a good unit on tour,' he says. 'Our manager, Vincent Meredith, had a rule that where

Doug Dalton, the North Island forward who roomed with Gilbert, the South Island back.

possible a North Island forward roomed with a South Island back. Hence Doug Dalton was my mate. We were all given a book of vouchers to use as our daily allowance. It was three-bob [shillings] a day, but the voucher could only be used in the hotel where we were staying.

'Mr Meredith was pretty keen on keeping the amateur ethic going. That was why we didn't play the French. At that time they had been booted out of international rugby for doing quite a bit of under-the-table professional stuff. Mr Meredith even moaned when a company gave us each a hat to wear. We had to make sure that we never had our pictures taken with the hats on, in case we were seen as endorsing the manufacturers. We played every game with the famous Gilbert brand of ball from the town of Rugby. Eric Tindill and I had our photo taken holding a couple of the Gilbert balls one day and Mr Meredith wasn't happy with that either!

'I clearly remember a couple of other things we did. We didn't do the haka on tour. We only had one Maori in our team, Tori Reid from Hawke's Bay, and Dave Solomon was a Fijian. The rest of us were all Pakehas. Before the tour, Mr Meredith said: "Look, we're over here to play rugby; we're not going to be dancing around like a bunch of whirling dervishes!" [Perhaps a remark Meredith would not get away with today.]

> ## We were all given a book of vouchers to use as our daily allowance. It was three-bob [shillings] a day, but the voucher could only be used in the hotel where we were staying.

'And our team contributed to a significant change in the All Black uniform. If you look at the pictures of us when we left New Zealand, there is nice white piping around our black tour blazers. But on tour it was the part of the uniform that we couldn't keep clean. So we had a team meeting and decided to all peel the piping off. You'll notice that at the end of the tour, our blazers are completely black. And that's how they've stayed for the All Blacks ever since.'

Talking about blazers, two gentlemen, New Zealanders named Barry and Small, were the only supporters who followed the All Blacks around on tour. Remember, the 1930s were tough times. The All Blacks were so pleased to have the two fellows support them that they gave them blazers and insisted that they be allowed to travel as All Blacks, or be listed for functions as 'members of the New Zealand party'.

Gilbert says his 1935–36 lads were a band of all-round good guys and should be remembered thus. Some from that team haven't spoken terribly kindly of the captain, Jack Manchester ('He was a snob,' one All Black told me). Gilbert says the only offence caused during the four-month tour occurred at a private zoo the team visited. 'There was a wild gorilla in a cage and we all jumped up and down in front of it, pulling faces and making a commotion. Boy did *he* get wild,' chuckles Gilbert.

As Gilbert recalls those far-off days, he beams with pride. It makes his treatment at the hands of the New Zealand Rugby Union all the more shameful.

Shield fever

Wairarapa had a tricky time of it in the 1920s, as far as the Ranfurly Shield goes. In 1927, there was the famous Battle of Solway match against Hawke's Bay, with the subsequent dispute over Wattie Barclay's residential qualification and the appeal to the New Zealand Rugby Union.

In 1929, there was another curiosity involving a big Shield game. Having regained the Shield in 1928 with a narrow win over Canterbury, the strong Wairarapa team reeled off eight successive defences before facing Southland at Carterton in August 1929.

Most locals considered Wairarapa would win comfortably. With 11 All Blacks in the side, including the legendary Bert Cooke, Wairarapa looked to have too many guns for Southland, who had just four national representatives, and had to take the field without several leading players.

News Media Auckland

Bert Cooke.

So confident were Wairarapa that they did not bring the famous Log o' Wood with them to Carterton. It had been on display up the road in Cooke's mercery business shop window, and that's where it was on the Saturday of the Shield game.

But Southland, not for the last time, put up a surprisingly plucky showing and held on against the fast-finishing Wairarapa to win 19–16. A local official was hastily summoned and asked to speed back to Masterton to pick up the Shield so it could be presented to the new champions.

38. Bugger!

The speech that stopped a nation

In conservative New Zealand of the 1950s the media was vastly different to what it is today. For a start there was no television. Radio, being government-owned, was careful and conformist, newspapers rarely gave by-lines to writers and bad language across any of the communications industry was unheard of.

That is not to say bad language did not exist in everyday usage. It did. For instance, men returning home from the rigours of their Second World War experiences spoke in very sharp terms about what had happened to them while in battle. But very few recordings of swearing ever made it to air in the 1950s. It just wasn't done.

There was one very famous instance, though. And, perhaps surprisingly, given the conservative times, when a dreaded word was dropped the whole country rocked with laughter. Hearing the same word today would not raise an eyebrow. And the dreaded word of 1956 was much milder than many that are heard today. Nonetheless it was outrageous in its own way.

The occasion concerned the end of New Zealand's most dramatic rugby test series to that point. The Springboks, under captain Basie Viviers and manager-coach Danie Craven, had just completed the fourth test of a three-month 23-match New Zealand tour.

To say the tests were epic contests is an understatement. Even today New Zealand men of a certain age recall those games with a sharpness that is amazing. There must still be thousands of scrapbooks lying in lofts and studies, kept by young kids at the time, and too precious to be thrown out.

The fourth test was a true pinnacle of a fiery series. New Zealand had won the first and third tests, South Africa the second. All the games had been close. So all of New Zealand tuned in to hear Winston McCarthy's famous radio commentary on fourth test day, with the nation hoping, and probably praying, for a New Zealand win. Then, and only then, could the All Blacks say for the first time: 'We have won a test series over South Africa.'

The Eden Park test unfolded and the country hung on McCarthy's every word. He was assisted in the broadcast box by the local Auckland commentator Colin Snedden. Slowly but surely the minutes ticked by and New Zealand's team, captained by Bob Duff, edged to an 11–5 lead. This was sufficient for the nation to think: 'They have to score twice to get the lead,' as a converted try was worth only five points in those days.

At one point the action became especially fierce and Tiny White, the New Zealand lock, was kicked on the ground. Two policemen came down to the touchline and stood close by in case they were needed to separate the players from breaking into outright affray.

Eventually the whistle went for fulltime and the game had gone New Zealand's way by that six-point margin. Could it be said that that result signalled a glorious day for New Zealand nationhood? Maybe so, for rugby was definitely King in those days.

People flooded onto Eden Park from all quarters. They rushed to a centre spot on the halfway line and looked up into the grandstand. There was no trophy presentation, but it had become traditional for each ground to farewell the South African team.

News Media Auckland

Peter Jones.

I can clearly recall the crowd chanting for the New Zealand players to come forward and take a cheer. There were two particular heroes — Don Clarke, the young Waikato fullback who was known far and wide as The Boot, and Peter Jones, a shy fisherman from one of the farthest north places you can get in New Zealand, Awanui, just by the famous Ninety Mile Beach. Jones had brushed aside Springboks after chasing a bouncing ball to score a breathtaking try; Clarke had kicked the rest of New Zealand's points, with a conversion and two penalty goals.

The chants continued after short speeches by New Zealand rugby officials and Danie Craven had made his famous, and very generous, remark: 'New Zealand, it's all yours.' The crowd gave an almighty roar when Craven uttered those words.

Then Peter Jones was pushed forward to the microphone and the crowd hushed to hear what he had to say. Colin Snedden adjusted the microphone, and Jones leaned forward. With sweat on his brow, he said: 'Ladies and gentlemen, I hope I never have to play another game like that in my life. I'm absolutely buggered!'

The words echoed around the ground to a massive shout of astonishment and approval. The noise was so overwhelming that young Don Clarke's simple 'thank you' could hardly be heard.

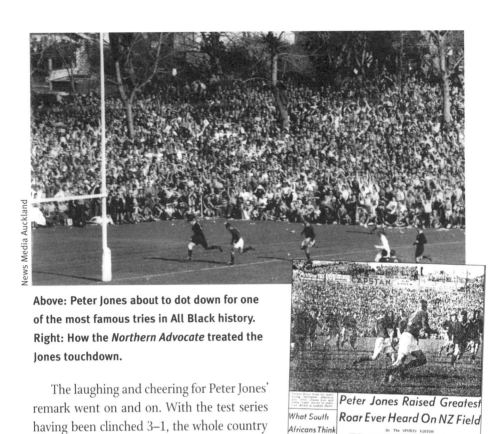

Above: Peter Jones about to dot down for one of the most famous tries in All Black history.
Right: How the *Northern Advocate* treated the Jones touchdown.

The laughing and cheering for Peter Jones' remark went on and on. With the test series having been clinched 3–1, the whole country was indeed 'vastly relieved', except Jonesy had said it better.

However, behind newspaper editors' desks and at broadcasting headquarters there was not such total approval. Terry McLean told me the *New Zealand Herald* decided not to publish the offending remark. And the Saturday night sports edition of the *Auckland Star*, the *8 O'Clock*, described the offending word as b———— in its story. The New Zealand Broadcasting Service phones ran hot as the bosses called in to say the remark by Jones must not be played again on the radio. The sentence was deemed distasteful to the audience's ears. The tape was not replayed until Peter Sellers, the sports radio historian from Dunedin, sought and was given approval for the remark to be played in a summary of Radio New Zealand Sports highlights nearly 30 years later.

But let's go back to the time. In 1956 you shouldn't really have said that word in polite company. But it was outrageously correct because it so perfectly summed up the nation's mood. The All Blacks had won their tests against their grimmest rivals and we, players and listeners alike, were exhausted by the build-up of the whole three months.

It is true to say the country was 'absolutely buggered' and we had Peter Jones to thank for saying it for us.

39. Thanks for nothing, Jock

Turning our backs on a rugby saviour

Jock Hobbs, former All Black captain, has been the victim of some outrageous treatment by the New Zealand Rugby Union. So poorly has he been treated that these days Hobbs has only a peripheral involvement with the sport, and that is a terrible waste of ability.

Hobbs was a fine loose forward, good enough to represent Canterbury through their golden Ranfurly Shield era of the early 1980s, and then to go on to not just All Black selection, but the All Black captaincy. From 1983 to 1986, he played 39 matches for New Zealand, 21 of them test matches.

His was an interesting career because in 1986 he was one of the players who toured South Africa in the Cavaliers team, and received a two-match suspension on his return. It seemed he was quickly forgiven because at the end of 1986 he captained the All Blacks on their tour of France.

However, he was forced to retire prematurely from the game because of health problems — he was getting concussed too often and was advised to give the game away. So shattered was Hobbs to be forced out of rugby on the eve of the 1987 World Cup that he did not remain in New Zealand during that tournament. He took a holiday in the Pacific Islands to try to get away from rugby and the disappointment of not being part of the first World Cup.

It seemed he would still make a valuable contribution to rugby off the field, though. He moved to Wellington and turned his attention to administration and coaching. He was the New Zealand representative of the Japanese company Mizuno, the contracted boots supplier to the New Zealand union. He became a successful club coach and coached the New Zealand Universities in 1992, 1994 and 1995.

In addition, he became a member of the New Zealand union council, where his stature as a player and his skill as a lawyer made him doubly valuable.

It was to Hobbs that the union turned in the middle of 1995 when the news broke that the All Blacks were on the point of defecting en masse to a private promoter, the World Rugby Corporation. Hobbs worked tirelessly for weeks on end. He moved out of his house and parked himself in a hotel so he wouldn't waste as much time in travelling. He drew up contracts and budgets, travelled up and down the country meeting players, negotiating, talking, discussing, cajoling.

In effect his job was to try to save New Zealand rugby. In his mind, that's what he was trying to do. He did everything he could to get the players to re-sign with the New Zealand union, and in the end he succeeded, though my impression is that the real power players were to be found in the upper echelons of the big television companies backing the rival rugby organisations.

News Media Auckland

Jock Hobbs . . . not paid a cent.

I was shocked to learn that for all the work Hobbs did for the New Zealand union, he was not paid a cent. He was offering players contracts worth many hundreds of thousands of dollars, he was endeavouring to save a deal worth $555 million to the New Zealand, Australian and South African unions. He stopped his own work and he devoted himself around the clock to the cause of rugby. For free.

During that frenetic month, Hobbs was dismayed to find some Rugby Union councillors were making proposals behind his back, suggesting compromise solutions with WRC without even running the ideas past him. I may be wrong, but I sensed a growing disenchantment in Hobbs.

This is perhaps best summed up by the fact that on the day when All Black captain Sean Fitzpatrick announced he and the team were staying with the union, Hobbs was nowhere to be seen. Fitzpatrick held a major press conference in Wellington. The media was there in droves. So were all sorts of rugby officials. Hobbs wasn't though. I know that because he elected to have lunch with me and a friend across town, seemingly relieved to be rid of the whole business.

We joked as we left the restaurant that Hobbs had been so busy he had not been able to even dress properly. He was still wearing his dinner jacket trousers and had thrown on a sports coat as he'd rushed out of his office. He was exhausted and had clearly pushed himself right to the limit.

I asked Jock a year or two later if the players were grateful for all he'd done for them. 'If they were, it was not evident, no,' he said. 'They may not have liked what I did because it was written that I helped save the All Blacks, which implied they were doing something wrong. They were on a particular course and wanted to see it to its end, and didn't, so there may have been some disappointment and frustration about that as well from the players' point of view.'

Astoundingly, after giving himself selflessly to the union, and for no pay, Hobbs failed to gain a seat on the new, smaller NZRFU Board the following year, after the old council was dissolved. It was a decision that was as callous as it was ungrateful.

It has clearly had an effect on Hobbs. He doesn't attend many major matches now, and if he does it's more often than not for work reasons. He is the Chief Executive of Strategic Ltd, and they have a box in the Stadium in Wellington. Outside work, Hobbs' involvement in rugby seems limited to watching and helping his teenage son Michael.

It all seems so wrong. As Phil Gifford once wrote, the New Zealand Rugby Union should have erected a statue to Hobbs and placed it outside the Huddart Parker building.

40. Chasing the big money
The great player (and coach) drain

For years, there had been rumblings within New Zealand rugby about the player drain — the vast number of players heading off overseas on lucrative contracts. The concern among those who followed these things closely was that a whole level of expertise — good, competitive provincial players, former All Blacks, potential coaches — was being lost to New Zealand rugby. But probably what shook up New Zealand rugby more than any player defection was the sudden announcement in 1998 of Auckland coach Graham Henry that he was heading off to Wales to coach the Welsh national side.

One day Henry was the Auckland coach. The next day he was holding a hastily arranged press conference and saying: 'Hooray. I'm off.'

News Media Auckland

The New Zealand Rugby Union did not react well to the news that one of the country's most eminent coaches was off to help another test side. They had Henry on contract, but Wales bought it out. The Rugby Union introduced a rule — often called the Henry rule — that people who have coached national teams overseas were ineligible to ever coach the All Blacks. This seemed a particularly petty reaction, hardly constructive, and certainly not a very clever way of dealing with a situation that was only going to get worse. I'm pleased the law has now been altered —

Graham Henry . . . 'Hooray. I'm off'.

hence John Mitchell, former England assistant coach, could be appointed All Black coach in 2001.

The drain on New Zealand rugby over the past decade has been incredibly dramatic, far more so than most people would believe. Every month there are reports of players and coaches heading to England, Ireland, Scotland, Wales, France, Italy, Japan, Fiji, Samoa, South Africa, even Argentina. Because the announcements dribble out in ones and twos, they do not make for dramatic reading.

And because most players are either past their best, or at least not star All Blacks, these things are generally accepted with resignation. It is the same with coaches, or it was until Henry was nabbed. Suddenly there was awareness that perhaps New Zealand rugby was losing far more talent than it could afford.

I am not talking about players switching to rugby league. That has gone on since 1908. In the first decade of this century, such great All Blacks as Charlie Seeling, George Smith and George Gillett had gone to league. Over the years many more were to follow, including leading rugby union figures such as George Nepia, Bert Cooke, Mike Gilbert, Joe Karam, John Gallagher, John Schuster, John Timu and John Kirwan. Once rugby went professional in 1995, this exodus largely dried up; if anything, the trend has reversed and I expect we will see an increasing number of league players swapping to union, which offers good money, plus a broader international horizon.

What is of more concern here is the huge amount of rugby talent nurtured by New Zealand and then lured overseas.

There have always been a few. Back in the early 1970s, current or recent All Blacks Chris Laidlaw and Earle Kirton, two lateral thinkers, based themselves in Europe. Laidlaw took up a Rhodes Scholarship in 1969, represented the All Blacks in 1970, then returned to Oxford University in 1971 and later played for Lyon University in France. Kirton, an All Black from 1963–70, took a post-graduate course in dentistry in England and played for the Harlequins, Barbarians and Middlesex, later becoming coach of the Harlequins and Middlesex.

Grahame Thorne, one of the most brilliant three-quarters to play for New Zealand, emigrated to South Africa shortly after touring there with the 1970 All Blacks. He represented Northern Transvaal and Natal and played in three Springbok trials. As Thorne was just 24 when he emigrated to South Africa, New Zealand rugby lost his best playing years.

A few years later a young All Black lock named Andy Haden decided to sample the delights of Europe and from 1974–1976 played club rugby in France, sharpening his French and also learning a lot about how things were done on the other side of the world. These lessons stood him in good stead over the next decade when he toured with New Zealand teams. Haden became a real pioneer, selling his rugby services in the New Zealand off-season. At one point, he was playing on Saturdays for the London club Harlequins and on Sundays for a club in Italy.

His future All Black team-mates Graham Mourie and Murray Mexted, two world rugby figures, also campaigned overseas, Mourie in 1977 for Paris University club and Mexted over a stretch of several years for club teams in France and South Africa. Neither, however, missed many opportunities to represent New Zealand.

The situation was still not really causing concern. Increasing numbers of lesser-known New Zealand players shifted overseas and were to be found all over the world. Murray Kidd, the former King Country player, became a coach in Ireland. Craig Green, the underrated All Black winger of the mid-1980s, moved to Italy and was lost to the All Blacks.

In hindsight, the drain on the pool of rugby talent in New Zealand was gathering pace, but because not many of these players or coaches were headline-grabbers little was made of the fact. One player who fitted this category was Brian Hegarty, who I still say was one of the first true professional rugby players from New Zealand. Hegarty, a solid Wellington player, was paid to play for France's Biarritz club and was twice named as a reserve (selection by convenience, rather than on merit) for New Zealand while it was touring France in 1977, one of the matches being a test match. In 1981, another New Zealander, Peter Hurley, filled a similar role, taking his place in the reserves on more than one occasion while the All Blacks were in Europe.

By the time Craig Green headed for Italy, the situation was becoming more serious. John Kirwan was spending his northern winters in

News Media Auckland

Grahame Thorne . . . New Zealand lost his best years.

Italy, and, as the saying went, 'He wasn't there just for the red wine and pasta.' It became clear that Kirwan and players like him were heading overseas to make money out of rugby as the game became ever more entwined in shamateurism. Kirwan, in fact, has campaigned extensively overseas. The great All Black winger played each off-season in Italy during the late 1980s, eventually marrying an Italian. After his All Black days were over, he turned to league for two years, playing for the Warriors. Then he had a stint as a player-coach in Japan, and after time

News Media Auckland

Craig Green found the lure of Italy irresistible.

coaching in Auckland, returned to Italy to be Brad Johnstone's assistant with the Italian national side.

The exodus began to quicken once rugby went professional in 1995 and today any players who have reached All Black status are fair game for overseas scouts and hundreds of provincial players look to cash in on their ability by making money offshore.

Here is a very brief overview of where some players and coaches have gone. It includes a few, such as Laidlaw, Kirton and Thorne, who made lifestyle choices, but you'll see that the vast majority have headed overseas simply to make money from their rugby expertise. It is, however, far from comprehensive and I have compiled it merely to give readers an insight into just how widespread the practice has become:

• **Ireland:** Murray Kidd, Warren Gatland, John Mitchell, Mike Brewer, Kurt McQuilken, Ben Willis, Jason Holland, Andy Ward, Mike Mullins, Sean McCahill, Ross Nesdale, Brent Anderson, Andy Leslie.
• **England:** Earle Kirton, Chris Laidlaw, Andy Haden, John Mitchell, Wayne Shelford, David Kirk, Zinzan Brooke, Bernie McCahill, Ian Jones, Simon Mannix,

Jon Preston, Inga Tuigamala, Stephen Bachop, Pat Lam, Ofisa Tonu'u, Josh Kronfeld, Angus Gardiner, Hika Reid, Andrew Blowers, Craig Dowd, Ross Nesdale, Wayne Smith.

- **Fiji:** Chris Laidlaw, Brad Johnstone.
- **Western Samoa:** Bryan Williams, Peter Schuster, John Boe, Michael Jones.
- **Tonga:** Jim Love.
- **Japan:** Jamie Joseph, Arran Pene, Andrew McCormick, Graeme Bachop, Scott Pierce, Kevin Schuler, Alan Whetton, Joe Stanley, John Kirwan, Filo Tiatia, Jason O'Halloran, Marty Brooke, Mark Finlay, Richard Turner, Liam Barry, Alama Ieremia, Willie Lose, Ant Strachan, Adrian Cashmore, Blair Larsen, Glen Marsh, Scott McLeod, Rob Gordon.
- **Canada:** John Gordon.
- **Hong Kong:** John Gordon.
- **Italy:** Andy Haden, John Kirwan, Craig Green, Brad Johnstone, Simon Mannix, Frank Bunce, Mac McCallion, Gary Seear, Mark Finlay, Kieran Crowley, Peter Barlow, Alan Crowley, Tommy Fern, Lee Lidgard.
- **Wales:** Graham Henry, Steve Hansen, Brett Sinkinson, Shane Howarth, Matt Cardy, John Plumtree, Hemi Taylor, Ofisa Tonu'u.
- **Scotland:** John Leslie, Martin Leslie, Sean Lineen, Tommy Hayes, Todd Blackadder, Brendan Laney, Gordon Simpson, Glen Metcalfe, Kelvin Howarth.
- **South Africa:** Grahame Thorne, Laurie Mains, Alex Wyllie, Kevin Eveleigh, Murray Pierce, Murray Mexted, Alan Sutherland, Kevin Putt, John Plumtree.
- **France:** Chris Laidlaw, Andy Haden, Graham Mourie, Brian Hegarty, Richard Loe, John Drake, Frank Bunce, Lee Stensness, Murray Mexted, Mike Clamp, Glen Osborne, Tony Marsh, Norm Berryman, Isitolo Maka, Finau Maka, Mark Mayerhofler, Tabai Matson, Gary Whetton.
- **Argentina:** Alex Wyllie.

Now please don't go ringing me up telling me I've missed out this player or that player. I stress, this is but a smattering of the vast number of players who have headed overseas. When you consider all the rugby knowledge that has been learnt in New Zealand and then been shipped overseas, it is mind-boggling. In previous generations, these players, and the hundreds more like them, would have finished their careers, put their time and energy into club rugby and possibly progressed through the ranks of coaching or administration.

Instead they have left a void in New Zealand rugby. New Zealand has become the great feeder of world rugby.

41. Money, money, money
When the game went professional

When I look back at those crazy, hectic weeks in mid-1995 when the evolution of professional rugby turned into a revolution, lots of images come to mind. There's Jock Hobbs, working around the clock on behalf of the New Zealand Rugby Union, trying to stop the leading players signing for a private promoter. There's Phil Kearns addressing the huge crowd after the Bledisloe Cup test in Sydney and making a strange, semi-coded 'farewell to rugby' speech. There's a scheduled video hook-up between the three test captains, Sean Fitzpatrick, Kearns and François Pienaar, in which Pienaar fails to front. In the middle of it all, there was an outstanding All Black display at Sydney, with Jonah Lomu reaffirming his sublime World Cup form.

So many people were in the headlines at that time for reasons only slightly related to on-field performance — Ross Turnbull, Brian Lochore, Rupert Murdoch, Louis Luyt, Jeff Wilson and Josh Kronfeld, Richie Guy, Laurie Mains, Kerry Packer. There were statements from everyone — Phil Kingsley Jones, Eric Rush, Simon Poidevin. Terms we'd never heard, or at least never really bothered with, became familiar: World Rugby Corporation, News Limited, SANZAR, Super League, Tri Nations, Australian Consolidated Press.

At the end of it all, what happened? Well, rugby, which had been existing in an increasingly 'shamateur' state in the preceding years, had gone professional. This wasn't a dip-the-toe-into-the-water exercise. Rugby had dived into the deep end. The game would never be the same again. Tradition, history, loyalty, pride . . . these things didn't suddenly become unimportant, but now money was the name of the game.

In hindsight, it's weird how it happened. After years of edging ever closer to embracing professionalism, it all occurred in a matter of weeks, in a swirl of meetings, contracts, press conferences, claims and counter-claims.

The rush to professionalism was brought about by a set of unusual circumstances. For years rugby league had been siphoning off a stream of good rugby union players.

In a nightmare month in 1990, Matthew Ridge, John Gallagher, John Schuster and Frano Botica all went the league way. Va'aiga Tuigamala, John Timu and others had joined them shortly after. Then in early 1995, the Super League war broke out. Suddenly there were two groups bidding for league players' services for rival competitions, and they were backed by television companies with big cheque books.

Rugby league players found to their delight that they were suddenly worth three or four times what they had been the year before. Their wages sky-rocketed.

League officials needed yet more good players to bolster their rival competitions. Not surprisingly, they looked at rugby union as a potential source of more talent. It was blindingly obvious that a lot more rugby union players would soon cross over. The money would be too attractive. What held the union players briefly was the fact that the 1995 World Cup was about to be staged in South Africa. The All Blacks' attitude seemed to be that they would wait until after the World Cup. Victory there would be immensely satisfying and would increase their market value.

At the same time, there were other possible destinations for All Blacks looking to cash in. Japan was becoming ever more attractive. Tales floated back about how Andrew McCormick, the son of a legendary All Black, but just a solid provincial player himself, was making hundreds of thousands of dollars a year. As it transpired, All Black halfback Graeme Bachop and forwards Jamie Joseph and Arran Pene all headed to Japan during 1995.

There were yet more options — Britain (especially England), France and Italy were all potentially sources of vast income for All Blacks looking to cash in.

Financially, things had never looked so good for New Zealand's leading players. It was as if all the hard work and great play down the years of Billy Wallace and Charlie Seeling, George Nepia and Maurice Brownlie, Kevin Skinner and Bob Scott, Colin Meads and Sid Going, Graham Mourie and Bruce Robertson, Gary Whetton and John Kirwan and all their famous team-mates was about to pay off, but only for the modern players. These players had for decades given the All Black name and image value and prestige and now it was ripe for picking.

Suddenly there were all sorts of vultures circling. The biggest early threat came from World Rugby Corporation, which claimed it had the financial backing of Kerry Packer's ACP organisation. WRC organisers put together a proposed world competition and were offering very fat pay cheques. At almost the same time, South African, New Zealand and Australian rugby bosses, realising their game was under threat (though they didn't know about WRC and perceived Super League as the major challenge) had devised two new competitions that we now know as the Super 12 and the Tri Nations. They had gone to Rupert Murdoch's News Corp and endeavoured to sell them to the television company, hoping that income would enable them to pay enough to hold on to all their players.

It is amazing, when we look back, to see how crucial the timing was. Richie Guy,

News Media Auckland

Photosport

Kerry Packer (left) and Rupert Murdoch . . . major players in the transition from amateur to professional rugby.

the New Zealand union chairman, had been told by senior players that he would have to pay each All Black $150,000 a year to keep them. He felt that a good deal with News Corp would enable the New Zealand union to offer such large contracts. But, unbeknown to Guy and his cohorts, WRC was offering even bigger money.

On the eve of the 1995 World Cup final, Louis Luyt was summoned to London to meet one of Murdoch's right-hand men, Sam Chisholm. They agreed that News Corp would pay $555 million over 10 years for the television rights to the Super 12 and Tri Nations. This was wonderful news for the traditional rugby unions. Everything was sweet, or so they thought.

But WRC had already approached leading players and offered contracts worth much more.

Guy and the rest of them were shocked to find the players' responses were at best lukewarm when they offered their professional contracts. Why were the players not excited to suddenly be offered this sort of money?

The answer quickly became clear as word of WRC and its plans leaked out.

There followed weeks of intrigue. The New Zealand union sought the help of Jock Hobbs, a lawyer, and the vastly respected Brian Lochore, to talk to their players, see what they wanted and retain their services any way possible. Australia had Poidevin acting in a similar capacity. In South Africa, Louis Luyt set about reclaiming the loyalty of Pienaar and the other springboks.

Hobbs worked tirelessly. Luyt took whatever means he deemed necessary. Nearly all the leading players in South Africa, Australia and New Zealand — plus a lot of Northern Hemisphere rugby stars — had signed for WRC. So the traditional rugby

François Pienaar . . . failed to front for a video link-up of the three captains.

News Media Auckland

officials were well off the pace.

There were secret meetings. Little things seemed to make a difference. Wilson and Kronfeld, claiming loyalty to their fellow Otago provincial players, signed with the New Zealand union. Pienaar failed to front for a vital video link-up of the three Tri Nations test captains. The chinks began to appear.

Though starting well behind the eight-ball, the three unions gradually won through and eventually signed all the players. The threat from WRC had been beaten off.

That's the story that came out, but I don't believe it.

My research into this subject leads me to believe that while Wilson and Kronfeld, Luyt and Pienaar, Hobbs and Lochore and the rest of them all worked hard, in the end they had no effect on the outcome of this rugby civil war.

The issue was decided by very wealthy men in dark suits meeting in secret in hotel rooms in London. I have been told that principals for the Murdoch and Packer organisations met to discuss the situation. For them, this was not about sport. It was business. My understanding is that they met and divvied up their goods. Not just rugby and league, but Asian horse racing, movies and other television fare.

After that meeting, WRC basically pulled out of the rugby war, which freed the way for the traditional unions to retain their players and for the $555 million deal with News Corp to be confirmed. Laurie Mains said as much to me when I interviewed him on this subject.

'At the end of the day,' said Mains, 'it was Packer who pulled the pin because of the arrangements he had made with Murdoch. I don't think any one person could possibly say they had a significant hand in it, other than Packer and Murdoch, although Louis Luyt was a huge deterrent to the Packer organisation — he was a very strong player. I had a ring from the WRC people the day before it collapsed and was told a deal had been reached between Murdoch and Packer. It was something to do with racing, and therefore Packer was withdrawing from this exercise. The Packer people didn't pull out because of the signings with the New Zealand union, or what was going on in South Africa. It was purely over Murdoch and Packer reaching a deal.

'There was talk about Jeff Wilson and Josh Kronfeld signing with the New Zealand union and all that, but that wasn't significant. The deal that Packer and

Josh Kronfeld, who along with Jeff Wilson, broke ranks in the pro battle.

Murdoch did turned everything around.'

Mains' views tied in with how other key players read the situation. Sean Fitzpatrick told me that the one thing WRC did wrong was that they didn't guarantee the money. Geoff Levy, a South African-born Australian who was the WRC lawyer, said: 'Even after the Springboks wavered, we could have gone ahead. We had more than five hundred players signed, four of the top Super 12 teams in New Zealand, plus the All Blacks. Whether Jock Hobbs and the union had signed up one or two provinces wasn't really a factor.

'I don't think it is right to say Jock Hobbs saved the game. We would have gone ahead had I not been asked to make the peace and had the financial backing remained.

'You've got to ask the people in the two organisations [Packer and Murdoch] what occurred. It's hearsay for me to state what happened in a hotel room in London. Certainly we noticed a lot of deals afterwards between the two groups. Whether they were related or not, you have to ask them . . . I did get a call saying, "Let's make peace. Let's do it in a way that we preserve the boys, get the best deals for them."'

So it ended with victory for the New Zealand, Australian and South African unions and an even bigger victory for the players. I am sure that when they signed with Murdoch, the three unions had no idea that so much of their television income would be required to pay the players.

It was interesting watching how various players carried themselves at this stressful time. My impression from the sidelines was that some of the veteran All Blacks, nearing the end of long careers, were primarily concerned with the money. The younger All Blacks cared about their international rugby futures. Some of the older All Blacks were predictably selfish, using the umbrella of team unity to try to induce their younger team-mates to go with WRC, which was initially offering more money.

It's no secret that when Kronfeld, who had played seven tests, and Wilson, 11 tests, signed to stay with the New Zealand, some older All Blacks were very annoyed. Zinzan Brooke later said he would think twice about helping out Wilson if he was at the bottom of a ruck and Kronfeld talked about receiving a hard time from his roommate Richard Loe the following year. It was a torrid time for everyone.

Remember, these were All Blacks, not lawyers. They were very good at playing rugby, but most were not used to reading contracts. Suddenly they had three or four organisations vying for their signatures and offering them vast sums of money. No wonder the signs of stress showed. There were players who cried during negotiations. Some signed at least two contracts, with rival organisations. Some went back on their word. Some seemed to be bought off. Some put the team first; others worried only about themselves. Some left everything to their agents and lawyers; others wanted to retain control.

It was probably the first time in New Zealand rugby history that the players, not the administrators, held the whip hand.

But in the end no one could beat the men in dark suits meeting to talk really big TV deals in far higher circles than anyone knew about.

Strange dismissal

There have been players sent from the rugby field for more than a century. Generally, they make the long march towards the sideline with head bowed, contemplating the ignominy of the situation. Occasionally, though, a player will try to brazen his way out of the situation.

The first recorded example of a New Zealand player trying to bluff his way to the sideline occurred in Sydney in 1893 when New Zealand were playing New South Wales. Near the end of the game, referee Edward McCausland, a member of the Natives touring team who had subsequently settled in Australia, was seen to be in earnest conversation with New Zealand forward William McKenzie.

McKenzie was quite a personality. He was the oldest of five brothers who all became leading rugby figures, as players, coaches or officials. William was known as Offside Mac, and was said to be the first New Zealander to hone the wing-forward position. After his chat with McCausland, he limped towards the sideline, where the large crowd of nearly 20,000, believing he had been injured, gave him a rousing ovation.

It was only after the game that it came to light McKenzie had been ordered from the field and had tried to disguise the fact by pretending to be injured. He was the first player to be sent from the field while representing New Zealand.

Ironically, McKenzie's career was cut short by rheumatism. He moved to Rotorua for treatment and later shifted to Australia for health reasons. He died in Melbourne in 1943, aged 72.

42. Grannygate

When is a Welshman not a Welshman?

It became known as the Grannygate scandal, it involved three New Zealanders, and it sent shock waves around the rugby world.

Aucklander Graham Henry was received as a conquering hero when he took over as coach of the Welsh national team coach in 1998. Welsh rugby followers, numbed by years of indifferent performances, loved the energy, optimism and discipline that Henry brought to the job. They felt Welsh rugby was getting a healthy dollop of the New Zealand way, and they were pleased about that.

Eventually they had too much of a good thing, though. Henry selected two former New Zealand players, fullback Shane Howarth and openside flanker Brett Sinkinson. Both claimed they were eligible to play for Wales because they had Welsh grandparents. Except, it transpired, they didn't.

Howarth was a good All Black fullback in the Laurie Mains era, but his aspirations of continuing to represent New Zealand were torn apart by Jonah Lomu in early 1995 in a trial match at Whangarei's Okara Park. The young Lomu ran through and around Howarth as if he wasn't there, and from that day Howarth faded out of the All Black reckoning. Sinkinson was a solid loose forward for Bay of Plenty.

Howarth turned to rugby league, playing for the North Queensland Cowboys, before returning to Auckland in 1997. He turned out in two matches for the Auckland Blues that year, then headed for Britain where he played for the Sale club. Howarth was in demand in Britain. He turned down an offer to play for England, before Henry snared him for Wales.

Sinkinson, while he did not have the reputation of Howarth, nevertheless made a good impression when he arrived in Wales, being one of the best-performed players in the club competition there.

The International Rugby Board's eligibility rules stipulated that players could represent a country if they had a grandparent who was born in that country. Both

Shane Howarth, an All Black who turned down the opportunity to play for England before switching his allegiances to Wales.

Flanker Brett Sinkinson (with headgear) was the other 'Welsh Kiwi' to become embroiled in Grannygate.

Howarth and Sinkinson stated they had a Welsh grandfather. However, an enterprising British journalist did some investigation and discovered this was not the case.

Sinkinson's grandfathers were born in New Zealand and England. Birth records showed that Howarth's were, too, but he then claimed his mother was born after a secret liaison between his grandmother and a visiting Welshman by the name of Williams. This prompted newspaper headlines such as 'Land of Our Stepfathers'.

Basically, Howarth asked to be taken on trust. As there is now a vast amount of money to be made in professional rugby, and Howarth's presence was depriving a Welshman of a test place, this was a bit rich.

Henry's role in the Grannygate affair was questioned, but he escaped relatively unscathed. The players were ruled ineligible to represent Wales until they had served the mandatory three-year residential qualification. By mid-2001, both had done this and Sinkinson had actually been pulled back into the Welsh test side, though not with any notable success.

What the scandal did was throw the spotlight on the IRB's slap-dash eligibility rules. These have since been tightened. Now players can represent only one country, at either test or second XV or national sevens level. The three-year residency rule still exists, and I would like to see it stretched to at least five years.

The rule restricting players to one country will have a big impact on world rugby, and one of the countries most affected will be New Zealand. Many All Blacks have gone on to represent other countries. To name just a few examples over the past few years, players like Frano Botica and Matthew Cooper have appeared for Croatia, Jamie Joseph, Arran Pene and Graeme Bachop for Japan, Inga Tuigamala for Samoa. In addition other All Blacks, such as Frank Bunce, Steve Bachop, Alama Ieremia, Ofisa Tonu'u and Michael Jones, first appeared at test level for Samoa. Other New Zealanders, including Andrew McCormick (Japan), Sean Lineen, Brendan Laney and John and Martin Leslie (Scotland) played at NPC level in this country before making

> **Basically, Howarth asked to be taken on trust. As there is now a vast amount of money to be made in professional rugby, and Howarth's presence was depriving a Welshman of a test place, this was a bit rich.**

their names as test players elsewhere.

Late in 2001, I myself played a part in a New Zealand-born player representing France. One night the New Zealand-born rugby writer who is a long-time resident in Paris, Ian Borthwick, rang me at home and asked if I could verify the career records of former Counties player Tony Marsh.

Marsh had been playing in France for three years and under residential rules had qualified to represent France, whose French selectors had started to take an interest in his form. However, Marsh's status was still not confirmed under the other part of qualification scrutiny. Had he disqualified himself by representing New Zealand, New Zealand A or the national sevens team?

Apparently the French Rugby Federation had faxed the New Zealand union and asked if Marsh had breached any of the above categories. The New Zealand Union replied by fax that indeed Marsh had toured Samoa with New Zealand A in 1998. It was an easy conclusion, therefore, that he could not play for France.

Borthwick asked me to double-check the information. So I did.

I have been keeping copies of that trusted New Zealand weekly *Rugby News* since its inception in 1970. They are stacked year by year in my library at home. After Borthwick's call, I looked through the paper's reports of the New Zealand A tour of Samoa in 1998. If Marsh had played just one game on that trip he would have to be out of contention to represent France. It was a three-match tour. And there it was. Marsh had indeed appeared in one game wearing the New Zealand A colours. It was the fixture against the Samoan President's XV.

But there was a catch. Apparently before the game it was agreed that the local team could field many more substitutes than the official laws of first class rugby allow. By law, the maximum of substitutes in any game is seven. A read of my *Rugby News* story showed that the President's XV ran on 10 players off the bench. The game should therefore have been classified as non-first class.

I reported back to Borthwick, who then wrote it up in his columns in that authoritative French daily sports paper *L'Equipe* and from there further inquiries came back from the French authorities to the New Zealand union. The union then confirmed that Marsh was not one of theirs after all, and that the French could claim him.

And so Tony Marsh, ex-New Zealand Maoris, ex-Counties and ex-unofficial New Zealand A player, was indeed eligible to set out on a new international career. He made his test debut for France in their win over South Africa in Paris on November 10, 2001 and the following week scored France's only try in their 14-13 win over Australia.

He could do so only because of three things:

• The Samoan President wanted to see more of his players in a game three and a bit years earlier.

• A French/New Zealand reporter wanted to thoroughly check out the hint of a story.

• A New Zealand reporter was able to justify to his wife why 30 years of aging rugby newspapers are still well worth keeping!

43. A tale of two stompings

The Ashworth and Higginson affairs

Now I would like to deal with two incidents that occurred during All Black tours of Wales. They happened two years apart, but I believe they were related.

The first happened in 1978 and reflected very poorly on the All Blacks. It has become known as the John Ashworth affair. Graham Mourie's Grand Slam All Blacks were well into their 1978 tour by the time they got to Bridgend. They had lost one match, to Munster, but otherwise had marched triumphantly around Britain. They'd been very fortunate to beat Wales in the dying moments, when Brian McKechnie had kicked a sideline penalty to give New Zealand a 13–12 win. The fact that most people in Wales believed referee Roger Quittenton had awarded the penalty only because of the blatant diving from the lineout of All Black locks Andy Haden and Frank Oliver made the defeat all the harder to swallow.

Anyway, by the time the All Blacks got to Bridgend, for their seventeenth (and second-last) tour match, there was a certain desperation for a Welsh team to beat Mourie's men. Bridgend were to be the last Welsh combination to confront the All Blacks during the tour, so the 15 players wearing blue and white carried the hopes of the whole nation.

Their aggression was met by a fierce All Black determination and a real dogfight broke out. From the kick-off, fists were flying everywhere, and boots, too. From high up in the broadcasting box, I saw clearly one incident: brilliant fullback John (J.P.R.) Williams went to the deck in a ruck and was stomped in the face by an All Black. In my commentary, I called it as I saw it: the act involved the Canterbury prop John Ashworth.

After the game, which New Zealand won 17–6, all hell broke loose. Williams, who at the time was one of the most famous rugby players in the world, had stitches

Above: Circle marks the spot . . . John Ashworth's boot and J.P.R. Williams' head are on a collision course. Left: J.P.R. and the bloody aftermath.

inserted in a big wound on his cheek and he protested to the media over the incident. At the official dinner afterwards his father caused a scene and some All Blacks stormed out.

The whole day had a nasty edge to it, nasty indeed. The British media went ballistic at the All Blacks. The team's management played down the significance of the incident, but I felt that much of the criticism of the New Zealand team was warranted.

For me, there was peace for a few days, because it took time for the video of the game to be flown home. But when it was finally shown, there was even more of a storm and I found myself at the centre of it. From being a TV broadcaster who had reported an event, I found I was now making the news as one who had dared to reprimand one of the All Blacks. In those days they were deemed to be above reproach.

I felt I took more heat for commentating in a straightforward manner about what had taken place than Ashworth did — and he had done it!

The final chapter in the Bridgend episode came when Ashworth was cruelly dealt to by two members of the British media at the end of the tour. The New Zealand management planned a farewell press conference at Heathrow Airport while the J.P.R. affair was still hanging in the air. True to form, the British media focused all their questions on the incident, but were gently deflected onto more pleasant subjects.

Two British reporters decided that rather than attend the press conference, they would go to a bar at the airport and ask their mates later what had been said. But they soon realised they had missed out on any quotes for their following day's stories and they knew their editors would be expecting something juicy from the All Blacks' departure.

So the pair agreed to simply invent some quotes from Ashworth. Those fake quotes were duly published in each of their papers with headlines screaming something along the lines of 'Ashworth Apologises to Wales over JPR Incident'. In fact, the All Black had not been in a position to say anything of the sort. The two writers presumed correctly that he would be on his way home by the time their works of fiction were published. Even if he did complain about being misquoted, the two newspapers on the other side of the world would have much greater legal backing

The whole day had a nasty edge to it, nasty indeed. The British media went ballistic at the All Blacks.

than anything Ashworth or the New Zealand Rugby Union could muster.

It was a good management team that year with Russ Thomas manager, Jack Gleeson coach and Graham Mourie captain. Three finer rugby people it would be hard to find. I still say, though, that they did not do themselves proud in their reaction to the Ashworth stomping.

Now, if we fast-forward two years to the All Blacks' 1980 visit to Wales, we will see the sequel to that business. The All Blacks were back in Wales to play a pivotal role in the Welsh Rugby Union's centenary celebrations. They played five matches in Wales, besides two in North America on the way over.

Mourie was again the captain, Ray Harper was the manager and by now Eric Watson was the coach. The team seemed to be going out of their way to make sure the tour was trouble-free. The 1970s had not been a happy time for Welsh–New

News Media Auckland

News Media Auckland

Above: Referee Alan Hosie checks with his touch judge before ordering All Black lock Graeme Higginson (right) from the field in the tourists' 1980 match against Llanelli at Stradey Park. He changed his mind and allowed Higginson to remain only after the intervention of Welsh great Phil Bennett.

Zealand rugby relations. Keith Murdoch's sending home in 1972 following an incident at Cardiff, then the 1978 tour business of the lineout dive and the Ashworth stomping had rather soured relations.

I got the impression that the All Blacks and their hosts were both at pains to ensure the 1980 tour went off harmoniously. The first match, at Cardiff, was no problem, but the tour nearly came off the rails at Llanelli, when, I believe, All Black lock Graeme Higginson became perhaps the first player in the history of rugby to be ordered from the field without having to leave.

Llanelli played extremely well that day, and led 10–3 at the interval before Mourie's team pulled them back (this second half revival was a trademark of teams Mourie led and was due in no small part to the captain's cool head and calming influence). With fulltime nearly up, New Zealand led 16–10 and were assured of victory.

Then Higginson was caught stomping in a ruck. The referee, Alan Hosie of Scotland, heeded the advice of his touch judge and called over Mourie. The crowd, sensing what was about to happen, began chanting, 'Off, off!'

There was quite some discussion and then Hosie stretched out his right arm and appeared to everyone watching to send Higginson from the field. All the good feelings about the Welsh centenary and the rehabilitation of the All Black image in Wales were about to go out the window.

I have seen many players ordered from the field and am in no doubt that was what was happening at Stradey Park that day. Mourie's shoulders sagged, Higginson looked resigned, and Hosie had the grimly determined look of a man doing what he had to do.

Then Llanelli flyhalf Phil Bennett ran up to Hosie and engaged him in a discussion that was so animated that Bennett was actually jumping off the ground. Llanelli captain Ray Gravell and veteran forward Derek Quinnell joined Bennett. Finally, Hosie closed the discussion by blowing his whistle to signal the end of the game.

The story afterwards, from the referee and both teams, was that Higginson had received a stern warning. Few of us there bought it. It seemed to me that Higginson had been given his marching orders, but had been talked out of such drastic action by senior players determined not to mar the All Black tour with one nasty incident in the dying moment of a game already decided.

44. Buck up or we're off

A near walk-off by Shelford's Maori

In 1982 I accompanied the New Zealand Maori team on a nine-match tour of Wales and Spain, covering the matches for Television New Zealand. The tour was not a total success, though five of the matches were won and another drawn. Paul Quinn captained the side and the Wellington loose forward struggled for his best form because of injury. Manager Waka Nathan and coach Percy Erceg had trouble maintaining discipline at times and overall, even though the team was eagerly received wherever it went, I didn't think it did a lot for the reputation of either Maori people or New Zealand rugby.

The next time the Maori team made an overseas tour was in 1988. This time Wayne Shelford was the captain. At that time Shelford was one of the giants of world rugby. He was the All Black captain and a genuinely formidable international No 8. I was interested to see if Shelford would be able to instill more discipline into a team that had not always been strong in that department. Looking at tour statistics, you would have to say he succeeded, for the Maori side won 10 and drew one of their 12 tour matches, losing only to a French Selection at Narbonne. They had a warm-up match in Auckland, then played matches in Italy, France, Spain and Argentina, so it was an all-encompassing tour.

The most curious feature of the tour concerned an incident that occurred in the match against a Southern French Selection at Rodez. The match finished in a 10–10 draw, and even now there is dispute about whether Shelford took his team from the field as a protest over some referee rulings he found unfathomable.

Tour reports indicated that quite early in the game, Shelford led his team to the sideline and had an animated discussion with the referee and the tour interpreter. This was a rare action for a rugby captain, and from a distance seemed to constitute either strike action, or at the very least the threat of strike action.

New Zealand Rugby Union chairman Russ Thomas wasn't impressed and

News Media Auckland

Buck Shelford . . . 'There was going to be a blow-up, so I intervened'.

suggested the action was inappropriate, and that Shelford had not acted in a way that was becoming of an All Black captain.

Shelford gave his version of events in *Buck*, saying one of the Maori props, Arthur McLean, was having trouble and wouldn't go down in the scrums. McLean apparently felt the referee was letting the opposition charge over the mark and wouldn't listen to attempts to talk over the new rules.

It was a tense situation, exacerbated by the fact that the referee spoke no English. 'There was obviously going to be a blow-up, so I intervened,' said Shelford. 'I told the referee if there was any more trouble, I would have to take my team aside. There was never any mention of leaving the field. Sure enough, there was another scrum and more trouble with the referee unable to sort out the situation, so I took the players to another part of the ground — which happened to be the sideline.

'I signalled urgently for our tour interpreter to come down from the stand and we spent two minutes with the referee, the interpreter, their captain and me in a big pow-wow. Finally, through the interpreter, I told the ref if he didn't sort out the problem we were going to leave the field. That threat worked and he let the scrums do their own thing from then on. There was no more silly business.'

Was it a walk-off? You be the judge. It was certainly among the most drastic actions I can recall being taken by a captain in international rugby.

45. The plight of the code hoppers

All Blacks who switched to rugby league

If there has been one thing that has stunned the average New Zealand rugby union follower over the years, it has been seeing an All Black switch to rugby league. Such players never actually switched codes; they 'defected', as if showing some unspecified piece of disloyalty.

The first All Blacks to switch were in 1907–08, when a group of eight of them signed up for Bert Baskiville's pioneering rugby league tour of Australia and Britain. At the time, they were called the Professional All Blacks and some time later became known as the All Golds, which these days is used endearingly about those hardy football pioneers. But when the pro-rugby union establishment coined the term, it was meant in a derogatory manner, casting aspersions on these footballers who had the temerity to want to be paid for playing sport.

There were some famous All Blacks in that 1908 team, flying winger George Smith among them. The best New Zealand — and perhaps world — forward of the era was Charlie Seeling, who'd been a sensation when touring Britain with the 1905 All Black Originals. Seeling didn't tour with the All Golds, but turned to rugby league in 1910 and established a massive reputation in England, providing yeoman service for the Wigan club.

Through the decades there has been a stream of players swapping codes. Karl Ifwersen, the brilliant Auckland back, was an exceptional case. He had a season of rugby for Auckland, then switched to league, representing New Zealand from 1913 to 1920. He was reinstated to rugby before the 1921 season and was at the centre of a storm when called into the third test of the series against the Springboks that season. Though he continued to play rugby union, the league slur remained with him and he

George Nepia and his wife Huinga pose with local rugby league officials on a visit back to New Zealand in 1937 after a stint in English league.

was ruled ineligible for selection for the 1924–25 All Black team to Britain.

Two of the greatest of all All Blacks, George Nepia and Bert Cooke, turned to league in the 1930s. Cooke, often touted as the finest second five-eighth/centre produced by New Zealand, represented the Kiwis at league against Britain in 1932 and Australia in 1935. Nepia had one league test, against Australia in 1937, on the same day the All Blacks lost the test series to South Africa.

Cooke and Nepia were two of a select group who gained reinstatement to rugby through what was known as a war amnesty. Others, such as Mike Gilbert, the robust and reliable fullback for the All Blacks through Britain and France in 1935–36, were not so fortunate and for the rest of their lives were largely spurned by the rugby establishment.

The attitude of rugby union authorities towards league is perhaps best summed up by this true story that emerged from England in the 1950s. Dartmoor Prison fielded a team in the local rugby competition. Now Dartmoor was a tough prison, housing murderers, rapists and other criminals of the worst kind. But the team came together well and played good rugby. All was well until one day it was discovered that one of the team had once been a rugby league player. He was immediately banned from the team forever. The rugby authorities didn't mind their code being played by rapists and murderers, but drew the line when the dregs from the very bottom of the barrel — a league player — tried to join a rugby side.

This was the sort of Neanderthal thinking that any player contemplating a code

Jimmy Haig kicks ahead for the South Island during the 1946 inter-island match.

switch knew he would encounter. Nevertheless, many of them still made the jump.

Jimmy Haig played two tests at halfback for New Zealand in 1946 and impressed with his speed and accurate passing. Soon after he was snapped up by league and represented the Kiwis with distinction from 1947 to 1954, a key part of one of the golden eras of New Zealand league.

For every successful code switch, there were many who failed to make the grade. Joe Karam shocked rugby followers by switching codes in 1976 when it was expected he would be the All Black fullback in South Africa. Karam played for the Glenora club in Auckland, but never seemed at home in league. Neither did lumbering forwards Kent Lambert and Graham Whiting, while in later years Doug Rollerson and Shane Howarth never shone as brightly in league as in rugby.

Mark Brooke-Cowden turned to league after the 1987 World Cup. I well remember Brooke-Cowden, when rumours of an impending change were put to him, denying the story, then the following day announcing the details. For rugby union players to even discuss terms with a league club put them beyond the pale and denials were routine until the final formal announcement.

There was a thawing out of this hostility of rugby union towards league in 1987. The two national teams were led by eminently sensible coaches, Brian Lochore (rugby union) and Graham Lowe (league). During the 1987 Rugby World Cup, Lochore and Lowe were in contact more than once and the world did not stop. By

1990, the two sports' administrators were working closely enough for a double-header weekend to be planned for Athletic Park, Wellington. It was a notable first for New Zealand sport, but hardly memorable in terms of results as, in bitterly cold conditions, both New Zealand teams were beaten by their Australian counterparts.

All Black rugby was severely hurt in 1990 when within a few weeks four fine backs, Matthew Ridge, John Gallagher, John Schuster and Frano Botica, all went the league way. Curiously, of the four Ridge had done the least in rugby, representing New Zealand but not in a test. Yet it was Ridge who prospered in league, playing outstandingly for Manly and eventually captaining New Zealand.

Interestingly, at a function in London in November 2001, I met up with Gallagher again and we spoke of his switch to league 11 years earlier. He firmly believes that the four All Blacks going to league in 1990 helped speed up the process of rugby union going fully professional. 'The union game then had no career path for its All Blacks,' Gallagher said. 'After we four went across and played professionally, they had to think, "What if this continues to happen?"'

Another back of the same period who really shone in league was Inga Tuigamala. Inga the Winger was a very popular rugby player, but did tend to be somewhat lazy in his training. Once he was bought by Wigan, though, it was a different story. He moved to centre and became a brilliant player, a powerful runner, a clever thinker and a great off-loader.

There were more switches to league in the 1990s, as players unashamedly chased the big money on offer in league. Marc Ellis, John Timu and John Kirwan were three All Blacks who swapped codes. All had their moments in league, but in truth none really looked at home.

In the early to mid-1990s, one area where rugby was well ahead of league was in place-kicking. Rugby union had a large number of extremely accurate round-the-corner place-kickers, this at a time when many league kickers still kicked with their toe. Therefore kickers such as Eion Crossan and Daryl Halligan, solid provincial rugby union players, became major league assets. Halligan, in fact, went on to have a wonderful league career, playing in the National Rugby League competition for North Sydney and Canterbury and eventually setting a points-scoring record that was finally topped in 2001 by Jason Taylor.

But the football world changed in 1995 when rugby union went professional.

Suddenly the motivation for swapping codes vanished. Rugby had always offered greater travel opportunities for it is more of a global game. But league's big carrot was money. Once rugby union could offer big pay cheques, the stream of rugby to league players dried up and now we see a trend beginning the other way.

Australian rugby is targeting high-profile league players. Willie Carne swapped codes, though not with any great success. Andrew Walker has quickly become an asset to the Wallabies, and now we see Wendell Sailor and Mat Rogers also moving

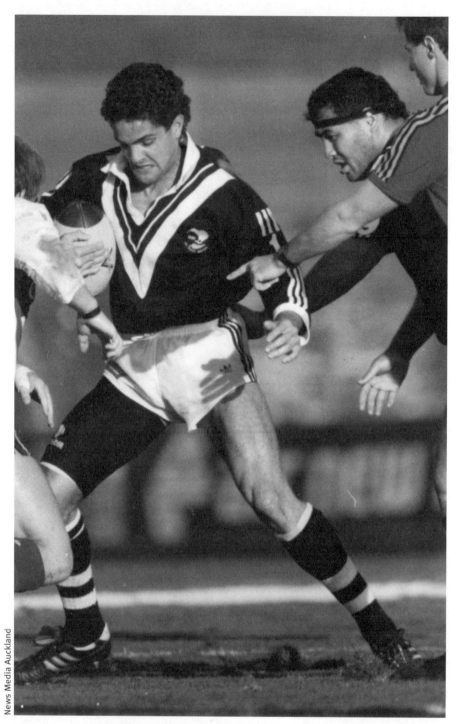

News Media Auckland

While he never tasted test match rugby for the All Blacks, Matthew Ridge had a distinguished international career for the Kiwis.

Players who have represented New Zealand at rugby union and rugby league

Opai Asher	John Hogan	Jim O'Brien
Frano Botica	Ned Hughes	Lou Petersen
Alphonsus Carroll	Karl Ifwersen	Matthew Ridge
Bert Cooke	Bill Johnston	Kurt Sherlock
Tom Cross	Herb Lilburne	George Smith
Marc Ellis	Dougie McGregor	Dave Solomon
Dave Evans	Duncan McGregor	George Spencer
Charlie Fitzgerald	Bill Mackrell	John Spencer
Bolla Francis	Hawea Mataira	John Timu
George Gillett	Harold Milliken	Jum Turtill
Jim Haig	Billy Mitchell	Eric Watkins
Harold Hayward	George Nepia	Edgar Wrigley

from league to union. The case of most interest to New Zealanders is Brad Thorn, the Brisbane Broncos star who played for the Crusaders and Canterbury in 2001. I judged Thorn's first season in rugby to be a success. He was a regular member of both teams and as he came to terms with the different requirements of a rugby union forward, he looked more at home. His ball skills, running ability and athleticism were big attributes for his rugby union coaches.

Thorn's selection for the All Blacks in 2001 was deserved, but for him to then announce he was undecided about his footballing future was grossly unfair to the rugby union scene. To be named in the All Blacks for their world tour and then pull out 24 hours later was virtually without precedent. To me it was a scandal. I hope no-one refers to Thorn as an All Black.

I've always felt it was easier for backs than forwards to swap codes. Big rugby forwards tended to struggle when faced with the amount of running and tackling required in league. That's not to say there weren't exceptions. I know Graham Lowe was extremely keen to sign Zinzan Brooke for Manly and I have no doubt Brooke, with his vast array of skills, would have been a sensational league player.

Generally, though, it's the good backs who have adapted best. Players like Ridge and Tuigamala have been able to use their speed and strength to become top league players. The requirements are a little different for backs going the other way. I wonder if league players, even talented players such as Sailor, have had enough practice at kicking, as they virtually never are required to kick in league. Also, outside backs in rugby touch the ball a lot less than in league, so the requirements of a winger are rather more different than would first appear.

46. The flight of the Cavaliers

Rugby's rebel tour of '86

It was probably the biggest scoop I ever had as a sports reporter. And easily the most nervous I ever felt about one.

In March 1986 a visibly shaking Keith Quinn went on nationwide New Zealand television to make a very significant announcement concerning the first news of an event that was completely outside the bounds of rugby correctness in New Zealand.

As I recall, the time allocated to me was just a couple of minutes and it came at the end of a day's play in a New Zealand v Australia cricket test from Auckland.

Over the previous few weeks several of us in the Television New Zealand sports office in Avalon, Wellington, had been gathering information about a secret plan by top New Zealand players to fly to South Africa for a rebel rugby tour. The word rebel was quickly used to describe the structure of the tour as its arrangements were outside the desires and official rules of the New Zealand Rugby Football Union. The tour was also outside the laws of the New Zealand courts. When the tour was formalised, it became known as the Cavaliers.

The early concealment of the tour's arrangements had been very deep, but as with many things in New Zealand, eventually whispers sneaked out. The clandestine word around our small country was that the players who had previously been announced as members of the official All Blacks tour to South Africa the year before were to be invited first to make up the new hush-hush touring team.

An official tour of South Africa in 1985 had been sanctioned by the New Zealand union, but was cancelled after court action scuttled the plans. South Africa was still a country in the grip of apartheid and there was widespread opposition to the tour throughout New Zealand. The players chosen to tour South Africa in 1985 were deeply

Breakfasting rebels . . . members of the Cavaliers shortly after their arrival in South Africa. Players, from left, are: Wayne Shelford, Craig Green (with menu), John Ashworth, Scott Crichton, Andy Donald and Bryce Robins.

angered that they had missed out on the tour of a lifetime and were reportedly only mildly satisfied with the replacement trip to Argentina. The key players, and Andy Haden was one of them, initially went about sketching plans for a surrogate trip to South Africa later in 1985, and when that was not possible, for another in 1986.

Early in '86 vague plans began to be mentioned behind cupped hands via contacts around New Zealand. Details were always sketchy. Trying to pin down just who of the current All Blacks might be available was made more difficult because of official arrangements that were put in place for a number of leading players to go to Britain to play several matches for a World XV. These were part of the International Rugby Board's Centenary celebrations. There was even talk of an official World XV game in South Africa.

The major breakthrough for us at TVNZ came at a sponsor's function in Auckland. The good people of Steinlager were laying on some of their finest products for Auckland players, officials and the media. My colleague, Gavin Service, and I thought it would be appropriate to find out just when the World XV game in South Africa might be played. It could be shown on TV One if we were able to obtain the rights. But we needed to know the date.

We agreed afterwards that it was strange how the leading players blanched when the match in the Republic was mentioned. No one wanted to speak about it to us. However, we thought of it as nothing more than curious behaviour.

It wasn't until we returned to Wellington that we took a call from Haden, who was ringing to ask a colleague: 'How does Quinn know about these games in South Africa?

There's going to be more than one, you know.'

'More than one!' we said to each other after hanging up, and for us the gossip suddenly moved up a level. We now knew some sort of tour was on. Then, quite innocently, the dates for the tour and, in particular, what we were told would be test dates dropped into our laps. They came via a New Zealand travel agent who was told the dates by a confrère in South Africa. The travel agent was told to start organising supporters' tour groups. The tour could be up to 12 matches long, said the South African. Now we had a tour and we had test dates and we had a duration. It became a chase.

The next act in the drama was that another source revealed that a previous rumour about the composition of the team was now confirmed. The team would be exactly the same as the one chosen to tour South Africa the previous year.

Something slightly unnerving crossed our paths next. We discovered that the prodigious and talented writer Alex Veysey of the Sunday paper, then called the *New Zealand Times*, was going to publish a story about a so-called rebel tour in the next weekend's edition. Apparently Veysey had also been working the story through what he knew. We respected him to be a very conscientious man with excellent backup. In the TVNZ office we then understood we had to confirm what information we had if we were going to expose it for a scoop before Veysey on Sunday morning.

I went home in a state of apoplexy. Nobody rang me to ask if I was right or wrong about the tour — I had no idea. Had I made a fool of myself?

That's why you would have seen the nervous Quinn go on TV when play ended at the cricket on Saturday, March 14, 1986. I actually had very little to go on, but there was enough. I mentioned first that a team of leading New Zealand rugby players, many of them All Blacks, would be leaving New Zealand in secret within the next few weeks to take part in a 12-match rebel tour of South Africa. I then listed the test dates when the team would play the Springboks. I did not know the names of the full list of players at that point, only that they came mainly from the New Zealand team that had been picked to go to Argentina the year before and who had largely comprised the team that had nearly made a rebel tour to South Africa in 1985.

After the announcement of this team — one hugely significant and controversial in New Zealand's rugby history — I had a feeling of tremendous nervousness. I went home in a state of apoplexy. Nobody rang me to ask if I was right or wrong about the

Peter Bush

Grant Fox sets the Cavaliers backline away in 'test' action from 1986.

tour — I had no idea. Had I made a fool of myself?

That night I tossed and turned. Finally I rose at some ungodly hour and drove around the neighbourhood trying to find a shop open early to see if indeed the *New Zealand Times* had run Veysey's story.

Talk about nervous! However, at a small dairy in upper Willis Street, Wellington (a long way from my residence in Lower Hutt), the first shop I found open had a stack of freshly printed papers. The nice man sold me a copy and I can remember clearly folding open the front page to see my friend Veysey's story. He and I were essentially saying the same thing. The rebels were a fact; they were going to happen!

The rest of the Cavaliers tour, which some might have called outrageous, went off from that double TV/newspaper release. The team played their 12 games. Wherever they went in South Africa, they were billed as the All Blacks, though they went without the blessing of either the New Zealand union, or most of the New Zealand public. On their return each player was suspended for two test matches and the coach, Colin Meads, an All Black selector at that time, was reprimanded. The Springboks were awarded full South African caps and won the home series 3–1.

Footnote: the name chosen by the players for their team was highly appropriate. At their first meeting in South Africa they called themselves the Cavaliers. The *Collins Dictionary* defines 'cavalier' as 'offhand, showing haughty disregard'. How true!

47. The (first) long walk
Cyril Brownlie ordered off

For nearly 100 years, the only two players sent off in a rugby test from any country were the New Zealanders Cyril Brownlie and Colin Meads. Their lonely place in rugby's hall of shame became ammunition for certain countries to view the manner New Zealanders played the game with a certain amount of glee. British people in particular believed the way Brownlie and Meads played 'rugger' was far outside the true and honourable way the game was played in the country of its origin. The British opinion was that it was always the colonial roughhouse chaps from the other side of the world who played outside the true bounds of decency!

On the other hand, rugby watchers in New Zealand have never accepted the manner and rulings that led to Brownlie and Meads being banished. While the Meads sending-off, which occurred in an All Blacks v Scotland match in 1967, was widely covered in the age of television, the Brownlie dismissal has remained largely clouded in the mists of time.

Cyril Brownlie was a giant of a man from Hawke's Bay. Throughout his rugby career he carried the nickname Lofty. He and his younger brother Maurice set off from Hastings with Cliff Porter's 1924–25 touring team to Britain and Ireland. This was a massive undertaking, the team having been chosen in June 1924, departing Wellington by ship on July 29 and not returning until March 17 the following year.

The Invincibles, as the team became known, played 32 games and won them all. Quite rightly they sit in New Zealand rugby history as one of the greatest All Black sides ever (alongside the 1905–06, 1956, 1967, 1987 and 1996 combinations).

Yet the sensational sending-off of Brownlie, the biggest man in the team, caused headlines that in their time were at least as big as those accorded to the Meads dismissal 43 years later.

Maurice Brownlie was a towering figure in the Invincibles and played 26 games out of 32. Cyril missed some early matches because of injury but still played 17 times.

Cyril Brownlie is directed to the sideline by referee Albert Freethy during the All Blacks' test against England at Twickenham in 1925.

Together the two became a massive force in the second row, with Maurice outstanding and Cyril not far behind. (Maurice went on to lead the All Blacks on the next major tour, to South Africa in 1928. Again Cyril accompanied him, the great combination continuing.)

The two names, Brownlie and Meads, had much in common when they made the biggest headlines from incidents they would prefer to forget. Just as there were two fine Brownlie forwards, so too were there two fine Meads forwards, brothers Colin and Stan. Both families had large followings from fans at home. That devotion has no doubt played a part in New Zealanders, at the time and down the years since, never accepting the reasons why the two refereeing decisions came down so harshly on the All Blacks.

Cyril's departure came during the test against England at Twickenham. By that time the British public were aware that the New Zealanders were something special. They were unbeaten in all 27 matches on tour. But England fancied themselves as well. With the leadership of the deeply-respected Wavell Wakefield, one of history's greatest forwards, England were also in middle of one of their golden periods. They were consecutive Five Nations Grand Slam champions in 1923 and 1924, and were unbeaten at Twickenham for 12 years.

So the clash with the All Blacks a couple of days into 1925 was like that of the immovable object meeting the irresistible force.

Alongside Wakefield in the English pack were a couple of rascally fellows who had

Central figures in the sensational ordering off. At left, Welsh referee Albert Freethy, who uttered the words, 'You go off', and above, Cyril Brownlie.

a reputation of never taking a backward step. One was Tom Voyce of Gloucester and the other Reg Edwards, a hard-as-nails prop forward who travelled from Newport in Wales to play for his native country.

The Brownlie brothers were never dirty players, but were immensely proud and strong. Locals would later recall that at home on their farm in the sunny fields of Hawke's Bay they could comfortably sling 70-pound bales high onto ever-mounting stacks of hay.

All thoughts of home were banished for the men of both sides on the fateful rugby day of January 3, 1925. When the game kicked off in front of a Twickenham record crowd of 60,000, there was immediately a crackling tension on the field. At least twice, maybe three times, there were explosions of fighting between the two packs of forwards. The Welsh referee, Albert Freethy of Neath, appealed for calm. In the first moments he spoke sternly to the two captains, Wakefield of England and the New Zealander Jock Richardson (who was regularly chosen as test captain ahead of Porter). At the sight of the scuffles, the crowds roared on their particular favourites.

Apart from the non-test players, there were also a number of New Zealand business people there and it is known that 12 sailors from the ship *Royal Sovereign* were in attendance. So there was *some* cheering for the men in black.

Here is a summary of the reporting from at least 15 newspaper accounts from the day. The Fleet Street pressmen were at Twickenham in droves and from their reports a quite brilliant souvenir scrapbook was handed at tour's end to the New Zealand player Neil McGregor. That scrapbook was passed to me for grateful permanent safekeeping in 1998. It is a superb record of a wonderful tour but, to be frank, there are wide contrasts in its opinionated writings about the Cyril Brownlie sending-off. These variances cast severe doubt on whether the New Zealander should have ever taken the long march that he did, head bowed in shame, passing under the Royal Box where the Prince of Wales sat along with British Prime Minister Stanley Baldwin. There is sufficient evidence to show that if the New Zealander had to be ordered off, at least one other player should have marched in humiliation with him.

To that point it was the most sensational incident in world rugby's young history. It occurred less than 10 minutes into the game (some papers say it was after only seven minutes). This was perhaps the third breakout of fighting between the two weighty packs. Then the whistle blew shrilly and, watching from the stands, the shouting crowds hushed.

Then they gasped and went into an eerie silence when they realised what they would now see. Dressed in his dark blazer with a white scarf and pocket handkerchief, Freethy could be seen with his finger pointing firmly towards the dressing rooms. Cyril Brownlie could be also seen beginning to walk away from the game. On the sideline from not more than 20 metres away a famous photograph recorded the incident. The New Zealander had been sent off, for kicking an England player on the ground.

'You go off,' were the reported words Brownlie heard from the referee. His stunned All Black mates saw one of the famous brothers trudge away.

No reasons for his dismissal could be given until the match had ended. Not one reporter of the 15 or so there has written as having seen anything definite with the naked eye.

> 'You go off,' were the reported words Brownlie heard from the referee. His stunned All Black mates saw one of the famous brothers trudge away.

So we shall leave that for the moment. Meantime there was a game still to be played and a test to be decided. While Cyril stayed out of sight in the dungeons of the dressing room under the grandstand of Twickenham, the remaining 14 New Zealanders took up again the battle to overcome the might of The Red Rose.

What transpired was one of the most famous of All Black victories. The 14 played for 70 minutes against 15 and won 17–11. No fewer than four tries did the All Blacks score, against only two by the English. The All Blacks raised their game and were magnificent, none more so than the man playing for the dishonour he believed had been delivered on his brother by the referee.

Maurice capped a triumphant day in All Black history by picking up a ball from loose play and rushing 15 metres to score. Not an England player could stop his surging charge. There is scratchy film of the run. Perhaps in keeping with his concentrating on correcting the injustice that he believed had been placed on the family name, he is shown on the film getting up from scoring and walking back, a picture of concentrated dedication.

The English team, under Wakefield, competed bravely but could simply not match the inspired New Zealanders. While they honoured 'Wakers' for playing so strongly against them that day, the All Blacks never quite forgave him for not appealing to referee Freethy to keep the dismissed Cyril Brownlie in the game. While Richardson had remonstrated keenly with Freethy, Wakefield stood nearby and uttered not a single word. In the grandstand, the Prince of Wales had asked officials if he could intervene on behalf of keeping Cyril on the field, but Wakefield did not.

According to the reports from the Neil McGregor scrapbook, there were no great celebrations by the All Blacks at the end of the match. In different circumstances they might have shouted to the heavens that they had gone through the best of Britain and Ireland unbeaten, but they were a downcast team at what had happened.

The reporters rushed to find their various angles on the incident and over 75 years later they add up to confusion of the highest order, not the least in the various utterances of the referee himself. Said Freethy in an official statement released at the ground after the game: 'Cyril Brownlie deliberately kicked on the leg of an English forward lying face down on the ground . . . I had taken my eye off the ball for a moment and therefore saw exactly what happened. I had warned both teams generally three times.'

That in itself sounds solid enough, but E.E. (General) Booth, the 1905 All Black, who was reporting for *New Zealand Truth*, dug deeper, writing that 'Mr Freethy could not name the England player reported by him as being kicked. There is no evidence of any player actually being on the ground at that time . . . And from information received from most reliable quarters it appears Cyril Brownlie was not one of those players previously cautioned. Actually it was Maurice Brownlie who had been spoken to'.

Initially Wakefield declined to comment beyond saying that he had 'witnessed the incident but preferred to say nothing'. This quote certainly appears in most of my yellowing clippings. But later at the official dinner at London's famous Café Royal, the England captain did become a little more expansive. He told another paper: 'Brownlie only had himself to blame. He was cautioned twice or thrice for swinging his arms and legs about and persistently playing the man instead of the ball. The referee finally caught him tackling a man five yards from the ball . . . we

BAD FEELING FOLLOWS THE ALL BLACKS SENSATION.

Teams Dine Together But——. | Why Brownlie was Sent Off.

" THE PEOPLE'S " WARNING IGNORED

Brownlie Ordered Off After Kicking a Man on the Grou

How some of the newspapers of the day treated the sending off of Cyril Brownlie.

SENSATION IN RUGBY TES

All Black Player Sent Off for Alleged Foul P
Referee's Explanation of Drastic Action

NEW ZEALANDER DENIES CHARGE OF KI

None of the remarkable incidents that packed the game
the All Blacks and England at Twickenham yesterday—the fin
of the New Zealanders' tour in this country—caused such a g
sation as the dismissal from the field of one of the tourists.

Cyril Brownlie was ordered off the field for alleged foul play ten
minutes after the start—an incident without parallel in a game of such
importance.

With only 14 men; the All Blacks secured victory by 17 points to 11,
and have thus won every game in their
strenuous programme.

The game was played at a fast, fierce pace,
and the excitement of the crowd rose to fever
heat. The Englishmen made a wonderful rally,
scoring eight points in the last few minutes,
but the spurt had come too late.

The Prince of Wales, Prince George, and Mr.
Baldwin were among the spectators. The
Prince shook hands with all the Blacks, and the
English team, the All Blacks, and the
referee dined together at the Café Royal last
night. Mr. W. S. Donne, president of the Rugby
Union, was in the chair.

OFF THE FIELD.

"ALL BLACK" FORWARD ACCUSED OF KICKING AN OPPONENT.

REFEREE'S CHARGE.

ENGLAND BEATEN BY 17 POINTS TO 11.

" WE DID JOLLY WELL "

English Players' Views on the Great Game

The following views of members of the Eng
land team were given to the *Illustrated Sunday
Herald* last night:—

W. Wakefield (the English captain): A splendid
match—hard and fast. I enjoyed every minute of
it and we were not quite out of the running to
the very last.

A. T. Young: We had no instructions to change
our usual plan of campaign. We played the
normal English game, trying to get the ball out
to our wings as quickly as possible.

What seemed strange to me—I don't know how
it struck the onlookers—was that in spite of their
eight outsides, we always seemed to have a man

REFEREE'S OWN STORY

Keith Quinn Collection

Hitchcocks FILM SERIAL

ENGLAND v "ALL·BLACKS"

AT THE KICK·OFF ENGLAND PROCEEDED TO DEMONSTRATE THAT THEY WERE A FIFTEEN TO BE RECKONED WITH .

NATURALLY THIS PUT A LITTLE GINGER INTO THE GAME AND FOR 5 MINUTES THE·ER·PLAY WAS SOMEWHAT STRENUOUS NEAR THE N·Z LINE –

WHICH RESULTED IN C. BROWNLIE BEING ORDERED OFF. IF FOR NOTHING ELSE THE REFEREE DESERVES A MEDAL FOR COURAGE – BROWNLIE IS 6 FT 3 IN HIGH AND WEIGHS 15 ST.

COVE·SMITH WAS FIRST OVER, AND THE CROWD WENT MORE OR LESS MAD.

THAT MADE N·Z MAD First SVENSON SCORED

can't stand that behaviour from any team.'

All that in perhaps just seven minutes' play?

Another player from the England team offered this: '. . . the incident followed an incident where Tom Voyce of Gloucester was hurt in the mouth.' My clippings also tell me that Voyce and Reg Edwards were openly using their fists and received a caution from Freethy early in the game.

Yet another Englishman spoke up at the dinner: 'It was Brownlie who foolishly gave backchat and that settled it. The referee then pointed to the pavilion.'

So we now must ask — did Voyce cop a punch in the mouth? Certainly he was outraged and swinging punches. Maybe, to be fair, it was a kick to the leg. But if that was the case how was he then 'hurt on the mouth'. Another paper reported: 'A.T. Voyce made a complaint to the referee and the matter was ended when C. Brownlie was ordered off.'

So now we have Cyril Brownlie sent off for either kicking a player (according to the referee's statement), or for tackling an English player away from the ball (Wakefield's view), or for backchatting the referee (from the unnamed English player). Or did in fact Brownlie go toe to toe with Tom Voyce and punch him in the mouth? After all, the New Zealander had been warned for swinging his arms about, had he not?

Freethy had a number of the British writers on his side. W.E. Hayter Preston wrote: 'The referee's action was justified there can be no doubt.' The esteemed Percy Rudd added: 'Had Mr Freethy overlooked such an offence the game might easily have become a freefight.' And this from an unnamed correspondent: 'C. Brownlie had to go from this incident which was without precedent in international rugby.'

But the New Zealanders also had their opinions. They knew their man. Cyril Brownlie was a towering figure at that time (his height of 6ft 3in would equate to 6ft 8in or 6ft 9in today) and he came from an impeccable family. It was beyond comprehension that he would go over the top in fighting and squabbling on a rugby field. Certainly he was a powerful man and it is true that the unbeaten record to that point on the tour created deep pressures.

Remember, they were trying to leave Britain with an unbeaten record, which would be one better that the famous 1905–06 Originals All Blacks had achieved.

But let the following quotes perhaps go part way to summarising this story, and to perhaps raise the question — did the venerable Freethy have any idea at all just why he had sent the New Zealander off on that famous day, to condemn him to a place of notoriety that he does not wholly deserve?

• **General Booth, _NZ Truth_**
'There is every reason to suppose that he [Freethy] was considerably overwrought

and overly excited about the fiery aspect of the opening play.'

• New Zealand team members (quoted at Café Royal dinner)
'Cyril Brownlie was not the aggressor, but he retaliated when struck by a player who had been warned three times.' Also: 'The incident took place at a lineout so no player was on the ground. The ref made a mistake.'

• Stan Dean, New Zealand team manager
'I had a long chat afterwards with Mr Freethy and asked him point-blank who it was who Cyril Brownlie had deliberately kicked. The Referee said he did not know.'

• The Brownlie brothers
At the dinner all Maurice would say was: 'Anything may have happened. But nothing deliberately.'

And according to one newspaper (the origin of which cannot be identified as its masthead has been clipped off) Cyril Brownlie himself offered the following observation about the incident that was to follow him until his death in Wairoa, New Zealand, in 1954: 'It was a piece of sheer ill-luck on my part. I found myself involved in a series of minor retaliations and was unfortunate to be dropped upon as the second man in the affair. I do think another man should have gone off the field besides myself.'

The famous New Zealand rugby writer Terry McLean has perhaps come up with the last word on the fateful skirmish. In his excellent work *New Zealand Rugby Legends*, McLean tells that when the brothers returned from the tour to New Zealand 'no-one, unless invited, ever spoke about it to any member of the Brownlie family'. Maurice, according to McLean, was 'keenly sensitive about the incident but harboured no grudge against Freethy.' Said Maurice: 'The best referee I ever played under was Albert Freethy of Wales; he was outstanding. And he was quite right about my brother, Cyril. Cyril did punch Voyce, though this was a retaliatory blow after Voyce had belted him.' Maurice went on: 'After the game I said to Freethy: "Why didn't you order the other man off too? They were both at fault." Freethy replied: "I'm sorry, I can only adjudicate on what I see."'

48. Night rugby . . . without the lights!

The darkest test in history

It was absurd that the New Zealand rugby team in Britain in 1978 had to play their international match against Scotland in such ridiculous weather conditions. It has become a classic memory for those of us who were there. We recall the abject gloom in which the all-important game was played. The video footage that remains in the libraries shows it *looking* like it was extremely dull weather, but to the 69,000 people who went to Murrayfield that day (night!) this was a test pretty much played in darkness.

The weather conditions could not be controlled, of course. We know that all weather is heaven sent. But in December in Scotland, temperatures can drop very low and are often accompanied by gloomy, foggy weather. December 9, 1978 was just such a day.

On the Friday before the Saturday fixture the weather was so bleak in Edinburgh that there was virtually total darkness by mid-afternoon. As the international the next day was set to kick off at 2.15 pm, inquiries were made by TV staffers about whether an earlier kick-off time might be contemplated. As Murrayfield then had no floodlighting, this was sound thinking. The no-lights attitude was part of the prevailing conservative nature of Scottish rugby thinking at the time.

There were sound reasons for having an earlier kick-off. Back then, TV schedules were not the critical jam-packed matters they are today. In Britain on the BBC, there was a *Grandstand* show which ran all Saturday afternoon, so bringing the game's start time forward would presumably have been a relatively simple matter for the programmers. The BBC could either have shown the game in an earlier time slot or recorded it for replay at its original start time. The other main carrier of the game was Television New Zealand. Across in the TVNZ world, a 2.15 pm kick-off in Edinburgh was a 2.15 am slot in New Zealand. Therefore shifting the kick-off to midday (midnight in New Zealand) would have been beneficial.

The game was particularly significant. New Zealand's All Blacks, under Graham Mourie's leadership, wanted the best possible playing conditions to give themselves every chance of victory. They were desperate to earn themselves the title of Grand Slam winners, having previously beaten Ireland, England and Wales during the tour. No other All Black team had achieved a Grand Slam.

But it was not going to be easy to shift the kick-off. On Friday, the murk set in around Edinburgh and the forecast for the next 24 hours ahead was for more of the same.

The match programme for the 1978 Scotland test.

So one enterprising TV type (actually it was me!) took it upon himself to phone the Scottish Rugby Union offices to ask whether they were looking at the weather and whether they were wondering if the game the next day could go ahead in such disastrously gloomy mid-afternoon conditions.

They didn't need me to, but I told them anyway that by midday on the Friday it was gloomy enough in Edinburgh for the lights down the famous Princes Street shopping precinct to be switched on fully; by 1 pm on the same day the famous Royal Mile could only be seen with the full distinctive street lamps showing the way; by the equivalent kick-off time, it would be a joke to begin a football game without lights.

The gentleman at the Scottish Rugby Union's office who took my call was the secretary, John Law. His tone was short and direct. 'Sir,' he said in an appropriately chilly tone, 'we are keeping an eye on the weather and if it is dark we will bring the kick-off of the international forward. Don't worry — we are mindful of the situation.'

I had to press on with him and ask the next question. 'If you do have to bring the kick-off forward,' I gingerly asked, 'by how much will you do it? As one of the TV stations taking the game I will have to ring my producer in London to alert him to booking an earlier satellite time for the transmission.' To that eminently sensible question I can still remember the curtness of the secretary's reply. 'If the weather is exactly like this tomorrow, we will bring the kick-off forward by five minutes.'

And so they did. I could not believe it. If anything, the darkness the next day at not 2.15 pm but 2.10 pm (!) was worse than it had been the day before. Thank you for the foresight, Mr Scottish secretary!

That Mourie's All Blacks went on to win 18–9 and claim the Grand Slam was cruel

News Media Auckland

Rival skippers Graham Mourie and Ian McGeechan after the 'night' test.

indeed to the honourable effort put in by the brave Scottish team. While it is true that neither side coped absolutely with the darkness, the game nevertheless had many fine moments.

Watching the game back on video, it gets to the point where even the false lightening of the picture image via the electronic cameras cannot escape the duskiness changing to murkiness minute by minute. The cameras desperately try to hold onto a lighted version of the late action in the game. A modern comparison of the night-vision of the cameras peering in at that far-off game at Murrayfield would be the images we saw looking into the gloom of modern night war action shots taken over the war in Afghanistan.

Perhaps Bruce Robertson's memory of the game emphasises just how dark it was. Robertson told me: 'The Scotland test sealed the Grand Slam for our team in 1978. It got darker and darker during the second half. We charged the ball down on our own 22, kicked it through and eventually I managed to score the try. It was amazing because even the players weren't aware of who'd scored. Graham Mourie went up to B.G. (Williams) and said, "Great try, Beegee."'

Footnote: In 2001, while on holiday in Scotland, I went to visit some friends I had made on my 1978 and other visits to Murrayfield. The famous ground was being renovated and the turf replaced. When the Scottish union learned a New Zealand reporter was coming, several of their staff kindly lifted a slice of the grass and presented it to me in a neat box. It was accompanied by a plaque which read: 'On this spot on December 9, 1978, Bruce Robertson scored the winning try for New Zealand in their 18–9 win over Scotland.'

It was a funny, kind and thoughtful gesture and I appreciated it, especially when they recruited the British Lions player Simon Taylor, who was there training, to present it me.

It was a great pity the foot and mouth scare prevented me bringing home the turf to New Zealand and actually presenting it to Bruce Robertson for him to keep at his home.

49. Silver ferns and golden wallets

1907: Professional rugby arrives

There have been traumatic years for New Zealand rugby, years that will never be forgotten. The horror years for the All Blacks were 1949, when they lost six tests, and 1998, when they lost five in succession. There were other disastrous years, such as 1981, when the Springbok tour split the country asunder, and 1986, when the rebel Cavaliers set off for South Africa.

But has there been any year that threatened rugby more than 1907, when a professional New Zealand rugby league team was formed and set off for a tour of Australia and Britain? This team, drawn from national and provincial rugby union representatives, was so successful that it launched a whole new sport in New Zealand, a sport that directly rivalled rugby union.

The team became known as the All Golds, a term bestowed on it by an Australian newspaper that was attempting to decry the players' endeavours to earn gate-money. In Britain, they were known more often as the Professional All Blacks. This was a pioneering team in every way and rugby league followers are understandably very proud of what tour organiser Albert Henry (Bert) Baskiville and the players achieved. Rugby league in New Zealand (and Australia) owes its genesis to this team, made up of players who had the courage to brush aside conservative sentiments and fierce opposition to found what they believed was an improved, professional form of rugby football.

The New Zealand rugby establishment reacted with hostility when news of Baskiville's plans to launch professional rugby leaked out. Baskiville was inspired by the breakaway in northern England in 1895 of a group of rugby players and teams who wanted to be paid for their efforts. This rebel group played what they called Northern Union, the game we call rugby league today.

Team photo of the 1907-08 All Golds. Tour organiser — and player — Albert Baskiville is seated third from left in the front row.

NZ Rugby Museum

Baskiville, only 23 when he set about organising the tour, found himself blocked at every turn. He became the first person to be banned for life by the New Zealand Rugby Football Union. At the 1907 North-South match, every player was required to sign an affidavit saying he would not switch to Northern Union. Not only did Baskiville have to battle rugby officials, who barred him from their grounds, but newspapers of the day were staunchly pro-rugby and were extremely critical of Baskiville. His activities were also frowned on by various central and local government agencies. For instance, New Zealand Prime Minister Joseph Ward wrote to the British government requesting that visitor permits not be granted to the footballers Baskiville was signing.

In spite of these difficulties, and the fact that communication was so rudimentary in the early years of the 20th century, Baskiville, who had been a good senior club player in Wellington, persevered. He was encouraged by the fact that so many of the rugby stars of the day were keen to join his venture. The 1905 Originals had seen Northern Union played and were not only impressed with the game but also with the fact that players got paid. That was a strong motivation for a lot of the poorer All Blacks to make the switch once they were approached by Baskiville.

The 26-strong team, captained by Wellingtonian Bumper Wright, eventually included eight All Blacks and 14 provincial players.

Baskiville's first coup was in signing George Smith, who was appointed vice-captain. Smith, a speedster of a winger, had been one of the stars of the 1905 Originals. In addition, he had been a champion jockey and a world-class sprint and hurdles athlete, good enough to set a world record. When he joined Baskiville's team, Smith gave the venture a great deal of credibility. Other All Blacks signed up — Edgar Wrigley, Jum Turtill, Tom Cross, Eric Watkins, Duncan McGregor, Massa Johnston and Bill Mackrell. Smith and Johnston, who both had immense standing among football players of their day, played important roles in organising the tour and recruiting other players.

Another significant name was Auckland five-eighth Lance Todd, who went on to become a revered figure in England. In fact, even today his name is remembered because the Lance Todd Trophy for the Challenge Cup player of the day is named after him.

Baskiville's team had tremendous depth, quite apart from its All Black stars. Many of the provincial players had established themselves for Auckland or Wellington in Ranfurly Shield matches. Baskiville was designated secretary-promoter, and the team eventually headed for Sydney, where it picked up a player named Dally Messenger. This was a pivotal moment. Messenger is still regarded as arguably the finest footballer produced by Australia and his decision to switch to rugby league (Northern Union, as it was then known) gave the venture the standing it needed in Australia.

To try to convey what Baskiville achieved, let me put it this way. Imagine a New Zealand promoter now deciding to field a team in a hybrid version of rugby and enticing Jeff Wilson, Leon MacDonald, Tana Umaga, Pita Alatini, Troy Flavell, Norm Maxwell, Anton Oliver and Mark Hammett to join him. Then imagine him signing up 14 more Super 12 and/or NPC players. Then he would look across the Tasman and get Stephen Larkham on board. His team would be so successful that it would provide the impetus for this new brand of football to prosper over the next century, to become a major sport in New Zealand and an even bigger one in Australia. That's what Baskiville did nearly a century ago. No wonder he rocked New Zealand rugby to the core.

Each player had to contribute £50 to the tour expenses before departing, a massive amount in those days, especially for the many who were far from well-off. The tour was such a success that it returned a profit of £3582, meaning each player earned enough to buy a house on his return.

On their way to England, the All Golds stopped in Sydney and won all three matches, one game drawing 20,000 people. They then played at Colombo, through Britain, 10 more games (including three tests) in Australia, and, finally, a benefit match in Wellington in memory of Baskiville, who tragically did not live to see the end of the tour. The young Wellingtonian's death was a shocking blow. He was immensely popular, respected and admired by the players for his organisation, fairness and energy. He contracted pneumonia and died in a Brisbane hospital on May 20, 1908, just before the team returned to New Zealand.

The All Golds' full tour record was: played 59, won 28, lost 24, drew 7. They played three tests in England, winning two. In Australia, they also won the test series 2–1.

The tour caused repercussions for rugby that are still being felt today. It is possible to make a case that if it wasn't for Baskiville, rugby league might not have taken hold in Australia. No All Golds, no All Blacks switching to league down the years.

Even though he undermined rugby union, I have great admiration for the energy and flair of the young Baskiville. The way he organised the All Golds tour was brilliant.

—

Walking stick attack

Rugby followers who hear the name of Michel Crauste recall the marauding, uncompromising French flanker of the late 1950s and '60s. But whenever I hear his name, I think first of a 56-year-old Oamaru grandmother, Mrs Hilda Marsden, and an incident that occurred during France's 1961 tour of New Zealand.

The French were playing South Canterbury at Timaru and Crauste had taken over the captaincy for what was expected to be a straightforward midweek fixture. Instead South Canterbury played like men inspired and the French tumbled to a 17–14 defeat. It was a rough match and fortunately the referee was Pat Murphy, one of New Zealand's best.

The penalty count favoured South Canterbury 17–3 (yes, Wellingtonians, they had lop-sided penalty counts even before the days of Steve Walsh!), and afterwards even the French did not try to excuse their savage tactics.

With 16 minutes left, Crauste was involved in a regrettable incident. After referee Murphy had turned his back, and several seconds after the whistle, Crauste punched Ted Smith on the jaw. Smith sagged to the ground and the players huddled around in concern. ('It was my fault,' Smith said later. 'I dropped my guard.') The incident, though missed by the referee, occurred in plain view of the spectators.

Suddenly out of the crowd marched quiet, retiring Mrs Marsden, who had for 35 years been an ardent rugby enthusiast. Bareheaded, fur-coated and utterly indignant, she marched up to Crauste, using a walking stick to help her mobility. She raised her right hand and punched him on the back as hard as she could. Then, still clutching her walking stick, she turned and stomped back to her seat as thousands watching roared with laughter. 'I didn't see a soul or think what I was doing,' she later explained. 'I just went out there to retaliate for what was done to that poor boy. I hit him hard, but I don't think it hurt. I think he got a bit of a shock, though.'

Mrs Marsden, who attended the match with her husband Rex, two boys Joe and Pye, and a nephew, Stu Birtles, added in her defence: 'It was not good for young boys to see that sort of play.'

Two policemen moved onto the ground to escort Hilda away, later declining to charge her because they felt that to have taken any action would have been ridiculous. Mrs Marsden died in 1988. For 27 years she had been 'the woman who hit the Frenchman'.

50. Pride and passion — the haka

The All Blacks' pre-game ritual

It has become fashionable these days to say the haka is overdone, that it has lost its impact through constant repetition. Let me say right now that I am a fan of the haka, but only when it is performed with meaning and emotion. In certain circumstances, it can be very moving for a New Zealander to watch a haka. By a haka, I mean the version that Wayne Shelford gave to the All Blacks, full of passion and really laying down a challenge to the opposition. Others, such as Steve McDowell, Taine Randell and John Timu have picked up the lead from Shelford and led the All Black haka with the same feeling.

I like to see a haka that is meaningful, not the 'white man's haka' of the 1970s and before. These were little more than exhibitions, a bit of a giggle, something to amuse the locals. They were not done well and generally some of the players looked embarrassed to be doing them.

Not any more. It's not only the Maori and Polynesian players who do a great haka. Sean Fitzpatrick used to get right into the mood and his haka repertoire was notable for the tongue-poking and facial expressions. Shelford told me: 'When I got into the All Blacks in 1985, a lot of players didn't want to do the haka. They asked Hika Reid to sort it out. I watched Hika taking a session and said, "If you're not going to do this properly, don't do it at all, because all

Hika Reid . . . was asked to 'sort out' the haka.

News Media Auckland

There were few more inspiring sights than Buck Shelford leading the haka. Here he gives it his all against Wales in 1988.

you're doing is embarrassing the Maori community." So we went to a team vote and decided to do it properly.

'From that time, in Argentina in 1985, the team started doing it correctly and with more passion. The stance became more correct and so did the hand movements. We had the likes of John Gallagher and Gary Whetton getting down and doing it correctly and knowing more about it. It is a war dance, a war chant and it's got to be done with pride. At the end of the day, guys like Gallagher and Terry Wright loved doing it because it made them feel so powerful and it was just that last edge before starting to play the game. A lot of teams over the years became very scared of the haka. We used it as in intimidatory sort of force, and it did work.'

The haka is a very New Zealand thing and, done well, can be so aggressive and have such clear intent that it brings out a strand of aggression in the opposition. It is quite difficult to stand impassively and watch a haka being performed and not register any emotion.

Until 1975, the All Blacks performed haka on the field only overseas. Even then, they didn't do them very often. Early touring teams, such as the 1905 Originals and 1924–25 Invincibles, were repeatedly asked to perform their haka and did so on trains, during evening functions, at factories they visited and the like. There are even references to the Natives team of 1888–89 performing their 'famous war cry'.

Into the 1970s, to see the All Blacks doing a haka before a match was still something of a rarity. Ian Kirkpatrick's 1972–73 touring team did only one pre-match haka on their 32-match, four-month tour of Britain and France, and that was before the Barbarians match at Cardiff. In 1976, Andy Leslie's All Blacks did just one haka, before the final test. The Cavaliers team elected not do the haka during their controversial visit to South Africa in 1986, at least until they got to Johannesburg for the final test. There, perhaps feeling they would need everything going for them, they performed their only tour haka. It wasn't enough — they lost that final match 24–10.

The first haka the All Blacks did at home, as far as I know, was before the wet-weather test against Scotland at Eden Park in 1975. It went down very well, though it took another decade before the haka became a regular sight at test matches in New Zealand. It is now impossible to imagine the All Blacks playing a test without doing their haka.

It has been interesting to watch the reaction of opponents. David Campese, the great Wallaby winger, sometimes walked down the field to his own goal posts and leaned against them, throwing a ball in the air to himself. It was a show designed to portray indifference. Campese explained: 'I respect the haka, but every individual's different. I've never been a person to stand there and watch it, because it intimidated me a bit. I did my own thing while they were doing the haka. I got letters from New Zealanders saying how dare I not respect it, but I didn't have to stand there. We decided that if a player wanted to stand there and eyeball them, great, but if you wanted to do something else, it was up to the individual.'

In his book *One Step Ahead*, Wallaby coach Rod Macqueen told of a plan he devised to combat the haka, which, he felt, was giving the All Blacks an advantage going into a match. Macqueen decided that after the haka, the Australian players would then form a huddle for perhaps 30 seconds of final instructions and re-commitment. The idea was that it would then be the Australians who were setting the tempo in the moments before the test began. The coach thought the tactic worked well and kept it throughout his time in charge of the Wallabies.

The aggressive nature of the modern haka has led to some near confrontations. Before the 1995 World Cup final, Jonah Lomu was throwing himself into the haka. Big Springbok lock Kobus Weise edged across and stood directly in front of Jonah, in a show of open defiance.

In 1989, Wayne Shelford and Mike Brewer led the New Zealand haka against Ireland at Dublin's Lansdowne Road and were confronted by Willie Anderson almost frothing at the mouth. Anderson gathered the Irish players around him, linking arms and edged towards Shelford. Referee Sandy MacNeill, fearing there might soon be some shoving and pushing, stepped forward ready to separate them.

At Old Trafford in 1997, referee Peter Marshall did actually separate Norm Hewitt and Richard Cockerill, the opposing hookers. Hewitt really looked the part of the warrior and Cockerill, never one to take a backward step, seemed to be going out of

John Timu was capable of leading a 'blood-curdling' haka for the All Blacks.

his way to be as confrontational as possible.

Perhaps the most stunning haka I have heard was at Agen in 1990 when John Timu led the All Black haka against the French Barbarians. It was a concrete stadium, about three-quarters full, and the French people had pushed a microphone in front of Timu, whose rendition of the haka therefore reverberated around the ground on the PA system. It was blood-curdling.

It must have been chilling to be confronted by the haka for the first time. Gavin Hastings, the Scotland fullback and captain, once explained to me: 'The first time, I thought, "What the hell's doing on here?" Half the Maori guys' eyeballs were popping out. I remember facing Inga Tuigamala one day and his eyes were popping out and I fixed my eyes on him. There was no way I was going to blink. Then at the end he jumped up, and when he came back down, he winked at me and we both laughed.'

The All Blacks made a big impression with their haka at the Olympic Stadium, Tokyo in 1987. It was pelting with rain and the All Blacks performed a particularly stirring rendition of the haka, then ran across to the opposite side of the ground to do one for the Japanese people.

> ## Perhaps the most stunning haka I have heard was at Agen in 1990 when John Timu led the All Black haka against the French Barbarians.

During my time covering the New Zealand sevens team, the haka has increased in significance. New Zealanders saw the magnificent haka the sevens team did after winning the gold medal at the Kuala Lumpur Commonwealth Games in 1998. Their pride in the silver fern was very evident.

These days, whenever the sevens team win a tournament on their circuit, they do a haka to each of the four corners of the ground. They are invariably incredibly well received by the crowds.

The haka used to vary from team to team. You'd see a group of New Zealanders at King's Cross, Sydney, or in Hyde Park, London doing a haka and chances are it was one they'd learned at school. These days, though, the haka that seems to be performed throughout the world is the *Ka mate!* haka, first performed by Te Rauparaha in the 19th century and popularised in modern times by the All Blacks. Most true All Black fans know it and are proud of it and are all too ready to perform it.

One of the special days of the haka was in 1996 before the All Blacks–Western Samoa test match, at McLean Park, Napier. There had been an arrangement made beforehand that the two teams' haka would be performed consecutively, not simultaneously. The New Zealand side duly set about their haka, only to discover the Samoans immediately bursting into theirs. The hackles rose on the back of the neck that day, listening to the two teams' haka being performed at the same time, with total vehemence. Truly, this was a case of each team laying down a challenge to the other.

One-way traffic

Imagine the All Blacks and the Wallabies playing a test that produced 60 points, all at one end of the field. Impossible, you'd think, but it happened at Carisbrook in 1997.

The All Blacks were on fire in the first half and by the interval led 36–0, having scored three tries, including a brilliant effort by Christian Cullen. Carlos Spencer had kicked the rest of the points, three conversions and five penalties, courtesy of the almost non-stop whistle of referee Joel Dumé of France.

It seemed like New Zealand would chalk up a record victory, but in the second half the All Blacks went off the boil and the Australians fought back, as they always do. Stephen Larkham (2), Joe Roff and Ben Tune scored tries and the Australians tallied 24 unanswered points.

So that was it: 60 points scored and all at one end. The odd thing was that it was a crisp, clear day in Dunedin, with little wind. The weather was not really a factor. The turnaround in fortunes can be put down only to New Zealand taking their foot off the pedal at the same time as Australia regrouped and increased their intensity.

51. A cell of a night for Joe and Andy

The jailing of Stanley and Earl

Quite apart from the infamous Keith Murdoch incident of 1972, All Blacks on tour in Britain have run foul of the law at least twice during my time of covering rugby.

In 1979, Marlborough winger Brian Ford was fined £10 for assault after a scuffle in an Edinburgh nightclub. Graham Mourie's All Blacks had been invited to visit a disco free one evening. The next night, Ford returned, but this time the bouncer turned ugly, aggressively telling Ford he had to pay. There was a bit of pushing and shoving and the result of the incident was that Ford was charged with assault, and had to pay the small fine.

The incident could have been blown up, but wasn't, mainly because of the way it was handled by manager Russ Thomas. In contrast to the 1972 Murdoch affair, when there was a gross overreaction from officials, Thomas stayed calm and in control. He called a press conference for the New Zealand media on tour, explained what had happened, and asked that reports of the nightclub affair not be blown out of proportion.

Ford, he said, was a good tourist, had learned from his mistake, and would be staying on the tour. The incident was quickly put behind everyone.

Ten years later, All Blacks Joe Stanley and Andy Earl found themselves in a prison cell in Llanelli after a scuffle with two Welshmen who seemed determined to cause trouble.

The All Blacks were back at the Stradey Park Hotel celebrating their hard-fought 11–0 win over Llanelli, mixing with some fairly disappointed local supporters. One man got involved in a slanging match with Earl and blew smoke in his face. That seemed the end of it. Earl left the bar and headed for his room. Stanley followed him soon after.

When Stanley reached the restricted part of the hotel where only house guests were permitted, he found the smoker from the bar was belting Earl, who said later he

News Media Auckland

News Media Auckland

Andy Earl (left) and Brian Ford . . . two All Blacks from separate tours who were involved in run-ins with the law.

had been hit from behind. The pair were still grappling when they crashed through two sets of doors and ended up outside. It became a serious fight, for the man who was attacking Earl was big and determined. Earl was having to fight for his life. Then the smoker's brother joined in, also hitting Earl. Stanley grabbed the second man and another fight was breaking out when big Gary Whetton arrived. At that point the two Welshmen thought enough was enough and scarpered.

But that was far from the end of the matter. At 5am the next morning, Stanley and Earl were woken by All Black manager John Sturgeon and a Llanelli detective and told complaints of assault had been made against them. The two players and the manager were taken to Llanelli police station. While the Welshmen were being questioned, the All Blacks were put in a cell, where they remained for a couple of hours.

The All Blacks were then asked for their side of the story. A key point was that the scuffle had broken out in a part of the hotel the Welshmen had no right to be. A couple of days later it was decided not to proceed with any charges.

Over the next few days parts of the story emerged slowly. 'All Blacks in prison' sounded like a juicy story. Manager Sturgeon would have been better advised to copy Russ Thomas' tactics and be upfront with the media, rather than remain silent and hope the matter blew over. In the absence of an explanation from the manager, some imaginations ran wild until the full story finally emerged.

52. Baabaas' black sheep
The Brewer-Barry Affair

One of the more outrageous All Black selections took place during the 1993 tour of Scotland and England. Mike Brewer, who was ruled out of the tour after a battle with injury that season, accompanied the team for all but the first week or two. He was travelling as the Marketing Manager of Canterbury International. Brewer was a close friend of coach Laurie Mains, and was a senior All Black.

Seeing Brewer training with the All Blacks each day lifted a few eyebrows, but it was what happened near the end of the tour that really raised the hackles.

The team ran into a slight problem over the last three matches because of an injury to loose forward Paul Henderson. The situation was exacerbated by a suspension, imposed within the team, on Jamie Joseph, for stomping on halfback Kyran Bracken during the England test.

There was still good loose forward cover, with both John Mitchell and Liam Barry among the 'dirt-trackers' who had been unable to break into the top side. This seemed an ideal opportunity for one of them, probably Barry, who was a flanker like Henderson, whereas Mitchell was a specialist No 8.

Instead Mains decided to bring in Brewer, who was named as a reserve for the England test, and again for the final tour match, against the Barbarians at Cardiff. When Blair Larsen hurt his ankle during the Barbarians game, Brewer jogged out onto the field. Skipper Sean Fitzpatrick, beaming widely, went over to Brewer to shake his hand, and then the game continued.

The selection of Brewer caused an outcry back home. Not only did Brewer get to claim $4000 as part of the tour payment handout, but his selection was seen as a snub to Barry, who came from a proud rugby family — his father and grandfather had been All Blacks, and his selection meant the Barrys were the first three-generation All Black family.

Both Mains and Brewer justified the selection in their biographies. They

Liam Barry (left) and Mike Brewer were the central figures in the Barbarians 'scandal' in 1993.

pointed out that the New Zealand Rugby Union chairman Eddie Tonks, tour manager Neil Gray, selector Earle Kirton and captain Sean Fitzpatrick had all been party to the decision.

On the team's return home, Tonks said he had not been happy with Brewer's promotion and Gray distanced himself from the decision. Mains did concede that while Tonks went along with the Brewer selection, he did express misgivings and was only lukewarm on it.

Mains said that using Barry was not a feasible option because he had been brought along on the tour just to develop him as a player, and that he did not have the physical strength to handle the big opposition loose forwards. The All Blacks were able to officially draft Brewer into the touring squad by using him as a replacement for the injured back Matthew Cooper.

Mains later pointed out the decision to go for Brewer was a democratic one, made by the entire tour management team. This may well have been so, but it was a poor one, and the New Zealand public knew it, to judge by the outrage it caused back home. Mains himself did not help matters when, after the Barbarians match, he was interviewed by my fellow TVNZ commentator Grant Nisbett. Grant mentioned that the media back home were making a storm out of the Brewer issue, and Mains replied that he didn't care what the public thought. Comments like that never go down well.

I thought the decision to draft Brewer was a terrible snub to a hard-working All

Black like Liam Barry. The 1994 *Rugby Almanack* summed it up with these words: 'The introduction of Mike Brewer to the reserves for the England international ahead of Liam Barry and John Mitchell, two fit loose forwards who were members of the touring party, was an insult to these players, and one of the worst selection decisions in All Black history. We have not spoken to one rugby follower who approved of the management's decision.'

At the time it was difficult to get a read on the reaction within the team. The players tended to remain loyal to Mains publicly, though I did detect resentment and anger at the decision. This was confirmed just recently with the release of Norm Hewitt's book, *Gladiator*, in which he said the Brewer affair contradicted the All Black camp talk about sacrifice and loyalty and sticking by your mates.

Hewitt had no time for Brewer personally, feeling he paraded his seniority and exhibited an arrogance that undermined the All Blacks as a team unit. 'When he was called into the ABs, I was pissed off', said Hewitt. 'The problem was that he was Laurie's boy — they went way back together at Otago — and All Black coaches do play favourites. Liam had been playing OK — not brilliant, but definitely OK. He was young, it was his first tour, no one else had gone much out of the way to help him — anyway, the next thing Mike Brewer is in the reserves and neither Liam nor John Mitchell are anywhere.'

The fact that for his few minutes of rugby Brewer then became entitled to, and claimed, a share of the All Black team fund, accumulated through such things as the sale of tickets, income from speaking engagements on tour and promotional activity income, rankled even further on Hewitt and some other All Blacks.

All in all, it was an unsatisfactory affair. I accept that Mains acted in what he felt were the best interests of his team, and that Brewer played only after being assured the selection had been okayed by all and sundry. But it showed a poor lapse of judgment all around. Barry, a very approachable young man, finished his career having played 10 matches for New Zealand, including one test, against France in 1995. The following year he took up a contract in Japan. He was just 25 and was not seen again in New Zealand until he reappeared for the 2001 NPC season, playing for North Harbour.

Despite his unique family rugby background, he is today recalled more for his part in the Brewer affair than for his own rugby.

53. Parc de Punch-up

Was our Bishop bashed?

Television audiences at home are being treated royally these days by technicians who plough ahead with advances that keep them right up with the play they are watching. The electronic advances have been staggering. Already, in the space of a little over a decade, the bulbous microphones that were suspended around a rugby referee's neck to relay his match calls have been miniaturised to a tiny lapel device kept in place by wearing a transmitting battery the size of a matchbox.

And whereas the early calls that came from the referee were only heard by the TV commentators, now referees can be heard — coughs, wheezing, warts and all — by anyone sitting around their television sets at home or watching live at the sports arena.

As an aside, this has brought about a change in style from referees. No longer do the players hear the salty language that was once used by some referees. In modern times, the ref has closed down any inclination to swear at the players lest he be criticised by the watching public, or worse, by his refereeing assessor listening in by earplug, too!

One former New Zealand test referee of the 1970s would hardly have survived in today's TV-and-microphone era. His language while controlling a game was of that kind that would have made a sailor blush. Similarly, what would the public have thought of the top World Cup referee of the 1990s whose words (going only to the TV and radio commentators) were so vulgar that they would not have impressed the South Wales Police, for whom he worked when he wasn't on refereeing duty?

So things have sure changed. This upgrading of refereeing gear means it is unlikely there will be a repeat of the incident that scarred a World Cup game in Paris in 1991.

It was after the World Cup quarterfinal between France and England. The game had been controlled by New Zealand's No. 1 ref, Dave Bishop, and had been a particularly violent affair. There were several outbreaks of scrapping and fighting. At one point, the game threatened to run out of control. Bishop tried his hardest to quell things and did a fine job in an electric atmosphere.

News Media Auckland

1991 French World Cup coach Daniel Dubroca.

High up in the towering grandstands of the Parc des Princes, the various teams of TV commentators from about a dozen different stations and nations had heard Bishop's refereeing calls through the match (including a high-pitched squeal of excitement as he ran onto the field — 'Hey Keith, say hi to all the family back home watching in Wanaka!').

There was an enormous amount of pride and ambition at stake in that quarterfinal. England and France had both started the game with high hopes of going right through and winning the World Cup. In the end, England got home 19–10 in a nerve-janglingly close contest.

In other areas of the grandstands, the stress and strain must have been having an effect as well. The French coach was Daniel Dubroca, the former captain, who just four years before had suffered the massive frustration of having led his country to a loss to the All Blacks in the first World Cup final, at Eden Park. To be part of a losing team in a World Cup four years on, especially on home turf, and after a match with so many controversial incidents was too, too much for him. He leapt from his seat and bounded down the stairs . . .

At the end of the game, most of the commentators pulled off their headsets, the ones through which they had been listening first-hand to the rugged contest, and raced downstairs to obtain the breathless quotes from players and officials involved in the dramatic encounter.

For some reason, I chose to stay upstairs and keep my headset on. Thus I could hear our man Bish as he came off the field, encountering all manner of pushing, shoving and shouting. I was able to eavesdrop on his friendly reaction to a number of the traditional 'thanks ref' calls he was receiving (mostly from England players, I supposed, according to my hearing anyway).

But then I heard another noise — the strangled sound of Bishop under attack. Suddenly my ears were filled with the offensive sound of scrapes, ruffling and scuffling. These new sounds were accompanied by throttled protests and angry yells.

The angry shouting came mixed with a strangled French accent voicing what was obviously very angry disapproval. By the tone of what I was hearing and by Bishop's own sudden shouts of protest, it could easily be deduced that the referee was the target of not just a verbal attack, but a physical one, too.

Sitting way up high in the Parc des Princes, this was a new experience for me. We

New Zealand referee Dave Bishop.

News Media Auckland

had seen attacks at rugby grounds before, but we had never 'heard' one. It was a new outrage of the techno era of the 1990s.

Of course, we now had concern for our fellow New Zealander. We all knew Bish and admired his refereeing talent greatly. He was a good bloke. One of us, so to speak. To hear him being the victim of such an extreme display of anger was a great worry.

Several of us TVNZ types dashed downstairs and made it through the numerous security barriers in place. We had other motives, it must be said. This sounded like a bloody good story, too! We eventually made it to Mr Bishop's dressing-room door in the stadium corridor just along from the players' rooms. We thumped on the door. We thumped again.

In the end, cheery old Dave emerged, smiling and as bright as ever. Hair combed, shirt and blazer now neatly in place. 'Scrap? What scrap?' he asked, grinning in his usual relaxed manner. All he offered was a shrug of the shoulders and a dismissal of the suggestion of a problem. Despite the fact that I told him I had heard him get attacked, he wanted no truck with an advance of that particular story, unsavoury though it sounded, into the media.

But it came anyway. Dubroca had apparently vented his spleen at the New Zealand referee as he walked towards his dressing room after the game. The Frenchman's actions were noted by a number of officials. The previously taciturn Dubroca alarmed everybody with his discovery of new depths of the English language as he abused our Dave for the way he had controlled the game.

Dubroca's emotional outburst stemmed, of course, from the fact that his team had lost a close contest in a stadium packed with home fans.

It was a strange old incident that one. Those few of us upstairs who had chosen to stay tuned to this new-fangled hearing device after the game became part of a strange piece of rugby history. These days, a decade on, everyone anywhere in the world can hear what the referee says, or what is said to him. But back in 1991, it was all new. Never before in a World Cup match had anyone been able to lend an ear, like listening through a glass at a wall, to those areas of the game that had previously been off limits to everyone, and especially, of course, to those of the dreaded news media.

54. Prop cops unfair media caning

Billy Bush hysteria in '76

While searching through some old clippings in researching this book, I came across many gems from the past. The story on this page, 25 years old, qualifies to be retained under the heading of 'outrageous' because it contains some of the silliest words ever seriously written and attached to the reporting of an All Black tour personality.

Of the millions of words written by thousands of correspondents, was there any more inane reporting by one man than that directed in this piece towards All Black Billy Bush on the 1976 tour of South Africa?

Some background first. Billy was a hugely popular member of that New Zealand team. He delighted the black and coloured populace of South Africa with the aggressive and combative way he faced the largely white opposing South African teams. Billy took no backward steps. The more aggressive Bill was, the more the non-whites in that apartheid time loved him.

It was a combination of his popularity and his warlike approach that eventually antagonised several of the South African touring news media, a media that was, of course, always of the white race in those days.

At one point one reporter, Paul Irwin, decided he had had enough. He was going to write a piece about Billy Bush which was going to condemn Bill for all time as not only a rugby player — but as a boxer as well.

Irwin's pièce de résistance came a couple of days after Billy had been in a bit of a dust-up in the game against a team with the unlikely name of North-West Cape/South West Africa. It was far from the first time on tour this had happened.

Irwin was obviously upset at what he had seen. But you might agree he actually struggled to write something that was going to dismiss Billy for all time. Rather than

News Media Auckland

Billy Bush (3) came in for more than his fair share of attention from South African refs in 1976. Here Piet Robbertse admonishes him in the Northern Transvaal match.

rubbish him for fighting on the rugby field, Irwin chose instead to dissect Bill's ability as a boxer. From the grandstand the strangeness (and silliness) of his report flowed thus:

'As one of rugby's knuckle men, given to throwing his fists at the slightest provocation — or even without it — the All Blacks' bearded and belligerent Billy Bush figures low in my ratings. Actually I reckon he fails completely to throw his weight. Having seen Bush in quite a few punch-ups on the current All Blacks tour, I can report that his fundamental weakness is his ability to get leverage into his punches. Like every boxing novice, he not only leads with his right hand, but throws his punches off his right foot as well, which is the wrong one.

'Besides making purists shudder, since a right lead leaves Billy the Beard wide open to a left hook if the other chap knows his business, [Billy's] clumsy method is about as effective as swatting flies. There is simply no weight behind his punches.'

So folks, you get the drift of Paul Irwin's silly stuff? His column actually raged on in total for 15 paragraphs under the heading 'Bush Throws his Weight About'. And it was published among the rugby summaries and reports.

I suppose back in South Africa in 1976, I must have felt I would get some mileage some time out of keeping the clipping. Now I can put it back into my filing system under S for Silly.

55. When Mum was swept off her feet

60,000 Athletic supporters

In these days of corporate boxes and luxury seating at the super flash rugby stadia springing up all over the country it is not wrong surely to hark back to simpler times. Like 1959, when the British Isles team was touring New Zealand. In every town or city, they received a rapturous welcome, and record crowds flocked to see them play.

It was a tradition outside some of the bigger grounds in New Zealand's major cities for the really keen fans to position themselves near to the entry gates at least 24 hours before kick-off. That meant an overnight sleep during some sharp New Zealand winters nights, but somehow a tradition built among the keenest rugby fans. After a sometimes restless night, the gates would be pulled open by officials mid-morning and a mad scramble would follow with those positioned closest to the turnstiles able to sprint to the best seats on the open terraces. None of this modern habit of arriving late after having coffee downtown.

There is one story of a group of young people who camped outside Athletic Park in 1959 hoping for a good position for the second test the next day. One of the lads offered a real advantage over other groups nearby. His mum lived just down the street.

At regular intervals during the night she brought to the huddled gang of friends such delicacies as tea, coffee, soup and the like. The waiting people were very grateful.

The next day the gates opened and the gang of friends raced to a perfect spot on Wellington's famous Western Bank. Their overnight vigil had been well worthwhile. They wondered how they could repay the kindness of their surrogate mum, who had allowed them to wake so fresh and sustained.

As game time approached, the old ground became completely packed. Indeed that test match day became famous in Wellington rugby history as the occasion when

Athletic Park's famous Western Bank.

Athletic Park was too small for the numbers who wanted to get in. It was the only time this had happened. A furore was created outside as the gates were closed on the disappointed fans who had not slept out. So they clawed at the wire fence and were amazed to see how easy it came down.

There was nothing to stop them walking in for a free look at a rugby test. So thousands did. It was estimated that more then 60,000 watched the test that beautiful winter's day. Not bad for a ground which normally held a shade over 50,000.

News Media Auckland

Our friends in the good position high on Western Bank did not know of the kerfuffle outside the gates, nor indeed did they care. That was until one of the group spotted the caring mother walking along the touchline *inside* the ground. She had apparently walked from home to see the crowds and seeing the fence was down had walked straight in, too. She was spotted without a seat directly in front of the vast, teeming embankment.

The lads tried to catch her attention. It was in vain until there was a momentary pause in the din, just enough hush for the cry of 'Mum!' to be heard down in front. Immediately hundreds were drawn to the plight of the lady as she stood at the bottom of the bank and waved. The group of friends waved back, but could do little else, as the aisles were jam-packed. There would be no way she could get up to join them.

So what did the resourceful people of that time do to bring together Mum and her brood? Some creative blokes at the front of the bank reached out and swooped Mum off her feet. They then raised her high over their heads and began to pass her up over the crowd, almost a 1959 version of Crocodile Dundee. Higher and higher she went still clutching her handbag and her dignity, until she reached the boys waiting at the perfect spot half way to the top. There, she was allowed to alight and watch the test from the best position one could ever have wished for.

It seems to me to be a perfect reminder of the spirit of rugby that existed in those days. And a reminder of how family support was repaid to people who helped in those far-off wonderful rugby days.

56. Now this was a bad day

All Blacks lose two on one day

To the modern breed of rugby follower, October 31, 1999 takes some beating as the nightmare day to end all nightmare days. The All Blacks, leading France 24–10 in their World Cup semi-final, crumbled and lost 43–31, a result that stunned New Zealand. That inglorious day cast into the shadows even August 29, 1998, when Australia beat New Zealand 19–14, so consigning the All Blacks to their fifth consecutive defeat.

But I've got news for rugby fans depressed about those two grim days. There has been worse. September 3, 1949 was, by my estimation, the worst day in All Black history.

On this day, the mighty All Blacks lost not once, but twice.

It happened like this:

New Zealand was touring South Africa, which took the top 30 players out of commission. From those left behind (which included Maoris Johnny Smith, Vince Bevan and Ben Couch — all ineligible for the South African tour), a New Zealand team was chosen to play two home tests against Australia.

The first was played at Athletic Park. New Zealand, captained by Smith, the wonderful centre, also included fullback Jack Kelly, whom most rugby writers felt should have been in South Africa as Bob Scott's understudy, promising lock Tiny White, and future All Black captain Bob Stuart. There were other good players, some of whom had been part of the famous Kiwis Army side.

But the New Zealanders were no match for Trevor Allan's strong Australian combination and lost 11–6, having trailed 11–0 at halftime. A loss to Australia. That made it a bad day for New Zealanders.

Action between New Zealand and South Africa from the third test of the 1949 series at Durban. The All Blacks lost this match 3–9 to complete an ignominious double of two test losses in one day.

Worse was to follow when that night New Zealand met South Africa in the third test, at the Kingsmead Ground, Durban, a match New Zealand had to win to keep the series alive. New Zealanders awoke in the middle of the night to tune in to Winston McCarthy's crackling commentary of the game. They were hoping for some good news, but it wasn't to be. New Zealand scored the only try, to centre Morrie Goddard, but Okey Geffin kicked three penalties and South Africa won 9–3.

Losses to Australia and South Africa on the same day. Imagine how fervent New Zealand rugby fans felt about that!

57. Kiwi Wallaby sent packing

The sending home of Ross Cullen

Memories of a major New Zealand rugby scandal came flooding back in 2001 when the former All Black Keith Murdoch emerged into the public spotlight again. Murdoch had been sent home from the 1972–73 All Black tour following a late-night incident in a Cardiff hotel. He chose to go into a self-imposed exile, living in virtual anonymity in the Australian outback.

But those who thought big Keith was the first New Zealander to suffer such dishonour on an international rugby tour are incorrect. That distinction fell instead to a New Zealand-born, Taumarunui-raised member of the 1966 Wallabies team. Not many New Zealanders will recall the headlines and fuss that surrounded the dismissal of the ex-King Country and Queensland player, Ross Cullen.

Back in the 1960s the interchange of players between New Zealand and Australia was not nearly as common as it is today. So far in the new millennium three players of Maori extraction — Glenn Panaho, Jeremy Paul and Manuel Edmonds — have readily been awarded Australian rugby colours. But with travel across the Tasman not as easily available in previous times, such appearances in the Wallabies by New Zealanders were rare. Ross Cullen was one of the exceptions.

The 1966–67 Australian team was set for a grand world tour. The team was captained by the great prop, John Thornett. The 30-man team set off in early October with 34 games ahead of them in Britain, Ireland, Canada and France. In those days, there being no such thing as test rugby representatives from ACT, the touring party was made up of three players from Victoria, six from Queensland and the remaining 21 from New South Wales. This was a reasonable representation of the strengths of Australian rugby at the time.

One of the Queenslanders was Ross Cullen. He was billed as a tough 26-year-old hooker, a tradesman by occupation with the Brisbane Harbour and Marine Development. It was expected he would appear only in the second-tier fixtures on the tour, as the top hooker was the 25-test veteran Peter Johnson.

Those were the days of true amateur rugby; only eight of the party were receiving any pay at all from their home employers and, of those, all were only on half or a third of their normal wages. The manager was a hard-nosed Sydneysider, Bill McLaughlin. He was happy to vigorously propound the amateur ethos of rugby that prevailed at the time, even insisting his players were not permitted to receive free cigarettes that were traditionally offered to touring teams in Britain in those pre-awareness times. The weekly allowance for each team member was £3-10-0.

Members of the 1966 Wallabies tour management pictured upon their arrival in London. From left, manager Bill McLaughlin, coach Alan Roper and captain John Thornett.

McLaughlin also demanded that his team play their tour games on some sort of lofty level of fair play. He declared that he wanted no truck with rough play and raised eyebrows when he assembled the media in Gosforth before the first game and announced that he would 'not tolerate dirty play of any kind. If I see a player do anything, whether the referee sees or not, that brings discredit to the team, [that player] will be expelled from consideration of playing for four games'.

McLaughlin went on to add that the heavy penalty would still take effect even if his player was provoked into a reaction. 'A hard tackle can be just as effective as a punch,' he said. 'In fact, it shakes every bone in his body, and not just his jaw.'

That announcement had the British press rushing to their typewriters. Here was a manager virtually declaring himself judge and jury of any incident on the rugby field. Previously, and until the arrival of television replays, it was a principle of the game that the referee was the sole judge, not a manager sitting up in a grandstand.

Whether such an imposition by McLaughlin put the Wallaby players into a state of excessive nerves or restraint is not known, but they promptly crashed to a 14–17 defeat at Gosforth, against the North-Eastern Counties. The team's first victory followed, against Midland Counties in Leicester. In those two games the newspaper reports show no record of any untoward incidents.

Cullen had made his debut in the first game and Johnson had played hooker in the second. Cullen was given his second chance in the third game, against Oxford

Ross Cullen.

University at the Iffley Road Ground.

This turned out to be a bright, exciting game played on a sunny day, and Australia came back bravely to win 11–9. Again, there were no apparent incidents of fighting in the game, though one newspaper report did make reference to the Irish forward Ollie Waldron having 'irked several of the Australian forwards during the game with his vigorous play'. Waldron was described in the same report as being a 'tough, ruthless forward . . . who had played second row for Ireland'. In this game he was propping for Oxford. Those words pertaining to the way Waldron played the game were to come back and haunt the match, and Ross Cullen's career, within the next 24 hours.

It seems that there was more to it when Waldron, the tough guy, was assisted off the field with seven minutes to go. As he left the field he was seen to be holding his ear. Soon allegations of foul play towards Waldron were being levelled at one of the Australian forwards. It emerged that Waldron claimed to have had his left ear bitten by one of the Australians in a scrum late in the game, to the point where the ear was left hanging on only by its lobe.

McLaughlin swung into action. He went down into the Oxford dressing room, then emerged to talk to the press, who had heard whispers of an incident on the field. McLaughlin would only say then that he would be issuing a statement some time the next day.

Some 24 hours later the full story broke. McLaughlin made the following statement: 'As a result of an incident during the closing stages of the match against Oxford University I have decided one of my players cannot be relied upon to carry out the firm decision of the Australian touring team management to play good, clean rugby during the tour of the British Isles. I have therefore made the reluctant decision that this player, R. Cullen, will return at once to Australia.' The statement ended with McLaughlin adding that he had the full support of his team coach Alan Roper and captain John Thornett.

It was a sensation. Cullen packed his bags and solemnly said farewell to each member of the team. Then, in scenes that were to be eerily repeated in the Keith Murdoch dismissal six years later, he departed the tour in a blaze of cameras clicking at London's Paddington station.

Cullen made few comments. All he said as the press crowded around was: 'This has all been very unfortunate. I accept the fact that I have been sent home. I don't want to say anything more.' Before he left London one other paper quoted him as saying that he 'did not want to ever play the game again'.

When Cullen arrived back in Sydney he also had a grim 'no comment' for local reporters before being driven away in a car accompanied by Australian rugby officials.

The repercussions over the Cullen incident were wide and deep. Among the reports of the time one stands out. One British paper called the Cullen style of play in the Oxford game 'a reflection on New Zealand's tough style of play'.

In Britain most of the broadsheet dailies came out in support of McLaughlin's action. The manager had given a lead to the rugby world, said one paper, which also asked that the rest of the expanding rugby world take note of McLaughlin's actions. It was also agreed in many papers that the onus was now on Britain, in particular, to clean up its own game as a result of the expulsion of the Wallaby. The style of the writing concerning the incident, so noble in its tone, seems almost quaint in the modern context of rugby play and reporting.

The British Press Association said: 'The Australian manager's action is deemed to have been one that British teams on this tour should now set an example to as well, and not provoke the Australians in any of the future games.'

Chris Lang in the *Daily Sketch* wrote: 'We must not provoke and incite these Australians.' Pat Marshall of the *Daily Express* wrote: 'Our players and officials must lean over backwards to ensure that the tourists get a straight fair deal from now on.'

But the jolly-old-school reaction from Fleet Street was not mirrored back in Australia. McLaughlin might have won plaudits on tour and from the conservative elements of the Australian Rugby Union, but at the grassroots level of Aussie rugby, there was much anger and resentment over Cullen's treatment. For the first time people spoke out strongly about the imposition of the no-retaliation rule on the Wallaby players on tour. Nobody liked it much. Australians then as now do not like taking punishment, unless they have a fair shot at dishing out some in return.

Within days of Cullen returning to Brisbane, his club side, Eastern Districts, unanimously re-elected him captain for the next season and the Queensland Rugby Union issued a statement in his defence. His Queensland coach, the former Wallaby captain Bill McLean, spoke out: 'Ross is a clean player, I can't make this decision out. If he did bite somebody he must have been severely provoked. A hooker has his arms bound in a scrum. If somebody is butting him and his props don't protect him there is not much he can do but bite, butt or kick back.

'In view of the fact that the match reports say the referee did nothing about the

Foul Play Charge Against Wallaby In Oxford Match

OXFORD, Oct. 26.—Allegations of foul play were made against an Australian forward following the Wallabies' 11-9 win over Oxford University today.

Oxford prop forward Ollie Waldron was led off the ground seven minutes from the finish with a badly-lacerated left ear. He needed stitches in the wound.

Later, the Australian manager, Mr. W. McLaughlin, said he would make a statement on the incident "some time tomorrow."

Not Named

No specific Australian player has been named as being connected with the incident.

Oxford University officials and players would not be drawn into open comment on the matter of Waldron's injury tonight, but team members were understood to have made the charge of foul play privately among

---

Row mounts over NZ rugby biter

LONDON (UPI), Saturday. — The row over Ross Cullen, the ex-New Zealand Rugby player who was banished from the touring Wallaby side and packed off home following an ear-biting incident, looks like developing into an international wrangle.

CULLEN BAN UPSETS WALLABIES' MORALE

N.Z. Press Association—Copyright

SWANSEA, Friday. — A heavy blanket of depression hung over the Australian Rugby Union team last night after the sending home of hooker Ross Cullen.

Ear-Biting Dismissal A 'Lead To Rugby World'

LONDON, Oct. 27.—The action of the Australian Rugby team manager (Mr. W. McLaughlin) in sending home the hooker Ross Cullen (see page 18) "throws out into the open and up for top-level argument the dirtiest play in the hardest contact game there is," Barry Newcombe wrote in the "Evening Standard" today.

ers, the spectators and the officials. But they carried on and would probably continue to do so until severe penalties —probably long-term or overall suspension—were imposed.

Newcombe said the problem in meting out punishment for Rugby offenders was to decide who was the aggressor and who the retaliator.

What McLaughlin had done

Not unexpectedly, the newspapers of the time had a field day after Ross Cullen was sent home from the Wallabies' tour.

Wallaby forward sent home

N.Z.P.A.-Reuter—Copyright

LONDON, Thursday. — A member of the touring Australian Rugby Union team, hooker Ross Cullen, 25, a New Zealander, has been sent home.

The decision came after an incident during the Wallabies' game against Oxford University yesterday when the opposing prop forward, Ollie Waldron, had the lobe of his left ear almost severed in a scrum.

The Australian manager, Bill McLaughlin, made the announcement to a meeting of the players today.

Soon afterwards Cullen left Oxford for London to join a flight back to Australia.

The Eastwood (New South Wales) hooker, Dick Taylor, will join the team in Britain.

Unprecedented

today and told him he was to be sent home.

The news was then broken to the other team members in an adjoining room, with Cullen present.

Each player solemnly shook hands with Cullen when they filed out. Cullen was not allowed to speak to the Press.

Cullen played one game for King County before leaving for Queensland two or three years ago.

A fast striker of the ball, he won a place in the touring side in the face of stern opposition from Taylor, his replacement.

Cullen played in the first

provocative football that Ollie Waldron had been playing during the whole game then the penalty on Cullen far outweighs the offence.'

At about the same time, the Wallabies had moved into Wales, where they lost a rugged match with the Cardiff club. According to one report, the Australians fell before a deluge of rough treatment, as they continued to heed their manager's no-violence call. Australian newspaper reports started to show resentment at how the Wallabies were being hamstrung. Said a Sydney sports editor: 'If Mr McLaughlin does not publicly withdraw his punishment edict against rough play by the Wallabies, members of his team can expect to be carried off in future games with fractured skulls.'

Indeed that almost happened after the Cardiff game. Brilliant halfback Ken Catchpole ended the game with his head swathed in a turban-like mass of bandages following the receipt of 10 stitches to a kick wound. The sturdy fullback, Jim Lenehan, was booted in the kidneys when he went down on a rolling ball. The referee spoke to a Welsh forward after that incident but no sending-off occurred. Wallaby flyhalf Phil Hawthorne was taken to hospital with a bruised lung after having spat blood throughout the second half. Four other players were so severely injured they were not available to play in the next game.

So where did it all end? And what happened to Ross Cullen? And, indeed, what happened to Bill McLaughlin and his honorable but hardly realistic pre-tour stance?

Cullen never played international rugby again. He issued a statement about the incident through his Brisbane solicitor. In it he detailed the aggressive 'boring in' scrummaging tactics of Waldron throughout the game; how he had warned him several times and indeed how he had nipped him several times on the ear with his teeth when the boring in underneath tactics from the Irishman continued. Cullen claimed that he had not been given a fair chance to air his version of the incident to McLaughlin. 'Until I was dismissed I was completely unaware that any action at all was being considered against me.'

Did the McLaughlin stance on behalf of clean rugby permeate into British rugby? Probably not, as British rugby has, in the years since, had as good or bad a record for rough play as any other place in the world. McLaughlin's Wallaby team plugged on, and while they had some excellent results (beating Wales and England), there were many losses. Not only did they fall to Scotland, Ireland and France, but in total they lost 14 games on tour. They had three draws and won only 17 times. Cullen claimed one of his Wallaby team-mates told him that after Cullen departed, 'while Bill McLaughlin was being patted on the back and called a great bloke, behind our backs they were laughing at us'.

The most curious end to this sensational incident came when the Wallabies returned home. For the first time, McLaughlin had to face the Australian media with their harder questions. It was four months after Cullen had been sent packing, but still the questions came thick and fast.

To the questioners McLaughlin made what was one of the most astounding claims of the whole story. Yes, he said, he had told his players before the tour they were ambassadors for Australia and that he would allow no punching from them in any game. 'But after a couple of games I told the boys they could punch back if they were hit.'

Confused? You ought to be. Isn't punching back retaliation? Australian rugby delegates were confused as well. They summed up what most of Australia thought and wrapped up the story by moving decisively to make their viewpoint clear on the performance of the leaders of the Wallaby tour.

The same day as the team came home the annual meeting of the New South Wales Rugby Union was held and McLaughlin was thrown off as the NSW delegate to the Australian Rugby Union board. At the same meeting Alan Roper, the touring team's coach, lost his place on a three-man ballot to retain the Australian coaching job.

Democracy had spoken, though it was little consolation to Ross Cullen.

Footnote: In 2001 while on a visit to Sydney, the 1972–73 All Black John Dougan (who remains one of my closest All Black friends) took me to The Rugby Club in Crane Place. While we shared a yarn or two with the locals I was introduced to Russ Tulloch, a loose forward from the 1966-67 Wallaby team. I hope as we chatted Russ was impressed with my knowledge of that tour. I had kept hundreds of clippings of that team's trip for 35 years but had never talked to anyone about them!

Russ confirmed that the Wallabies players on that tour were absolutely amazed and distraught when Ross Cullen was sent home after the Oxford University incident with Ollie Waldron. The Aussies were disappointed to say the least at the team management's heavy reaction. It was confirmed that from that point the team did not regard Mr McLaughlin or his managerial style highly.

Russ told me that through the 1970s and '80s most of the team had not seen Cullen at all. But when the team had a 30-year reunion in 1996, Cullen turned up and was a very welcome inclusion in the team's celebrations.

58. The mother of all tours
The 1888–89 Natives tour

New Zealanders with an eye to rugby history are understandably very proud of the Natives team of 1888–89. When John Mitchell took his All Black team overseas at the end of 2001, he had a contingent of 30 players and 13 support staff for five matches. The Natives, comprising 26 players and a manager, played 107 matches over a period of more than a year, playing in England, Scotland, Ireland, Wales, Australia and New Zealand. In addition, the Natives played eight Australian Rules matches during a three-week stay in Melbourne.

The Natives won 78 matches, drew six and lost 23, and drew large crowds. The team comprised almost all Maoris and played an attractive, physical brand of rugby.

But it wasn't always easy for them. They struck the British class system and had to put up with some superior and condescending attitudes. The *Daily Telegraph* wrote at one point: 'The Maoris have progressed since Captain Cook found the neatly tattooed ancestors of our visitors eating each other in the bush.'

In addition, they didn't always get kindly treated by referees. For instance, they opened their tour in October against Surrey County and Rowland Hill, secretary of the Rugby Football Union, refereed the game without a problem. Four months later Hill refereed the test against England, but this time the Natives had much cause for complaint.

Before halftime Hill awarded England two controversial tries, twice ignoring the fact that Natives players had touched down the ball in goal. Things got much worse in the second half.

Andrew Stoddart, who captained England at both cricket and rugby, dashed down the touchline and had his shorts torn in a desperate tackle by Tom Ellison. The players formed the customary huddle around Stoddart while he awaited a new pair of pants. In the meantime, the referee allowed play to continue and Frank Evershed picked up the ball and crossed the line unchallenged for a try that broke the Natives' resistance.

Team photo of those great rugby pioneers, the 1888–89 Natives.

Three of the visiting team walked off in protest and the match resumed with England playing 12 men. Not surprisingly, England won comfortably. The Rugby Football Union demanded an instant apology from the Natives, the demand coming from none other than Rowland Hill, who was wearing two hats quite comfortably.

The apology, when it was sent, was deemed inadequate and local officials threatened to cancel the rest of the tour by forbidding clubs to play the tourists. In the end, Edward McCausland wrote a second apology to Rowland Hill: 'I beg to apologise to the Rugby Union committee for the insults offered by my team to their officials on the field of play on Saturday last.'

The apology satisfied the Rugby Football Union, which was hardly surprising as it was dictated by none other than Rowland Hill.

The Natives enjoyed popularity throughout Britain, but apparently not from officialdom. When they returned to London late in the tour, they were ignored and there was no official send-off when they left in April 1889.

59. For autograph hunter, read photographer

It's the age of the digital camera

Many thousands of New Zealanders of all ages can reach onto the shelves of their homes and find on the curling pages of autograph books the scrawled signatures of their sporting heroes. For some people the collecting of signatures is a serious obsession and some collectors have literally thousands of famous people's own version of their name written down.

An appearance in public by any highly profiled sports stars can mean battling through a wave of jostling fans, who are thrusting books and pens at them. Many sports stars cope admirably with this, showing remarkable patience, signing over and over every day. Others consider autographs a problem and deal with their public's adulation in only a very cursory way.

In the new millennium I believe there is now a new scourge for sports stars to cope with. While there are still thousands of autograph books in the world I did notice while on the 2001 All Black tour of Britain and Argentina a new weapon of ammunition

Fotopress/NZRFU

Jonah Lomu . . . major target for autograph hunters and digital paparazzi.

for ravenous sports fans to carry. The thrusting, pushing fan now comes armed with a digital camera.

For Jonah Lomu, Tana Umaga and Anton Oliver in particular, life on the 2001 tour was constantly halted while the young, and not so young, asked, and sometimes demanded, a photograph be taken with their new gear.

Usually the camera operators these days work in pairs. First the famous player must be stopped, which I am proud to say the New Zealand rugby stars on tour generally did. Then the player had to pose with fan number one while the second fan became camera operator. That pic having been made, the fans then quickly asked if they could change places and a second pic was then taken.

This sounds simple enough and can be achieved in just a few seconds perhaps. But given the rising number of people in the world who own the new cameras, there will be many new types of stoppages for sports stars to cope with in the future. The digital camera is only half of the story.Within minutes the photos taken can be rushed home, or back to the office, and emailed to friends anywhere in the world.

Jonah Lomu, in particular, continues in his public career to show amazing tolerance with his thousands of fans. Very, very rarely does he not oblige fans with autographs. On the 2001 tour the All Black management had to put into place some level of security at hotels and grounds just so he could be normal to some degree.

There was one afternoon we of the travelling rugby media observed Lomu in the foyer of the Sheraton Hotel in Buenos Aires. The All Blacks were on some sort of free afternoon. Lomu had decided to go for a walk outside. He might have assumed that if there was one place in the rugby world where he could stroll and not be hounded by fans then Buenos Aires might have been that place.

But no. No sooner had he arrived in the foyer of the hotel and tried to exit by a side door than two men in suits rose quickly from their lobby chairs and chased him. He stopped and posed for the obligatory two pics; with this one first and then that one which followed. Several more autographs and photograph posings with other people took place as Lomu walked towards the outside door. Then we watchers saw Lomu stop and make a personal command decision.

Seconds before leaving the hotel, he no doubt thought, 'Those damned digital cameras.' We saw him turn and walk quickly back across the foyer, into the lift and out of sight.

Two things conclude this story: the two pictures taken of Jonah that day were no doubt within minutes emailed proudly across the country of Argentina or perhaps out across the world. It is the world we live in now.

For Jonah Lomu, and others like him in the glare of modern sports technology, a lifetime of new pressures from digitally aware fans lies ahead in life.

●

60. They call you what?

Nicknames – the good, the bad . . .

The nicknaming of our top rugby players — the All Blacks — has almost been an art form as long as the history of the team itself. Some of the names have been obvious, some curious and some outrageous. It has to be said, though, that the quality and appropriateness of All Black nicknames seems to be slipping as a tradition. Perhaps a rallying call needs to made to improve modern All Black players' nicknames. Otherwise dull, logical and unimaginative names will become the norm with the team. Surely the young players of today can do better than the 'Fitzy', 'Foxy', 'Zinny', 'Cully', 'J.K.', 'B.G.' and 'Mehrts' nicknames of recent years.

In the history of the All Blacks it is the province of Taranaki which has comfortably lead the way in providing appropriate nicknames for their top players. When Peter Burke reached All Black status in 1957 it was noted by his friends that he did possess a slightly larger probiscus than most. He was therefore tagged, superbly, 'Bugle' Burke.

Roger Urbahn, the fair-haired and slim Taranaki halfback, was named 'Spider'; his provincial halfback rival of the time who also made the All Blacks, Kevin Briscoe, was therefore appropriately called 'Monkey'. So that when the two were being judged together as to who should play they were 'Spider' and 'Monkey'. (As in 'Spider-Monkey' one supposes.)

There are other excellent Taranaki examples: 'Goss' Mourie (after Gossamer — the very finest silkiness by which he played the game), 'Legs' Eliason (yes, they were very long and shapely for a man), John Major ('John Colonel' to his closest friends and 'John Ma-jaw' to others who recalled the way he was addressed by stuffy English people while on the All Blacks tour of Britain in 1963–64).

Taranaki also gave the rugby world Dave 'Trapper' Loveridge, Bryce 'Cabbage' Robins, Ross 'Pascoe' Brown, Brian 'Jazz' Muller, Kieran 'Colt' Crowley, Terry 'Tee Pee' O'Sullivan and many others. Well done Taranaki! Keep it up.

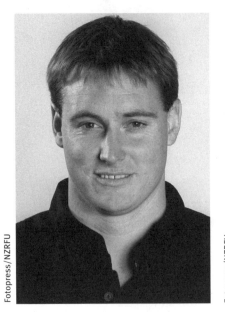

Andrew 'Mehrts' Mehrtens and Jeff 'Goldie' Wilson.

The All Blacks of 2001 did have some in their ranks some who showed imagination in their nicknaming. Jeff 'Goldie' Wilson is one name which lives on from the flying winger's early days of fame. Mark 'Sharkey' Robinson, Tony 'Claw' Brown, Mark 'Rigger' Cooksley and Scott 'Razor' Robertson are all worthy of the tradition.

But the folklore of many nicknames must never be forgotten; indeed they must be nurtured and encouraged to continue. Where would New Zealand rugby be without names like Colin 'Pinetree' Meads, Billy 'Carbine' Wallace, Joe 'Clock' Karam, Fred 'The Needle' Allen, Keith 'Killer' Arnold, Don 'Camel' Clarke, Ian 'Chutney' Clarke, Tom 'Angry' Cross, Bruce 'Diesel' Deans, Mark 'Bullet' Donaldson, John 'D'Arcy" Dougan, Kevin 'Hayburner' Eveleigh, John 'Bones' Fleming, Peter 'Tiger' Jones, Gary 'Axle' Knight, Brian 'Colt' McKechnie, Mark 'Twig' Sayers, Mark 'Cowboy' Shaw, Charles 'Bronco' Seeling, Alistair 'Ack' Soper, Ken 'Balfour' Stewart, Kerry 'Tumbles' Tanner, Barry 'Bear' Thomas, Kelvin 'Bunny' Tremain, Alex 'Grizz' Wyllie and many others.

In fact, a fair number of former All Blacks have lived their whole lives with a nomenclature which is just their nickname. A good rugby trivia question might be: name the first Christian names of these All Blacks — 'Red' Conway, 'Tuppy' Diack, 'Kit' Fawcett, 'Jock' Hobbs, 'Jock' Richardson, 'Bam' Koteka, 'Buff' Milner, 'Rusty' Page, 'Joey' Sadler and 'Ranji' Wilson.

A 100 per cent correct answer of the above paragraph means you are fighting hard too, to keep the tradition of All Black nicknames going.